VIOLENCE, BLUNDERS, AND FRACTURED JAWS

Violence, Blunders, and Fractured Jaws

Advanced Awareness Techniques and Street Etiquette

Marc "Animal" MacYoung

PALADIN PRESS
BOULDER, COLORADO

Violence, Blunders, and Fractured Jaws:
Advanced Awareness Techniques and Street Etiquette
by Marc "Animal" MacYoung

Copyright © 1992 by Marc "Animal" MacYoung

ISBN 13: 978-0-87364-671-0
Printed in the United States of America

Published by Paladin Press, a division of
Paladin Enterprises, Inc.,
P.O. Box 1307
Boulder, Colorado 80306 USA
+1.303.443.7250

Direct inquiries and/or orders to the above address.

PALADIN, PALADIN PRESS, and the "horse head" design are trademarks
belonging to Paladin Enterprises and registered in United States Patent and
Trademark Office.

Visit our website at www.paladin-press.com.

CONTENTS

PREFACE

> "In any art, the principles are few,
> the techniques are many."
> —Dale Carnegie

"An armed society is a polite society." Thus spoke Robert A. Heinlein years ago in the book *The Day after Tomorrow*. In it, America had returned to a dueling society, in which one's very words and actions could cost him his life. The other guy had to consider the fact that the person he challenged was just as likely to dust him. These guys were duelists, willing to fight to the death over their words and actions. Needless to say, nobody wanted to start the party.

While Heinlein's book is science fiction, it does point out some serious problems with the society we face today. His book is about the social dynamics that lead to violence—and so is this one. Contrary to what most people believe, hardly any violence is the "jump out of the bushes and grab you" variety. Usually, someone says or does something wrong and gets punched for it. By wrong, I don't mean "who's to blame" wrong. I means "oops" wrong.

To illustrate the difference, imagine three doors. Behind door number one is a lovely lady with strong oral tendencies. Door number two holds nothing—if you go through it, nothing good or bad happens to you. Behind door number three is a hungry tiger. Choosing that third door is the kind of serious "oops" I mean. Not that there is any blame, but this mistake turns violence from a potential threat into a serious reality. Something led to that encounter with a hungry tiger. It was not just an unexplained phenomenon.

But there's good news, folks. If you play your cards right in situations like the one above, you can avoid violence altogether most of the time. What's more, you can do so without having to back down or feeling like a wimp. These are the social dynamics this book is going to teach you.

Years ago, I had a smug businessman lean back and, with a smile, tell me that "with a corporation, you're safe. If something goes wrong, they can't touch you because you are not personally accountable." Just recently, I ran into someone else who was very worried because the situation had changed. In California, at least, banks are setting it up so that if something goes wrong with a business loan, they're coming after *you*, corporation or not. Your house, your car, your equity. This is a very unsettling concept for businessmen. Aww, poor babies.

American business has screwed the pooch in a number of ways. One of the ways that it affects you most is with the corporate attitude of "Hey, I'm safe" that has infected America. With this attitude, people believe that no matter what they do, the trouble will be passed on to someone else. The long and short of it is that businessmen think they can be assholes and not pay the price, that the worst thing that could happen to them is that they get fired.

This mentality causes people all sorts of pain when they step away from the office. They don't understand that outside the work world, they are held accountable for their actions. How much damage is done depends on where they are. I have been in and seen hundreds, if not thousands, of scraps, jams, fights, altercations, and situations over the years. Violence— and situations entailing the possibility of violence—has been my profession for a long time. Again and again, I have seen the "I'm not accountable for my actions" mentality as a major contributor to violence. Our society teaches this lesson not just in its corporations but also in its schools. Well, what's taught in school seldom has any resemblance to real life. The truth of the matter is, in a great number of places, not watching your ass is the best way to lose it.

Let's go back to the dueling society for a moment. Here are guys who put their lives on the line daily with what they say and do. Unlike the so-called gunfighter, these guys aren't hired guns. They are part of an armed populace. If anybody gets out of hand, the locals take care of it. Stop and think of what it means when everybody is armed. Do you want to be the one starting shit? Hell, no! Armed people quickly become polite when everyone else is, too. Most shootings and stabbings are one-sided affairs. One guy has a weapon; the victim doesn't. It's an entirely different ball game when the other team returns fire immediately.

The yearly increase in the body count of young Americans disproves the idea that youth is immortal. Sooner or later, people realize that the other side is shooting back. This is where *Violence, Blunders, and Fractured Jaws* comes in. For every two young bucks on the street, there's an old dog sitting back watching. These old dogs are the guys who made it through the crazies of hormones and have settled in. They'll leave you alone, but if you cross them, they'll tear you up. This book is about how the veterans act, what systems they use to keep violence down to a minimum, and how you can get to the same place in your life.

When I was a little squirt, I made a vow that I would survive. Whatever it took, I would make it. By promising myself to survive, rather than just to be tough, I kept open all doors as to how I would make it. As I progressed, I kept my eyes open. I went out and started learning everything I could. My lessons came not from the bullshit that is taught in school, but from the real world. Theories and hypotheses are fine and dandy, but what do the guys who are actually surviving the streets have to say about it?

Over the years I assimilated information, from my own experiences and from the experiences of others. Unfortunately, the guys in the field weren't really good at expressing overviews, but as I progressed, I began to notice patterns and systems of behavior. I conducted research and organized the information I had assimililated. This led me back to theories of human interaction and, finally, back to the dreaded school. I was less interested in the so-called facts these people were trying to stuff down my throat than the way they organized their files. In time, I found that there were names for some of these patterns and systems of behavior I had observed in action. Sometimes I learned some new things; other times, I wrote their theories off as bullshit.

In any case, I learned as I survived. In time, I began to look for the core of the system, its essence. Assimilate the principles (or, core) of a system, and you can tack on the details later if you're interested. At first, I concentrated on self-defense. Yet, since my goal had always been to survive, I realized that just being able to hit people was not enough, that other things were involved as well. The other thing that I realized is that the major league dudes knew this as well, but when I'd talk to them about it, they'd talk in a vague slang that really didn't make much sense to me.

Well, a few trips to hell later, I graduated to the big leagues, and I realized what these guys had meant in their cryptic lingo. Realization came like a 2 x 4 across the kisser. These street-smart veterans knew this shit, but they don't know how to talk about it! If you ask these old-timers for advice, they kind of group around for a minute and then say something like, "Keep your shit wired tight," or "Don't step on your dick," as if that explains everything! Sheesh! Ask any veteran street fighter what it takes to make it out there, and I will guarantee you that he will talk about awareness. It may not sound like it, but that's what he means.

Then came a day when I looked around and realized that people were coming to me for advice on self-defense. What shocked me was what I had to tell them, that self-defense seemed to have less to do with hitting and punching than knowing how to avoid stepping on your dick. I checked into it again and again, and the answer always came up the same: *Awareness is the key to self-defense.*

It all boils down to personal responsibility, how you behave and what you don't allow other people to do to you. In short, don't step on other people's toes, and don't let them step on yours. As a fourteen-year-old kid, having made a decision not to put limits on surviving, I had stumbled onto the closest thing to a cosmic truth I have ever found. *Awareness,* take it as deep or as shallow as you want, but take this one.

This book is going to be different from my other books in that it isn't going to tell you how to crack, crunch, slice, dice, smash, or bash someone. It deals with the interactions between people that lead to violence. It is a disturbing fact that most violence is committed by people who know each other, and this is especially true with murders and rapes.

This is the most advanced book I've ever written. At times, it will seem like what I'm talking about has very little to do with self-defense or street survival, especially in the first few chapters. Bear with me on these because they set the stage for everything else.

This is also the hardest book I've ever written. Society is purposefully blind when it comes to violence. Violence is never a pretty thing, but society would like to think that it has no connection to it. That's like saying you have nothing to do with your own shadow. If you weren't there, it wouldn't be either. Society and violence have a lot to do with each other.

Violence occurs for many reasons. In the scope of things, what is considered by most people as a "fight" is actually a very small portion of the violence that actually occurs. There is much more going on beneath the surface that people have no real concept about. What I've written here is an overview of various operating systems that normally lead to violence.

Learning about these other operating systems will keep you from being blindsided by them. To many people wake up in hospitals going, "What happened?" because they didn't know what to look for. If you learn how to read the different operating systems and how they affect people's behavior, you will be much safer.

An operating system is simply the accepted values and rules by which a group governs itself. The primary purpose of a group—any group—is to keep itself going. If you learn nothing else from this book, remember this. It is the axis upon which the whole shebang operates. A group wants to continue, and it does this by having operating systems that will ensure its survival. Individuals come and go; the group remains. The underlying assumption is that people are expendable, the group is not. This is the basis for 90 percent of all the rules that exist in an operating system. The other 10 percent is sheer profiteering by some power clique in the group.

(This, of course, reflects the group's attitude; my attitude as to exactly how expendable I am is considerably different. I assume that your attitude follows a similar vein as mine, with a different focus as to who isn't disposable.)

Basically, there are three primary operating systems that shape the behavior of each of us: cultural, family, and personal. Each of these will be discussed in detail in later chapters. Right now, you just need to know that each one of these has helped shape the punk who is eyeing you from the corner of the bar.

A large operating system consists of smaller networks and stratas. Each network consists of different communities or clusters that are based on the network's core assumptions, or principles. Individuals act out certain roles in each particular group.

There are two types of laws that must be understood: deep surface, which often are unspoken and unwritten, but which the group feels most strongly about; and surface, which often are either written or at least understood by the members. The trick to surviving anywhere you go is to be able to read both the deep structure laws and the surface rules. Once you understand this technique, you can mimic any operating system that you find yourself in. It is always important to realize that people attack what is not familiar to them. This knowledge allows you to hot wire, short out, or D-watt a situation rather than having to fight your way out.

I have included not only the systems of adolescence—a painful, chaotic period during which violence is prone to flare up seemingly out of nowhere with terrifying speed—but also other systems that deal with violence as a normal, ongoing part of life. Without an understanding of how these systems are organized, you'll never understand how they work. If you don't understand either, you can easily become a victim of the violence generated by one of these systems.

You are not expendable. The John Wayne macho attitude is the best way to get yourself killed. Yet it is what we are taught. It is also the fastest way to the trash can. To keep from becoming a statistic, you have to use more than just your testosterone. If you use your wits, knowledge, and awareness, as well as your right hook, you will be more likely to live long enough to celebrate your old age.

To write a book about furthering awareness as a way of avoiding violence, I had to delve deep into the psyche of these systems. The bad news is that most systems which use violence are a few bricks short of a full load. In many ways, probing into them is like diving into humanity's cesspool. I normally try to make all of my books as funny as possible. In many ways, I feel I haven't shot par on this one. Paddling in a cesspool does that.

Violence is growing like a berserk cancer in America. What once threatened only a few now looms over most of us. The human sheep in middle America think that the government should do something about this violence. They don't (or don't want to) realize that violence is born and bred in them, in the operating systems by which they are raised. Government can't do anything about violence because it's not a political issue—it's a social one. Most people don't want the personal responsibility of dealing with violence when it lands in their laps.

The good news is that violence is much like a volcano. There's a recognizable buildup long before any eruption happens. To avoid being consumed by violence, I truly feel that you have to know what's going on underneath and what leads up to the eruption. If you can read the signs beforehand, you won't get caught flat-footed. As with Mount St. Helens, you can get the hell out of there before it blows. The intent of this book is to teach you how to read the signs that predict a violent reaction.

In *Fists, Wits, and a Wicked Right* (available from Paladin Press), I spoke of violence being like a door into a person's reality. I stated that most people didn't know that the door even existed. Because the person didn't know about it, he left the door unlocked for violence to enter. In *Violence, Blunders, and Fractured Jaws*, I'm going to tell you where to find the doors through which violence enters.

I survived the streets of Los Angeles. I have been a drug dealer, bodyguard, special-muscle event security man, and bouncer. I also pulled a stint as a director of a combined state and federal correctional center in Los Angeles, where I got to examine the criminal element from the other side of the fence. Talk about a learning experience. I have survived being on the hit lists of white, black, and Mexican gangs. I have experienced more than my share of violence, as well as seeing the reality of the operating systems of the "streets."

The truths that I will be talking about in this book are not fun. But if you understand them and apply what I talk about, you will have the basic skills to survive in any potentially violent situation or system. Whether from the pits of Hell's Kitchen to the waves of a holy war, you will know what to look for, and from where it's likely to erupt, in order to survive.

Wait a minute, I want to mention one thing before we go toddling off into La La Land. I want you to know that I've included a bibliography in this book. Some of the most profane and radical ideas that I'll be talking about are backed up by these books. In some cases, they're more articulate than *moi*; in others, they'd knock an insomniac on his ass. Also for shits and giggle, I'm going to try something different: footnotes at the end of each chapter. Gosh, I feel like a real writer!

ACKNOWLEDGMENTS

Ordinarily, I work alone when I write, relying on what I know or have done or seen. When you're talking straight self-defense, that's easy. Did it work on the drunk biker I had to toss out? Had I seen someone else do it? To write this book, however, I double-checked everything I knew, thought I knew, or even suspected. I interviewed experts in certain fields and rattled my friends' cages about their areas of expertise. We ranted, raved, bitched, and snarled at each other in homes, cars, and coffee shops. I interviewed other people in some unique situations which I won't go into here.

It is with great love and respect that I thank those who helped me with this book:

My stepfather, Richard "Silky" Nelson, FBI retired
My clan brothers, Tim "Silent Wolf" Toohey
and Richard Dobson
Ina Gregory, M.F.C.C.
Gary "Rowdy" McClure
Peyton Quinn and Mike "The Amazing Eagle" Haynick
Alex Holub, Ph.D.
Dwight Rodgers, "Rolling '60s OG"
Lorenzo "Moon" Holmes
Jon Ford, Editorial Director at Paladin Press, whose prodding finally got me off my ass to write this book
And, of course, my lady, Tracy David

INTRODUCTION

> "It's just common sense. If a guy tells you that his wife's got a great pussy, you don't agree with him."
> —Bob Gibson on Texas etiquette

I was sitting across from one of those vicious motherfuckers who enjoyed cutting people up with his wit. A cat isn't vicious when it plays with its lunch; it's operating on instinct. This guy was being vicious. He'd slip up with his rapierlike wit, slash a few times, and then slip back going, "Ah, ha, ha, ha!" from a safe distance.

Everyone saw what was happening, but nobody mentioned it. He was a friend of the husband of the household. The wife really didn't like the guy, but hubby kept on inviting him back. So everyone was basically in one of two camps: ignore the guy and hope that he didn't come after them or sit and enjoy the show.

I was the new dude in town. I had just started dating the best friend of the wife. So off we went to meet her social group—fun, fun, fun. (The only thing worse is meeting a woman's family.) Now mind you, where I'm from, people who use wit as a weapon usually end up with an open mouth around a curb until someone kicks the back of his head. It's called the Berkley stomp and is used to show the joker how much you appreciate being attacked verbally. It fractures jaws and knocks out teeth. So while I had fast and vicious down, it wasn't with words.

Well Mike (that was his name) decided to see how much fun he could have with the new meat. He came over and joined the conversation. We were talking about life, the universe, et al. All of a sudden, *zing*—a verbal arrow. "Hmmm," says I, "old Mikey here just took a potshot." I decided to ignore it; throwing another guest out of a third-story window isn't the best way to get invited back to a place. Well, like most of these bozos, Mike decided that since I hadn't responded, I was too dumb to come back at him. Ergo, I was fair game. Silly boy.

For about five minutes, this guy ran with everything I said. His fan club was eating it up; everyone else sat there looking uncomfortable. I looked over at my date, who had this "Mike's being an asshole again" expression. Right, time to put a stop to this one. Old Mikey hadn't pushed it far enough that I could justify stuffing him down a toilet. Those sort of people never do, and unless they really get out of line, people remember that you threw the first punch, not that he was being a prick. It looks bad on you in court.

Since the conversation was dealing with social convention, anyway, I eased it over into my line of attack—sort of like easing a saber out of its scabbard.

"One of the problems with social convention is that people think they're safe when they really aren't," I said with all the innocence of an alligator.

"What are you afraid of, that someone is going to plant a bomb under your bed? Isn't that a little paranoid?" replied witty (and also real predictable) Mike. Step into my parlor, motherfucker.

"No," I said, "people rely on social mores too much. They think that keeps them safe. They don't realize that those things are nothing but air."

A third party asked for an explanation. God, I love straight lines.

"Society's rules are nothing more than a group of people getting together and saying this is the way it is. Those rules aren't real; they're an agreed-upon convention."

"Are you trying to say that society's rules are fantasies?" The way Mike asked, I knew he was winding up for another zing, not only by his tone, but by the fact that he had leaned forward for the kill. Too late, mofo.

"No," I said, turning toward him. "What I'm saying is that there is nothing between you and me but air . . . If I wanted to reach across this table and rip your throat out right now, there is nothing to stop me but social convention. And that ain't nothing but air."

Captain Wit's eyes suddenly got real big as he realized that he was on the wrong side of the fence with a large predator. Oddly enough, he chose to freeze rather than withdraw. He must have thought that his response was sufficient, "Well there would be the police."

Ooooh, I'm scared; see me quiver. Why do people always say that?

"Wouldn't do you any good," I continued. "The court would put me in prison for what I did, but you would still be dead. Besides, the prisons are overcrowded; I'd be out in seven years or so. But that's what I mean by social convention being just air. There's nothing to stop me if I decide to kill you right now. (Get the point, dickhead? Now it's time to take it back to conversation.) That's what people are relying on, air. It doesn't do the victim any good to put anybody in jail afterward; the damage has been done already. But people still think that social convention will keep them safe. That's bullshit!"

Mike had begun to lean back by now, but he was still in reach. His next attempt was to find out if I was bluffing. "Well, tearing someone's throat out—you'd have to be pretty damn good," he said.

Ah, the last trap. He was expecting me to go off on a bout of macho. He thought that by bringing up the subject of my proficiency, he could snipe at me while all I could do would be to flex my muscles and look tough. All I was going to say was a noncommittal "Uh-mmm," then continue being perfectly civilized. "He could do it!" my date piped in to Mike. Hallelujah and praise the Lord! Third-person backup was better than anything I could have said. We both just smiled at him. We continued with the conversation about social convention, and after a few moments, Mike got up and left.

Now, officially, I didn't threaten Mike. Under the guise of civilized conversation, I had made a point and used him as an example. In reality, under the same rules that allowed him to be an asshole and get away with it, I had just threatened his life—but nothing that could be interpreted as hostile, no "I'm gonna kick your ass" threats or long, drawn-out verbal duels.

Later, the hostess came up to me and congratulated me on dealing with Mike. She'd never seen him turn tail so fast. Mike never fucked with me again, even though I saw a lot of him when wife and hubby moved in with my date and me later on. Although looking back at the way our relationship turned out, maybe I should have saved myself a lot of trouble by throwing Mike out the window when I first saw him.

• • •

Why was I able to handle Mike without violence or real ugliness? Because I knew the rules by which we were both playing. They are what I like to call "street rules," and they apply everywhere, in living rooms as well as dark alleys and street corners. They are as follows:

1) *Life is predatory.* Where do you sit on the food chain, bucko? Contrary to popular opinion, the food chain is a little more complex than predators and food. It's like a row of fish, each one about to get eaten by a bigger fish. In some cases,

you eat others, and in other cases, you get eaten. On the street, you are both the hunter and the hunted. This makes street people both alert and aware to see whether people are potential victims or hunting for them. Like a lizard, if it's smaller, eat it; if it's bigger, run from it. Pay attention to this rule; it's a biggie.

2) *Human life is cheap.* This applies to both your own and someone else's. While you try to hold on, kicking someone off for a better meal ticket is acceptable. This includes everybody—children, elders, and women. Most people on the street know that there is a silver bullet out there with their name on it. Since they know that they ain't going to make it, they aren't afraid of death. This often makes them both dangerous and foolhardy.

3) *You fight to win.* Honor, fair play, and nobility are things that you use to wipe your ass with. Second place is in the morgue. You strike first and hard enough so the motherfucker doesn't get up. If the SOB is too tough to take out up front, hit from behind. You do what you have to do to win, without risking your own ass too much.

4) *Civilized boundaries don't exist.* The only boundaries that exist are the ones you can enforce with violence. If you can't back it up, it'll be crossed. Street people grew up with no boundaries except those enforced with violence. Al Capone's immortal line of "You can get farther with a kind word and a gun than you can with a kind word alone" doesn't exist in the street. It's pure how fast will you shoot someone? If they don't fear you, they will cross boundaries.

5) *If you want it, and you can get away with it, take it.* Since street people feel they have been "suppressed," they feel that this entitles them to grab whatever they can get. The only thing that stops them is the likelihood of getting wasted for their attempt. This is why you always keep your awareness up, because the other guy is always looking for a chance to snake in on you.

6) *Altruism and charity don't exist, betrayal and backstabbing do.* Honor among thieves is bullshit. Deals and alliances are based on profit and mutual self-interest between two parties. Once there is no more benefit, or a more pressing problem shows up, sellouts and betrayals are the norm. This includes family.

7) *Jail is nothing more than a pain in the ass.* The threat of being sent to jail is like threatening to send someone to his room. Often it is the cost of doing business. Many prefer staying in jail to facing the complexities of life in the world.

8) *They are scum.* People who live there have extremely low self-esteem. Theirs are what are called sham-based personalities. Down in the sublevels of their subconscious, these people think that they are trash. They are damaged people, the ultimate dysfunction. They reason that, since they are shit, they are going to act like shit.

9) Since they are damaged, *they feel that the world owes them something.* Whatever they can steal, con, or do is all right because they are underprivileged. They use this self-righteousness to justify whatever they do. Nobody can hold them responsible for what they do. "Yeah, I raped her . . . but you shouldn't be hard on me." I swear, I once heard that from a crackhead facing a prison term.

Those are the underlying core assumptions of the street. I hope I managed to get across the idea of how fucked up it is out there. It is a jungle. From the outside it looks as if there are no rules. It looks like you can do whatever you want. It's sex, drugs, music, and being cool, with no one there to pass judgment on you or to put you down for doing your thing. That is a fatal assumption.

Not only is the information contained herein crucial to surviving on the streets, but it also helped me to leave the street once I was done there. Believe it or not, if you become good enough to survive the streets, there will come a time when you ask yourself, what's next? This book will help you to step away when you're done.

When I look back at the number of my friends who bought it along the way, what scares me is that at least half of them were good, damn good in fact. But after a while they got tired and wanted to leave the system, and that's what got them. It wasn't going fast that killed them; it was trying to slow down. They hesitated when they shouldn't have, they tried to walk away at the wrong time, or old enemies showed up looking for vengeance and caught them unprepared. I am not talking about one or two deaths here. I have buried dozens of friends, and of those trying to slow down, I can say without exception that the reason they are dead is because they changed their reflexes but not the games they were in. It does no good to quit a gang but stay in the same neighborhood. You'll get dragged back into the game.

The games I talk about in this book are very real and, in some cases, deadly. You have to understand that to leave a game, you have to do more than just stop in the middle of the playing field and say, "I don't want to play anymore." Imagine doing that in the middle of a football skirmish. You'd get creamed. That's essentially what my friends did—they quit playing before they got off the playing field. Believe me, the field is bigger and deeper than you think.

If you're good enough to survive, you're going to have to accept that down the road the game changes.

I can't tell you every rule and aspect of the system—or game—you're operating in or that you might find yourself in. I can, however, give you the same tools I used to figure the systems out. I believe that this constitutes one of the core issues behind survival in general and street survival specifically. From personal experience, I can tell you that failing to conform to the rules can and will result in violence. Most violence comes from some sort of infraction of these rules.

You can look at this book as a guide to avoiding fights. I'm not talking about what to do when the guy is in your face—by that time, it's kinda late. What I'm talking about are the systems and behaviors that lead up to someone getting pissed at you, which is about eight steps before the first punch is thrown. If you know how operating systems work, you can avoid situations in which fights are possible. I'm talking about awareness.

Awareness is what separates warriors from soldiers or fighters. Soldiers follow orders and fight. Warriors don't need orders because they know what needs to be done. Nor do warriors fight for petty reasons; their job is to maintain and protect the tribe. Once you lose sight of what is going on, you slip into either soldier or fighter mode. That's not good. A soldier blindly follows orders, even if it means getting killed. If the people giving the orders have gone bad, the amount of damage can be unbelievable (look at Nazi Germany). A fighter, on the other hand, is like a rabid dog; he's hurt and fucked up and wants to share the wealth. Toe tags are not fashionable jewelry, but being a fighter or soldier usually leads to them. Unfortunately, our culture generally gives you a choice only of being a fighter or a soldier. This book tells you what you need to know to be a warrior.

As you probably know by now, I have a habit on pissing on conventionality. (Don't be surprised, you knew that already.) If something is taboo, by God, I want to see what the fun is that everyone else is missing. I admit, when I was younger, I was a bit of a rebel. I guess I was about twenty-five before I realized an important thing: It's not that I have a problem with rules, I just have a problem with authority. If I understand the reason behind a rule (and agree with it), I'll follow it along with everyone else. It's just when somebody tells me, "Because I told you so!" that I have a problem.

One of the biggest "because I told you so's" in society is the one with which yours truly has a major hard-on. What's amazing about this rule is that people don't even know consciously that it exists, yet it is the kingpin that keeps millions of people chained down. The rule is simple, and incredibly insidious: "Thou shalt not question the operating system thou art given!"

What's weird is that you can rebel against the system, but you can't question it. Questioning is considered much more dangerous than rebelling. You were shaped by your operating system so it knows how you're going to react to various provocations. The system, therefore, can set traps to catch you when you rebel. These traps are much more insidious than you think. They include the attitudes behind the system—not just cops, judges, and prisons, but the self-righteous clucking that goes on during the bridge club. It is the attitudes that will nail you in the long run.

If you're under twenty-five, everything you do is attributed to "just being young," and the system has ways of trying to bring you around through various attitude-adjustment techniques. If, however, you are a little too rambunctious or you persist in your rebelliousness, the system has a convenient way of dealing with you. The system has a trash can waiting for you to jump (or be pushed) into. From inside a trash can, you can't threaten the system. That's because the system can sit there and "tsk, tsk" about "wasted lives," while sitting nice and safe. Once you're put in the trash can, the system can write you off. For example, if you develop a drug problem, everything you say can be written off because you are in the trash can.

This is what happens when you just rebel. Drug addicts, convicts, alcoholics, prostitutes, and section eights (crazies) are folks who rebelled without ever really knowing that they were set up from the get-go. That these people ended up in the trash can is as predictable as a correctly made time bomb going off. The operating system programmed you to rebel in certain predictable ways, and it had safety measures in force to trap and remove you.

If, however, you question how the system works, you are going to expose all sorts of people with their pants down. It is here that you will discover exactly how ignorant and sheeplike people really are. While this may seem like fun at first, I guarantee you that you will win no popularity contests if you go after the system.

Six times out of ten, if you press for logical explanations of a system's taboos, you will end up with a "because I told you to!" What this message really means is: "I don't know, I never questioned it, and I'm uncomfortable with your questioning it."

Two times, you'll end up with a woo-woo explanation, which is either somebody making up something to shut you up or somebody trying to sell you something. Remember when you were younger and somebody told you something that was complete bullshit just to get you out of his hair? The explanation may also be something so far out that you end up scratching you head and going, "What?" Like the time the priest told me that "God allows terrible things to happen to test if mankind loves Him." (I still haven't figured that one out.)

The other two times, or about 20 percent of the time, you'll get either one of two answers. The first one is a technical explanation that is valid for the here and now. "We wear lead suits to protect us from the radiation so our dicks don't fall off." Okay, that makes sense—at least on the surface.

The last kind of explanation is one that made sense five hundred years ago. My favorite is the orthodox Jewish eating habits, 90 percent of which were designed so people could live in the desert without refrigeration. And believe me, Bucko, they work. The other 10 percent of the laws were designed to keep the kids away from the neighbors. (Food is a big part of social interaction, as I'll explain later in Chapter 3.) These are solid reasons although maybe no longer applicable.

The problem about questioning authority is that, unless you find a rare bird who can (and is willing) to tell you the truth, you're going to end up rattling cages. I cannot overemphasize how much importance is placed on this rule of not questioning the system. See, if you never question the system, it'll never get challenged.

For good or bad, these rules of the operating system keep everyone in line and playing the same game. Some sections of society get screwed in the deal; others get a better deal. Society has some harsh ways to keep the game afoot, including choreographed violence and antagonism. Remember, in the long run, *all* players are expendable. Players may be on different teams, but they're playing the same game. Oppressor and oppressed are just different sides of the same coin. As with a boxing match, the game has rounds; unlike a boxing match, it has no end. The system is playing for a victory of rounds, not total victory. Total victory would end the game, and that would be bad. That's why Hitler was such a mad dog. Instead of following the normal oppressor/ oppressed game, he went for total victory within his regime. Instead of oppressing the "undesirable" element, he went for eradication of those too far out of his system. This was unacceptable. So much so that now, nearly fifty years later, you still can't turn around in America without getting some form of propaganda about it.

Anytime one team gets far enough out of line to really threaten the system, the other side reacts violently. Look at the French Revolution—the upper crust got out of hand, and *blamo*, the lower castes went ballistic on them! Then the peasants went too far themselves. *Wham bam!* Things even out. Here in America you had the Watts (Los Angeles), Detroit, and Kent State riots in the late 1960s. The rioters pushed, and the establishment began shooting them to show how amused it was about being pushed. These are examples of the group using violence to protect its precious hide.

For the group to survive, it must make sure that everyone plays the same game. While the overall game is the same, the subsystem's (or network's) rules vary wildly. Just as with the operating system, subsystems also keep their players in line by not allowing them to question the system and by attacking anyone or anything that might threaten their status. This is where self-defense comes in. You can get wasted if you're not on your toes—not only for crossing another subsystem, but for pushing too far in your own.

If you don't know about these sort of subsystems in the group, you might go into unfamiliar territory and cross some unspoken lines. In this case, where you are determines how bad the damage will be. Another way to get hurt is to find yourself in a situation in which acceptable behavior in your system means you're dinner on the hoof to someone else's system. The third and most common route to violence is when you set sail on a course of action that inevitably ends in violence. This last path is twofold. One, you eventually step over the lines of the system, and it breaks your nose. Two, that path is one of the system's predesigned traps that lead to violence.

It's important to understand that these systems were given to you. They really aren't yours. The strata and culture you were born into determine what you were taught as reality. Most people never question the underlying subsystems. They raise hell about all sorts of surface stuff, but they never get down deep to the core. This is the never-question rule in action. The people pass the old system on for generations. They don't even know what they're passing on. It becomes a sacred cow. Nobody touches it—they let it wander around shitting all over the place, while people starve in the streets.

To look at advanced awareness techniques, we're going to have to knock over some sacred cows. While I admit that it's fun to pop other people's bubbles, you're probably going to find out that you've bought into a sacred cow or two yourself. I'm not advocating throwing out all the rules, nor am I advocating my own set of rules for your life. (The Pope I'm not.)

It's your life; do what you want with it. If you want to keep something, go ahead. If, on the other hand, you discover that there are things that you don't want, drop 'em faster than an annoyed tarantula.

There have been times in my life when I have had to knowingly and directly cut across somebody's operating system. I knew where I needed to go, and I knew the risks I was taking by doing so. (Of course, other times I was just being an asshole.) The key reasons I could do this and stay alive is that I was aware of what I was doing, and I did not do it unless it was necessary. Yet I have seen countless people blindly cut across operating systems for no reason. Not only did they not know what they were doing, they didn't even know they were doing anything wrong. The lucky ones are still wondering why they were the featured guests at an aggravated assault; a lot of the unlucky ones are dead.

One of the things that I insist on doing is not only showing you things that are applicable on the street but also adding hints about what is waiting for you if you go deeper into some of the things I talk about. A whole lot of what I'm saying here is not only going to be applicable to what works on the street, but also to life in general. This is some powerful information I'm giving you. Like everything else, I'm not giving it to you without warnings.

This can be dangerous stuff, but knowing something is dangerous makes it less so. This is why I wandered off into La La Land there for a while. If you take this stuff past street survival, the rules change. The systems stay pretty much the same, but the techniques are radically different. What's more, you can end up just as dead, set up, or, more commonly, cut off and impotent. Maybe what I'm saying doesn't apply now, but in a few years it might. Stick it in the closet for a while and let it sit. If it never works, throw the damn thing out and find something that does.

I've spent a lot of years cutting across territories I was told not to enter. Sometimes, the naysayers were right. I really shouldn't have gone there, and I usually realized this when there were illegal amounts of lead emissions in the air (bullets). All too often, though, what the people telling me not to go somewhere meant was that their system said it was wrong and they had never questioned what was on the other side of that hill. Other folks told me I shouldn't go because if I did, they couldn't control me anymore (awww, too bad!).

I will tell you, though, that I don't regret a minute of all those years I spent kicking around. Some were fun, some were pure hell, but it was all one excellent adventure. So it doesn't matter if you have itchy feet, want to get away from a fucked-up scene, or just don't want to get your head knocked in while having a good time, let's go see what's out there.

CHAPTER ONE

How Operating Systems Work

> "New points of view are not, as a rule, discovered in territory that is already known, but in out-of-the way places that may even be avoided because of their bad name."
>
> —Carl Jung
> *Synchronicity: An Acausual Connecting Principle*

I ended up rewriting this chapter because of a friend. I had originally written it as a long diatribe that was designed to distract you from the fact that I was planting seeds of suspicion not only about what you were taught, but also the way in which you were taught. When I handed a rough over to *mi hermano*, Richard Dobson, for review, I got an arched eyebrow and the comment of "serious soapbox." All right, all right, back to the drawing board.

You may be wondering why such a little thing would send me galumphing back to the 'puter. Simply put, Richard is one of the sneakiest, most double-dealing, manipulative, slickest sons of bitches that I know. He also happens to be probably the best fucking teacher I have ever met. If this guy hands you something, look at it in at least ten ways, knowing that it probably has more levels than the Empire State Building. Unlike many people I know who do this sort of stuff, he's not going to hand you a gift-wrapped grenade. We operate well together in messing with people's operating models.

So here I am faced with the job of trying to point out to you that you've been lied to. Actually, out-and-out lied to is not exactly right; you've been told only half of the story. The real bummer is that most of the people doing the lying aren't really aware that they're doing it. So if you get pissed at them, they get self-righteous, and the whole thing turns ugly. However, not all liars do so unwittingly; a certain number purposefully stomp on the truth to cover their asses.

Now this almost sounds like I'm talking about global conspiracies and secret societies. Nah. What I'm talking about could best be summed up by the major-league guy in the aerospace movement who described our space program as, "The closer you get to the top, the more you realize nobody is driving."

To show you how an operating system works, let's take a look at the game of basketball. It begins with a certain move called the tipoff. The referee throws the ball in the air, and two guys jump to try and knock it over to their team. Pretty simple, eh? The ball goes one way or the other. But let's make it a little more complicated. Instead of two teams, there are ten. Now which way does the ball go? Let's make it even more interesting, and within each team let's add factions. While they want their team to win, they also want their own clique to get the ball. The ensuing free-for-all would be a blast to watch if you ask me.

Well, folks, I got some news for you. That's what is going on right now in thousands upon thousands of games, from big to little, from multinational corporations to family squabbles. Everybody is scrambling for the ball. They're in a game, and everybody is going for the points. When the game was just between two teams, the rules were simple and easy to enforce. Now that it's every man for himself, there is a mondo amount of rule-breaking going on. With everybody's eyes on the ball, nobody is calling foul about elbow shots to the ribs and knees in the groin. If an actual fight breaks out, then people notice. However, the quick sucker punch under the basket has become a very real factor to contend with in the game.

With all these cheap shots going on, you definitely need new players on a regular basis. So off the team goes to recruit new players. But here's the rub: the cherries are only taught the old game's rules.

(To introduce a new—but more powerful—analogy into the conversation, how'd you like to be a military recruiter, telling a kid what war is really like? Instead of telling the kid that it will make a man out of him and that it will entitle him to all these GI benefits toward college, you gotta tell him that if he doesn't get killed, there's a good chance that he'll get his legs blown off and spend the rest of his life in a wheelchair. Or just as much fun, that there is a good likelihood that he's going to get splattered with the guts and gore of a person he's grown closer to than his brother. Shit, if you told the truth about MREs [Meals Ready to Eat] alone, nobody would join.

One of the worst things that happened with the Vietnam War was that the kids who went over there were totally lied to during recruitment and boot camp. They were not taught what it took to survive over there. When they got to 'Nam, they died like flies. Most fatalities in Vietnam happened within the first month of a tour. It got to the point where the rookies were called the Fuckin' New Guys [FNGs]. You didn't want to get close to a FNG because you knew he was going to die, and if he did something stupid, he'd take you with him. The people who made it were the ones who could drop the indoctrination of boot camp and adapt to the reality of the situation.)

The same is true with the mutant basketball game, except it's on a different level. When you get into the game, you're not signed up with a faction. You're just put on a team and let loose in the game. The problem is that you are playing basketball and the rest appear to be in a free-for-all. Needless to say, you're going to get knocked on your ass. As you sit there wondering what the fuck just happened, you'll probably notice that what's going on has very little to do with the game you were taught. Often what happens is that you grab hold of the nearest friendly looking person and ask, "What the hell is going on?"

Suddenly, you're recruited by a faction. It is now that you begin to learn an entirely different set of rules. You may or may not become proficient at these rules. Many people don't; they want to play the game that they signed up for, not basketball from hell.

Many people end up hanging on by the skin of their teeth for most of their lives, dreading the thought of getting taken out of the game. Others learn just enough to protect themselves and spend all their time covering their asses. Some folks, however, thrive in the game; the sociopathic part of them goes, "Wheeee!" and cuts loose.

The real reason that it's the basketball game from hell is that *it's for life!* There is no other game that you are allowed to play, and if you try to leave this game, you'll be trashed. Seriously, this is part of the indoctrination. Every player is absolutely convinced that he has no choice but to play that particular game. The only other option is the "trash can," and nobody wants to go there. After a while, people believe that there is literally no place else to go.

Let's look at another complicating factor here. Not only is the reality of the game different than what you were taught, but the situation changes from game to game. If you were to look outside, you'd see guys playing soccer from hell or football from hell.

Initially, we are going to get an overview of these games (read: operating systems) and then work toward specific games. If you get the general idea of how these games work, you can analyze the specific games you find yourself in. Once you can spot these systems, you know when to protect yourself and when you can relax. Nothing hurts more than a sucker punch. It's the guy who gets you in a tender spot when you're not expecting it who is dangerous.

Another key aspect here is that the games have evolved into something a lot more serious than your teachers prepared you for. One of the things you learn in boot camp is that it's the other side you have to watch for. That may have been true once upon a time (bullshit), but now the people you have to watch for are on the same team.

Let us take a gander over to the *1989 Uniform Crime Report (UCR)*.¹ The *UCR* is a compilation of all the reported crimes in America for a particular year. Like anything else from Big Brother, you should look at the numbers with a serious hairy eyeball. One, it contains only reported crimes. A thundering herd of stuff goes by unreported. Two, it has been through some interesting number crunching; not exactly falsifying statistics (the best way to lie is with statistics), but it is close. Categories get hazed out and smudged into other categories. So, as a rule of thumb, the report should be considered questionable. However, having said that, we can still get some interesting info out of it.

In the beginning of the movie *Cobra*, Sylvester Stallone lists how frequently crimes happen by using the *UCR*'s crime clock, which entails taking available time in a year and dividing it by the number of reported offenses. By doing this with the *1989 UCR* findings, you end up with statistics like:

- Every two seconds there is a crime.
- A property crime occurs every three seconds.
- A violent crime happens every nineteen seconds.
- An aggravated assault occurs every thirty-three seconds (this includes everything from attempted murders to punchouts).
- One robbery occurs every fifty-five seconds.
- One forcible rape every six minutes. (This is where the statistics are really off.)
- Every twenty-four minutes, someone is murdered. (That makes me sleep well at night.)

Want to know something scary? Most of these violent crimes are committed by someone the person knows! Yes, indeedy do, folks, forget strangers jumping out of the bushes; you are more likely to be murdered, raped, or assaulted by someone you know. According to the *UCR,* 39 percent of the 21,500 murders in 1989 were committed by someone the victim knew, and 15 percent were committed by family. That's 54 percent that authorities knew about. In 33 percent of the murders, the relationship between victim and assailant was unknown—that's the body-in-the-alley situation that nobody knows who killed. Only 13 percent of the murders were committed by a stranger. This makes me look suspiciously at that 33 percent unknown figure. If the same proportion holds true inside that 33 percent, you have about a 75 percent likelihood of getting offed by a friend, partner, lover, or family member.

Rape crisis centers figure that 75 percent of all rape victims know their attackers. The *UCR* is way off base with the rape numbers because it includes only violent rapes, not date rapes, and most rapes are not reported to the police at all. Some are reported to rape crisis centers with a request for silence. Even though a rape crisis center gets more victims than the police, a lot of women limp home and hide after the experience, and their rape goes unreported to anyone. The statistics get shakier and shakier.

Aggravated assaults made up 58 percent of all violent crimes in 1989—951,707 to be exact. That's nine hundred fifty-one thousand, seven hundred and seven reported assaults. Want to guess the number of unreported attacks? I don't. One of the scariest aspects about the way *UCR* statistics are compiled is the operating rule: no autopsy, no foul. It's attempted murder to the courts, aggravated assault to *UCR*.

I have been shot at more times than your average Vietnam vet, not including all the knife, club, and out-and-out fights I've waddled through, and I've got to admit that I never went to the police about anything. The same is true with my friends; hell if we could avoid it, we didn't even go to the hospital. Hospitals have a bad habit of calling cops. Now the intelligence of this is questionable, I'll admit, but if faced with a choice of sewing ourselves up or facing the cops, we'd opt for knitting class. So question any crime numbers you read.

Another thing about the aggravated assault numbers that you should look at is the geographic distribution. Certain areas prefer certain tools. Over the past ten years, guns and knives have run about 20 percent each in the nationwide picture of aggravated assaults. In the Northeastern states, the numbers were 16.3 percent guns to 22.5 percent knives, whereas in the Southern states, it was 25.3 percent guns to 22 percent knives. Oddly enough, the West had 19.5 percent guns and 15.4 percent knives—kinda low numbers. The leading category was "other weapons." This means clubs, blunt objects, chains, etc. In the Northeast, 34 percent of all ag asses were committed with these other weapons. In the Midwest, these accounted for 32.9 percent, while the South and the West were neck and neck with 30.7 percent and 30.1 percent respectively. The two regions you were most likely to get punched in were the Northeast and the West.

The *UCR* calls this next category "personal weapons"; I call it unarmed fighting. It entails using arms, feet, and other areas of the body as weapons. The West led all areas with 34.9 percent of the crimes committed with personal weapons, with the Northeast following at 26.3 percent. The West has Texas to throw the curve off.

I want you to sit there and think about all of these numbers. Let's take a guess and say that 75 percent of all assaults were committed by someone the victim knew. This may not be the exact number, but it's pretty close. Of those assaults, a good 80 percent were with weapons of some form. We're talking about people who knew each other! Somebody did something so far out of line that a person who knew him was motivated, damn near three out of four times, to pick up a tool and fuck him up. This is serious shit here!

A lot of times this is the result of people getting into a game from hell without being informed of what is really going on! Further, you are told that you can't question the system that results in such a high body count. The questions you are allowed to ask have incorrect answers coming back. So let's stop here, look at the bodies, and say, "Wait a fucking minute! If there are that many casualties, something is wrong!"

We've all heard that history is written by the winner. This is true in places where power comes out of the end of a gun. However, often what we don't hear is "He with the loudest media coverage wins." This is especially true in a so-called democratic society. Whoever can get more followers into his camp scores the most points.

There are some reports of smaller numbers beating a larger army in a toe-to-toe. Well someone went back into history (a reliable source, that's who) and gathered up the exact number of times that happened. It amounts to about 3 percent of the time. The other 97 percent of the time, the weaker side lost. On a much more personal level, the son of a bitch who tells you that size doesn't matter is lying out of his ass. When size doesn't matter is when skilled meets unskilled. I speak from experience on this one. As a skilled fighter against an unskilled bigger opponent, I kicked ass. As a skilled smaller fighter against an equally skilled bigger opponent, I got my ass kicked. That's why I lean toward weapons. "God created all men equal; Smith and Wesson guaranteed it." If size didn't matter, there wouldn't be different boxing weights.

If it is such an obvious lie, why do people still promote it? It's important to remember, most people in the game still think that somewhere there is a real sweetness-and-light, aboveboard game, where the rules really work and the game is played the way it's supposed to be. They think that they just fucked up and ended up in the wrong place. Very few people have ever actually stopped and compared notes from different games. They don't want to face this ugly reality, because if they did, they think they'd have to accept that there is no nice place.

The fantasy of a nicer place has kept a whole lot of people on a string on this planet. They convince themselves that although the current situation may be bad, it is just passing, and the real cookie is still up ahead. Then, one day they wake up and realize that they've been had. There was good and bad all along the way, but because they were looking for the good somewhere else, they never got the good that was there to be had.

The other reaction that many people have is to catapult themselves into the shit. They reason that it's all bad, there is no hope, and nothing good will ever come. The nastiness of the games from hell is all they expect from life.

So when you're out trying to find the truth, all you're getting is one side or the other. You're never told the full story. One side tells you never to look into the dark, and the other tells you never to look into the light.

Just as you are not to question the rules you are taught, you are not to second-guess the motives behind those who are teaching you. The "master" is beyond question.

Let's look at this in one specific area, the martial arts. I've fired off what is wrong with the martial arts in America elsewhere. I'm not going to do it again . . . well, maybe not as much. Ever notice how the instructors always look so confident? Strutting around the dojo in their crisp clean gis, they just ooze confidence, don't they? Understand, they are in a structured operating system there. They are surrounded by people who are not as well trained as they are. They know what is going to be thrown at them. They have nothing to worry about.

God help you if you question the efficiency of their moves. The instructors will show you how effective they are, all over your precious body. Whamo blamo! You now know that it works with a skilled opponent against an unskilled one, when the former is ready for the attack and the latter cooperates. What you don't know is whether it will work in the street against someone of undetermined skill and reaction.

All sorts of bullshit gets taught in these circumstances. Masters are teaching calligraphy when, in the streets, you need to know shorthand. In a real jam, fighting the way they teach will get you killed, while the streamlined version, which is very real and exact, can save your ass. Peyton Quinn and Mike "The Amazing Eagle" Haynick have an akido move, called the "Alien from Hell," that will put anyone on his ass ninety-nine times out of a hundred. The formal eight-step move will get you mauled in a barroom brawl, however. So they've reduced the formal move down to three quick, precise steps. Basically, it involves just grabbing the guy's face and pushing. It works for damn near everybody, while only a master can get away with the formal technique. (The shortened version is demonstrated in the video *Barroom Brawling: The Art of Staying Alive in Biker Bars, Beer Joints, and Other Fun Places*, which I collaborated on with Peyton and Mike. It is available from Paladin Press.)

Okay, let's expand on the situation of the teacher demonstrating on your head, the most common reaction you will encounter in any learning situation. That's not teaching; it's bullying. They have questions that are allowed and questions that aren't. The disallowed questions are heading into areas where their system doesn't work so well. How many times have you had questions answered with more force than is necessary? Yes, they're answering your question, but they're also backhanding you for asking it. After a while, you learn not to ask those kind of questions. Stick with a system long enough, and you forget those kind of questions even exist. Understand, I'm not talking just about the martial arts here. I'm talking about all aspects of your life.

In the real world, those questions you weren't allowed to ask *do* exist. In fact, they're often critical to making it without getting your nuts blown off. It's like boot camp again. You get trained not to ask questions and to follow orders, yet when you get out in the field, if you don't drop what you were taught, you end up a statistic. The other side of the coin—the side that keeps operating systems intact— is that, by teaching you only one way, the system ensures that you can't make it anywhere else. So you are stuck playing in that game, in that operating system.

The problem is, if you want to make it out in the borderlands, you'd better relearn to ask these questions. There is a great dedication in Ken Kesey's *One Flew over the*

Cukoo's Nest: "To Vik Lovell, who taught me dragons didn't exist then led me to their lairs." First teachers spend years pounding into your head that dragons don't exist, then off you go into the very home of *draceaus biggus*. While you're there, climbing the walls and freaking out about the dragon, they're standing there calmly wearing sunglasses, smiling, and lecturing that dragons don't exist. When, safely ensconced under a large rock, you query them with a cool calm, "*What the fuck is that then?!*" They either say, "It's a figment of your imagination," or "It's a dog." In the meantime, old brimstone breath is trying to dig you out to invite you to lunch.

This is an ugly scene to find yourself in. What's really bad is that everyday this scene is acted out in countless ways. How many times in your life have you been told that something is one way, while you're staring at something entirely different? If you're like most people, when you mention that something is amiss, you get slapped down, either verbally, emotionally, or physically, or told that you're nuts or stupid.

I used to think that I had been set up when this happened to me. I thought that people knew the dragons existed, but they lied to me. Part of me even suspected that they were working with the dragons. Needless to say, I was an angry young man. Using me for dragon bait pissed me off.

After a few of these little forays into dragons' dens, I had the opportunity to slay one of these pesky dragons. "Ah ha," I says to myself, "I've got it now. This is an initiation!" So I toddled over to the guy and said, "I have slain the dragon! I have passed the initiation!"

To which he replied, "What dragon?" It was then that the sickening truth dawned on me. These people *really* didn't see dragons. They didn't know that dragons exist. It's not out of spite, malice, or Machiavellian intent that they tell you that dragons don't exist. It's because they really don't fucking know! To them, dragons don't exist. *Draceaus biggus eatus youius* doesn't exist in their operating systems. If it's outside of their operating model, they don't see it.

After doing some research, I discovered that these people are made in such a way that they are not allowed to ask certain questions. If as a kid, they see a dragon, they get smacked for asking about it. Once they forget that these sort of questions exist, they are given a pair of sunglasses. These sunglasses are ultraviolet- and dragon-blocking. Put them on and you don't see dragons. Isn't that special?

These sunglasses, in reality, are various operating systems. Take this operating system and you won't see dragons. Take this one and you won't see violence. Take this one and you won't see drug/alcohol abuse. This way people can wander around happily not seeing things. If this kind of person happens to wander into a dragon's den, nine times out of ten, the dragon is going to be so confused by this nut blissfully wandering through its den that it won't eat the schmuck. People don't enter dragons' dens who aren't A) trying to slay it, B) bringing it a sacrifice, C) trying to cut a deal, or D) trying to commit suicide (it should be noted that all the others constitute the preliminary steps of D). That some bozo is walking through singing "Zippity Do Dah" puts the dragon on "tilt" status.

This is no shit. I've seen it happen. I was working in Compton (L.A.'s equivalent of Harlem), striking a movie set in a cemetery. I had a work crew of ten people, all very white. Included was a pale-skinned, red-headed Irish Teamster from the San Fernando Valley. He was about forty and not too bright. What's more, he had an attitude about me. We'd gone round-robin about loading the truck. Technically, he was right from a loading standpoint, but the way he wanted to load it buried the things we needed first deep inside the truck under everything else. I pulled rank, and we did it my way. He'd been pissy ever since.

So there we were, striking this set when a groundkeeper comes tearing by in stark terror. As he flew by, I got one sentence out of him: "*Gangbangers are coming!*" I tore across to where the rest of the crew was working, bellowing for them to lock it down and get their asses inside the mausoleum. I told white boy to get the truck locked down and moved out of the way. He copped an attitude, saying that I was overreacting. (I had two trucks, ten people, and about $200,000 worth of equipment to protect, and he tells me that I'm overreacting. Sheesh!) I told him to shut up and do as I said. The fool dragged his feet and didn't move the truck in time.

About seven hundred Crips pulled into the cemetery to bury their leader who had been blown away a week before during the incessant gang wars. I got everyone else into the mausoleum and started trying to figure out a way to tell the local Teamsters that their driver had committed suicide. The fool got out of his truck, stuck his jaw out, and walked dead center through one of the bloodiest Crip gangs in Los Angeles County. What's worse, the motherfucker was coming over to our hiding place! Yikes!

I sat there and watched as literally hundreds of Crips looked at this crazy-assed white fool. They were so shocked to see the guy walking blissfully through them that they didn't know what to do. I mean, they were dumbfounded. If the guy had shown one ounce of awareness or fear, they would have ripped him apart. Instead, they let him through.

He walked up to me and said, and I quote, "See, if you leave them alone, they'll leave you alone." The guy was so far out of touch that it saved his ass. The only person more surprised than the Crips was me.

That schmuck had the best pair of dragon-blocking sunglasses I've ever encountered.

How does this relate to self-defense? Let's take a look at those *UCR* numbers again. Do you think that the people who ended up adding their blood to the columns of numbers wanted to be there? Pretty fucking doubtful. However, somewhere along the line, they made a decision that put them on those stat sheets. It is my guess that one of three factors played a part in that boo boo.

1) *They were not familiar with the actual operations of the particular system they were messing with.* These are the guys who come from places where they can say things that are out of line and the worst thing that happens is they aren't invited to the next cocktail party. Then one day, one of them lips off to some guy on the street corner, and the next thing he knows, he's picking up his front teeth.

2) *They were familiar with the system but miscalculated the results of their action.* This is the most common form of suicide on the streets. Someone messes with someone else, but instead of staying alert to retaliation, he relaxes. Next thing he knows, boo ya! Permanent vacation. This occurs a lot with rip-offs and hustles. Someone thinks that he's come up with a way to get away with something, he gives it a shot, and, too late, he discovers that he was wrong.

3) *They thought they were untouchable.* This is closely related to number two, but it is more obnoxious. This is the guy who thinks that because he knows someone, he can be an asshole to him. Or the guy thinks that his dick is so big nobody will mess with him. There was a true-life TV movie not too long ago about a serious asshole in a Missouri town. The guy had been running amuck for years; then one day somebody shot him dead in the main street in the middle of the day. It's

funny, all those people standing there cheering and nobody saw who pulled the trigger. Imagine that.

The more common version is that someone has had enough shit and takes action. It's like the big brother who is always beating up the younger brother. One day the younger brother picks up a kitchen knife and plants it in the older brother's chest.

Actually, all three factors overlap, but for definition purposes, it makes sense to separate them. The bozo with the mouth thinks he's untouchable. He thinks he can use words to hurt people, but nobody can use anything else on him. I've seen this happen a lot with traffic accidents. The owner of the more expensive car gets verbally abusive and then discovers himself on the ground. Or a hustler comes down into a rural area and starts running shit on the locals. He thinks he's hot shit. He also thinks that people in the country react the same to getting conned as city folks. The police find him sitting in his car on a back road with his head blown off. Ooops. Or some white redneck who fucks with the Indians in town. One day he goes into an Indian-owned place in their territory and starts trouble. Damn, where'd he go?

One of the most common (and most often fatal) mistakes that people make is thinking only about the moment. The person planning the rip-off can see only the money that he'll get. He doesn't see that he'll have to be on the lam for a long time, in some instances, for life. This is especially true about rip-offs in the drug world. The guy who lips off isn't thinking about what is going to happen in a few seconds or when he walks out of the bar. The situation that really amazes me is the one in which a guy stomps someone and then thinks that it's over. No, no, no, no, no!

This is the thought pattern of the soon-to-be victim. However mistakenly he arrives at it, he comes to the conclusion that there is not going to be any ramifications for his actions, or he underestimates the reactions. A bully expects a person to fight back, but he also thinks he can overpower any resistance. Nine times out of ten, he doesn't expect the knife in the gut that he gets. If he had, he wouldn't have gone about it the same way.

A variation of this involves the guy who doesn't expect to get beaten off the draw. He gets his dick knocked out of joint and then comes back for a supposed one-sided rematch, but unfortunately—for him—the would-be victim is quicker. This amuses the shit out of me. Andrew Vachss is one of my favorite authors because he's real about the streets. I almost fell of my chair when I was reading *Blossom*. A grizzly old lawyer is explaining life to a young buck who is talking about proper law for someone who got blown away in a bar dispute. The young buck points out that the stiff only had a knife. The old guy tells him if you threaten a man in a South Bronx social club and come back with your hand in your pocket, you're supposed to get shot. That, he maintains, is the law!

I cannot come close to saying it any better. Yet you would be amazed at the number of times I have seen some fool think that he's going to get the drop on someone just by walking up to him. The person is so wrapped up in the moment that he doesn't realize he is about to commit murder or suicide.[2] If it's street against street, it's even money as to which one it'll be.

Remember, your would-be victim is not going to volunteer to be sent into the void. The farther you get from white upper-middle-class suburbs, the more likely that the guy will be ready for you. The flip side of that coin is if you jam with someone, you had better fuckin' expect him to back up on you. Thinking that he won't is the fastest way to the hospital that I know.

I really don't know what it is about the way men think, but I find that so many times men have this attitude of "It's over, I won." That's fine and dandy, but most times it isn't true. It isn't the first round that counts; it's the total at the end that decides the winner. It must be that men mistake the round for the whole match. I think this is one of the big differences between men and women. Women play for the whole match, while men go for winning the initial round. This is called endurance training. A man says, "No!" and he thinks the matter is settled. Later on, the woman comes at him again with the same idea. He says, "No," again, and this goes on until the man runs out of steam and says, "Gawd damn it, just do it and leave me alone!"

BUILDING AWARENESS

This type of awareness-building is not something that you do just once and walk away from. It's like exercising a muscle; you can build for one-shot strength like a power lifter, six hundred pounds in one shot. You can build for show—sculpt and puff—with very little real strength, or you can build for endurance, which is strength that does not wane.

On the physical level, I used to win most of my fights through endurance. I did circuit-training workouts, which if you've ever experienced them, you know are an absolute bitch. I would work out for three hours every day—an hour each running, with weights, and on the heavy bag. When I fought someone, he'd come on strong for the first minute or two, then he'd tucker out. They'd have shot their wad, and I would be standing there, smiling over their forthcoming attitude adjustment.

Where endurance really counts, though, is in the awareness area. By not realizing that things are going to last longer than the immediate moment, people disregard all sorts of important behavior—behavior from which they could have gathered enough clues to save their lives. You have to develop the ability to go a number of rounds not only in body, but in spirit, awareness, and emotions as well.

Understand, what I just said is sort of like saying all you have to do is move the mountain. Nothing like this is taught in standard Western culture. In fact, it's pretty much dormant in most folks today. You don't get awareness endurance sitting in a high-rise office staring at a list of numbers for twenty years. But the good news is that being dormant does not mean bred out. The fact that you are sitting here means that for at least two million years your ancestors had this sort of awareness. It kept them alive long enough to breed more of your ancestors. Those who didn't have it got eaten by lions, tigers, and bears. All we're going to be doing here is directing this awareness in a particular area. However, once open, awareness does have a habit of trickling into other areas.

Hyperawareness

At first, you are going to get your awareness in little spurts, which, like erections, will eventually falter. Don't worry because, like the aforementioned, awareness will rally back with a mind of its own once you pay some attention to it. At first you will go into states of hyperawareness. Behind each bush is a ninja; each rustle in the night will herald the attack of a drug-crazed serial killer. When you get into this state, your awareness is going to go batshit. It is this hyperawareness that explains the stories you hear about "masters" getting into fights, and the other person seems to be in slow motion while the masters have all the time in the world to move. Ah, young grasshopper, the awareness will be jumping big time.

There's a problem, however, with your awareness being that high—you eventually end up as jumpy as a man who came home with his wife and discovered his mistress had a surprise dinner waiting for them. You can't stay up that long, or you'll burn out. It is important to take it to the extreme for a short period. It's better if you can do it when you aren't exactly in the shit.

By doing it that way, if you ever end up in a code ugly, your body will know how to react. This is one of the goals behind boot camp: installing new physical imprinting. It's amazing how deep this imprinting must go. I still flinch every time I hear gunfire. My hermano Tim got onto a helicopter for the first time in twenty years. As they were flying toward their destination, he asked the pilot, "Is this LZ secure?" It's been many miles since Vietnam, and that motherfucker still rabbited off that Huey as if he were landing in a hot LZ. The nonvets looked at him as if he were nuts; he was looking for Charlie. This is the type of physical imprinting that is necessary.

In time, however, you begin to ease off the throttle as you realize you know what to do if necessity ever raises its ugly head. What you need to do to keep from burning out is to ease back to a place where an unconscious part of you is always scanning your surroundings. In time, you think about it as much as you do smoking a cigarette, chewing gum, or chewing tobacco. Really how much attention do you pay to the mechanics of chewing gum? When something comes up, you pay attention to it, but most of the time you do other things and let the part of you that deals with gum-chewing do its stuff. The same thing happens with your awareness.

Using Radar to Pick Up Trouble

Let's call this your radar. It's important to realize that it really is more like radar than defenses. The defenses are all there, but they are on standby. Face it, running defenses takes a lot of work and energy. When they are on standby, they're less likely to turn your ass into a frazzle. If you end up fried by having your defenses up when you don't actually need them, you won't have enough lead in your pencil to dick 'em, deck 'em, and dunk 'em when the shit hits the fan. This is what battle fatigue is all about: guys who have had to keep their defenses up too long. In World War II the shit got ugly but for set periods of time. You'd fight, win, rest, and move on. The guys in Vietnam were at defcon four all the time. They always had to have their defenses up. ZZZZZZT! Burn out!

The purpose of radar is to give you a warning that something is coming toward you. That gives you time to scramble your defenses up to the appropriate defcon level. General (later President) Ulysses S. Grant summed it up precisely. He posted a string of cavalry around camp at night. An aid asked him why he did that since any attack would surely blast through such a thin line. He responded, "They buy us time. That way we don't wake up with the bastards in our tents."

Here's step two about using radar rather than other defenses. Let's get our little poker hats out here and dangle our cigarettes from our lips as we ease the cards across the table. Now I'll tell you the truth, I'm shitty at poker because I don't know the odds and the probabilities of the various hands. What I am good at, though, is maintaining a poker face and bluffing.

If I have what I consider to be a hell of a hand, I'm not going to let everyone know exactly what I've got. Say I'm playing a-buck-a-hand poker. If I got dealt a flush and shoved fifty dollars into the pot up front, the only place you're likely to see faster folding is a kid ditching a *Playboy* when someone walks into the room. Anyone who decides to hang is going to be one of two things: a fool or someone who's going to be an absolute cocksucker to beat. Now if the kid's a fool, that's one thing, but if you're looking across the cards at someone who is downright frosty, you better start wondering.

Here's an important safety tip: *On the street only a fool shows what he has up front.* It's real simple. If you have all your defenses up and I check them out, I know how hard I have to hit you to beat you. Do you really want a full-scale blitzkrieg coming at you? You might as well be standing there pointing at your dick shouting, "Hit me here!" This is the main weakness of people with the "my dick is bigger than your dick" syndrome, usually young bucks. To show everyone, they have to leave it flapping in the breeze. They broadcast both strengths and weaknesses for everyone to see.

By using radar, you extend twenty miles out from your defenses, and you sprinkle that twenty-mile buffer area with booby traps, mines, and patrols. Anyone who gets close enough to know what you have in your arsenal must risk a recon, and recon teams have a habit of not coming back. Even if he gets into one part of your perimeter, he still doesn't know what you have over there. He can move into your space, but he's doing it blind. Only bozos move blind. With all those miles between your outer perimeter and your heavy-duty defenses, you can tear his shit up before he even gets close to your big guns. If he tries a stab at you, the next thing he knows he's got a 150mm landing on his ass. Oh, is that why I didn't want to be here? Remember, it is critical for this guy to be sure that he can get away before he moves. *If he isn't sure, he's not going to move ninety-nine times out of one hundred.*

By extending my territory with radar, I can foil, fuck up, sabotage, bushwhack, and rip the shit out of someone eighteen different ways before he ever gets close enough for me to use my big guns. Most people give up long before I ever get seriously ugly—the ones that are dumb enough to push in the first place. Those with some street smarts take a look and say, "There are easier people to fuck with; let this one alone." The pros walk up, look at the perimeter, and say, "I'm not touching that without a very good fucking reason."

Radar, then, is the first step in making people decide that it's not worth it to mess with you. It puts doubt in their minds. Remember, these people have to be selective about whom they fuck with. In a knife-fighting class I once taught, I made a comment that made ears perk up. I said, "I used to hunt the people who hunt you." Suddenly, everyone was all ears. Reaching quickly into my biological bag of tricks, I brought forth the concept of middle-line predators. These people are not only the hunters, they are also the hunted. These people are not invincible or untouchable. You have to realize this because, when you do, you can start sending out the real danger signals that these people understand and avoid, rather than macho fantasies.

Not Breaking under Abuse

Let's mosey back to sacred cows for a minute and take a look at some issues about life, the universe, and everything else. Most of what I'm talking about here is stuff you most likely have seen but probably did not notice, or it's things that you've noticed and gotten slapped for mentioning. Remember, slaps can come in all forms. The favorite is the backhand while answering the question in some fashion. This can come in a lot of forms: physically, emotionally, spiritually, and mentally. How the blows will come in any of these areas depends on where you are and who is doing the punching. Every time you take a shot, it affects all the other areas.

For instance, if you ask a question and get nailed verbally, it's going to affect you mentally. Then you'll feel stupid (emotional). If you get nailed enough, it will stifle you spiritually. There is nothing more pathetic than a person or animal that has been so beaten that its spirit is broken. This is the hardest part of teaching self-defense. By nature, a person wants to fight back and hold his territory. Only by years of training can someone be taught that he must take any abuse heaped on him. The fact that you are reading this book indicates to me that the system hasn't managed to break you, that you are fighting back the best you know how. Well here's some more ammo.

Beware, Logic!

Let us look at one of the keystones by which Western civilization holds the system together and the people subservient: logic! (Gasp!) I personally don't have as big a hard-on with logic as I used to. I consider logic to be like a roundhouse kick: limited in use and effectiveness, predictable, easy to defend against, and just generally tired from being overused. I was fourteen when I discovered that every bozo and his brother who had some martial arts training threw a roundhouse. The same can be said about logic. You can bet that anytime you start sniffing around the doors that lead outside of the normal way, someone is going to come up with something that he claims is logic to keep you where you are.

First off, let's look at what sometimes passes as logic. The truth of the matter is, you're more likely to encounter a bumblebee fart than you are true logic. What you encounter more often is a blend of logic and emotionally charged buzzwords. Most of the time the idea is to have you look toward a particular area rather than at the whole picture. This is what is involved in training you to march to the selected tune.

Logic is used to shoot down more ideas and realizations than anything else. See, we're taught that logic, science, math, reason, and rationality are what our system is based on. If something is real, it can be proven by math, science, or logic. If it can't, then it isn't real. To this system, feelings, hunches, or intuitions don't count. The idea that you have to be able to prove something for it to be real has run amuck in our judicial system to the point that these days you damn near need a videotape to get a conviction. This is the great bastion of logic and science. Prove it!

Here is another important safety tip, folks: *A logical argument can proceed from a false assumption.* Logic doesn't prove if something is right or wrong. All logic does is show if it is a self-consistent argument on a theoretical scale. Or in other words, does the argument contain any inherently inconsistent elements? Do you know that I can logically and mathematically prove that the world is flat? No shit, I had it done once to me by a woman showing me about logic. Unless you can pull up examples of physics to counterargue, I'd eventually make sense about the world being flat. Truth be told, you'd be sitting there going, "Bullshit," but you couldn't figure out what was wrong with the argument. This is logic run amuck.

Logic is like a karate tournament. The people in charge take away all sorts of effective moves and counterbalances and then play for points. The other issues that determine the outcome of a real fight are not addressed—issues which are critical if you want to survive. What's really sad is that after a while people forget that there is more involved and begin to think that a tournament is the real thing.

The same thing happens with logic. By taking away the real life checks and balances, you end up in La-La Land. From there on, it's a downhill slide. Unless you check it against reality every step of the way, you end up in left field. I'm not talking about checking logic against itself; I'm talking about putting it in the river and seeing if it floats. I heard a story about the first jet skis that illustrates this point well. The engineers had gone to elaborate measures to build these things so they would be unsinkable. They tested these skis against everything that they could think up to sink them. Everyone was really impressed with this little fact. Well, when they then went out to shoot the commercial demonstrating the ski, they had a cute model in the bikini to have her boobs wiggle as she rode it. It took the model exactly thirty seconds to sink the fucking ski. The fault was not hers; it's that the engineers had planned for the way *they* think, not anyone else.

What I'm trying to say is that logic is only one of the tools that you will need to master the skills in this book. What I'm talking about has less to do with a guaranteed response than what the hell is happening to you right then and there. That means that a full three-quarters of the information I'm talking about has zippo to do with logic as you were taught. What I'm talking about does not come from the part of the brain that deals with logic. How logical do you think Mr. Spock is during a fight with Klingons? When you got a 280-pound Klingon jumping your shit, another part of you has to be in control, not logic. Our society has taught you its version of logic so you won't apply real logic to some areas it wants to keep your inquisitive mind away from.

The reason is because *it ain't logic that ruins the system.* If society has convinced you that it is, you aren't going to notice what's going on in other areas. This is the "ignore the man behind the curtain" routine of the *Wizard of Oz.* Fuck that; we're going to look behind some curtains here. No more pissing down your back and logically explaining to you that it's merely precipitation.

What all of this leads to is that we are going to examine issues that are going to rattle some cages. A major point of resistance you'll run into is the person who is doing just fine with the system the way it is. This is the twit who Eric Hoffer described to a "T" in his book *The True Believer.* This is the guy who joins a mass movement less out of a sense of getting anything major out of it than just in getting a place to belong. These are the people often referred to as the masses (as in "The masses are asses"), the populace (as in "The denser the populace gets, the denser the populace gets") and, of course, the sheep (the little baa, baa, baas).

Believe it or not, these are the easiest people to deal with. You just nod your head and smile, and they do all the work in convincing themselves that you're one of them. Learn a bang word or two, and they go into a spasm of liver-quivering joy that you are one of them. The only time that they generally cause damage is if they get a tiger cub and raise it as a sheep. Then you usually end up with one fucked-up tiger. The other time that they can be dangerous is when they stampede. Nazi Germany was a particularly ugly example of what happens when the masses get out of control.

Your questioning the logic of some particular system or action can lead to trouble when you encounter someone who is benefiting from the system just the way it is. If every time a bell goes off, everybody jumps to the left three times and hands over a dollar, the guy who is collecting the dough isn't going to want anyone questioning what is going on. This one goes real deep and real wide, folks. Not all payments are in cash, either. There's a lot of currency in this world: power, control, ego gratification, and imagined safety can all be used as benefits. Watch this one, it can—and will—kill you if you're not careful. We will be treading close to these people's toes with this book. These are the people who know dragons exist but tell you they don't so they can turn a buck.

Who Benefits from the System?

There are two ways of benefiting from maintaining the status quo: direct and indirect. A direct benefit is when some guy gets glory, power, or moolah from a system, sometimes all three. Here you have your dictator, gang leader, evangelist, or unquestioned leader of a family. This situation is relatively easy to handle because you know who and what you're dealing with. The bad guy from the movie *Roadhouse* was a good example. He had the town wrapped up and wasn't about to change a good deal. It was pretty cut-and-dried: take him out and the system collapses.

The indirect situation is a real mofo to deal with. That's when someone or some people are benefiting from behind the players in the spotlight. These are the people who collect the dough when Simon says, "Jump to the left and hand over a dollar." Simon may get a cut, but the real collection is going on over on the sidelines. These situations are hard to deal with because—unless you know what to look for—you'll be watching Simon and the behind-the-scenes players will send someone along to take you out. This is the proverbial "power behind the throne" syndrome. These people won't come after you directly—they'll send assassins. These are the government and big business that stand behind the lab boys in science. The lab boys get the rah-rahs while the agency gets the bennies of the lab boys' work. This is also the mega corporation behind the lab boys, which makes sure that they don't come up with anything that would threaten the corporation's monopoly.

If you think I'm making this up, look up the life of Nikola Tesla, the grandfather of electricity. Tesla was the fair-haired boy of the early electrical power companies until he came up with a system that plucked electricity from the air. His discovery would have meant there was no more need for power companies. Tesla was stripped of his wings and halo and cast down from the heavens. His fall from grace happened in just three weeks. His theories were quickly discredited, about half of his plans and patents were "lost," and his name was deep-sixed. A guy named Thomas Edison went on to collect the fame and fortune. We now have a centralized electric system, which one atomic bomb would destroy—bringing the entire Western United States to a complete standstill. Gosh, that sure makes me feel comfortable.

Having a hidden faction benefiting from a system is real scary. It works from the very big to the very little—from multigenerational conspiracies designed to control mankind to the girl who is pissed at you and, by wiggling her tits, gets some knuckledragger to kick your ass. Someone is getting something from a system in either a nondirect or a nonpublicized way. These people will fight you the hardest in all manners and levels. Depending on where you are and who you are taking on, you can end up anywhere from ostracized to dead. They aren't fighters, but they send a seemingly endless supply of fighters after you. They profit without running the risk of getting shit spattered on them. Someone else will go down if you prove to be too hard of a nut to crack.

It is always important to watch who is standing behind the throne and profiting. Nine times out of ten these people will be the ones actually responsible for taking you out. Somebody else will pull the trigger, but they either set it up or approved it.

Listening and Learning about the System

Another important point this book addresses is that you can learn about these operating systems if someone is willing to talk about them. These lessons are not esoteric or obscure, no more than a dragon is really invisible. They do exist; most people just don't talk about them. You can learn about these things with out a Ph.D. (Piled Higher and Deeper). All you have to do is keep your eyes, ears, and, most importantly, your mind open. If you know about these systems, you can prevent yourself from crossing them unintentionally. Or if you have to cross them, you'll know what you're letting yourself in for, and you can cross them without getting your head blown off. Of all the victims in the *UCR* that we talked about earlier, the one thing I can say absolutely is that these people—someway, somehow—made an error with some rule of somebody else's operating system. Even a robbery gone wrong usually results from someone jumping the wrong way. A serial killer's motivation is in his own head, but his victims do something that makes the bell go off inside of that looney-tune melon.

This chapter was intended to wash some of the shit off the tools that we're going to be using in this book. Every day of my life, I see people flinch away from these tools because some asshole nailed them when they were younger for playing with the tools. Logic is not intrinsically bad; however, too many people have been kicked in the balls by someone who is hiding behind "logic." It is absolutely amazing what the illogical part of your brain is capable of doing, but society tells us not to look there. Yet we know that advertising relies on manipulating that part of your brain to sell products.

What really makes me want to rip my hair out and scream is that every day I see people use these very tools in a natural and healthy way; yet when I mention it, they freak out. Either they really are not aware of what they are doing, or they're using these tools in the dark for nasty purposes. Most of the time it's because they've been burned by someone using these tools clandestinely, and they don't want to think that they could be doing the same thing. In the second case, the person is using it as a weapon. If you turn on the lights, everyone will see what bastards they're being.

I've said it before, and I'll say it again: dysfunctional systems keep going by making sure you never question the rules or the definitions. Well, guess what, folks? I'm going to put on my little Pope hat. Okay, I'm the Pope, I speak for

God, and what I say is this: *"Question the rules, question the system, and most of all, question the definitions you were given.* Do not allow anyone to piss down your back and tell you that it's raining anymore. Amen!" Okay, my Pope hat is off now.

This includes questioning me. Look into what I'm telling you. Don't take anything that I say as gospel. Go out there and see if it works. I came up with many of these theories in the field. Check them out yourself. Even if you disagree; go out and disprove them. I have bellowed again and again that I do not know everything. Where you are is different from where I am. But probably not that far; that's why I can leave road maps. I've walked through these territories before. I give you what I have seen and learned. Take it and run with it.

Notes

[1] Unfortunately, the library, if it has it at all, is usually a few years behind in getting this exciting piece of literature. This is no real surprise since it is published by the U.S. government, which doesn't get its shit together with publishing it until August of the next year. Distribution is a joke.

[2] The main difference between a buck and a veteran is that there comes a point with a vet when he realizes it's no longer a game. Something clicks inside him, and he goes into combat mode. This is different from a "killing rush," which is a one-sided power trip that bucks mistake for combat. Real combat mode is *knowing* that, if you don't kill him right then and there, he's going to do you. A vet goes into the shit knowing that he's just as likely to die as the other guy; therefore, he's not going to start a fight for fun and games. Most bucks don't realize that they can get hurt or killed, and until they do, they'll jump in your face at the drop of a hat.

CHAPTER TWO

Cultural Operating Systems

> "All of your ideas come from one place. As long as that is true, you'll never be able to survive anywhere else. You will be stuck in whatever particular hellhole gave you your reality."
> —Me, lecturing at a workshop

The Chinese have a symbol called the yin yang. You've probably seen it; a local surfwear company adopted it as one of its logos. The yin yang is a circle with a white and a black teardrop making up each side. If you were to draw a circle and then draw an "S" through it, you'd get the basic idea.

This symbol is a whole lot more than just the logo of some clothing company, however. It represents the balance of opposites. Without one, you don't get the other. Things are defined not only by what they are, but what they aren't. You don't get high, unless you have low to compare it to; no light without dark; no hard without soft; etc. Neither is better than the other. They both are part of the whole. The point most people don't know is that this balance is always spinning round and round; it is never static, always changing.

Another thing the yin yang stands for is the balance between masculine and feminine. In case you haven't noticed, women are a little different than men, physically and psychologically. They mature at different rates, they operate differently, they have different senses of humor, and they have different priorities. It's amazing to see the differences. A woman will do things one way, and a guy will do them another. The problem arises when each side thinks that the other is totally nuts.

Tell me if this sounds familiar. You do something that is perfectly normal to you. The next thing you know your girlfriend is all bent out of shape about it. You sit there and wonder what the hell she is so upset about—you didn't do anything wrong. You try to explain why you did what you did in the best way you know how, and she looks at you like you've grown another head. What you did was motivated by a premise so basic that you're amazed she can't understand it. You look toward your buddy to see if you're explaining it wrong. He knows what you're talking about. Why can't she?

Well, guys, the answer is because she's a woman. And here's the catch: you do the exact same thing to her all the time. She gets just as exasperated with your not understanding what she's talking about. All of her friends know exactly what she's talking about, why can't you?

I cannot tell you the number of times I have sat there hunched over, with knitted brow and my tongue sticking out of the side of my mouth, trying to understand what a woman is talking about. It's less work understanding the outcome than it is trying to figure out how you got there.

Fortunately, I ran into a woman a number of years ago who looked at me in pity, patted me on the head, and said, "It's a girl thing."

I hate to say this, but women look at us with the same confusion, wondering, "How did you come up with that?" The basis of understanding is so totally different sometimes you think that we must be different species. Fortunately, I have a male equivalent of the "it's a girl thing." Now when I get that "I'm sitting next to a Martian" look from a female and what I'm talking about is something that any guy would understand, I say, "It's a dick thing." That let's the person know that what we're dealing with is totally foreign to her. It's not right or wrong, just totally different. Once that is explained, all sorts of relief comes flooding in. When a woman tells me "it's a girl thing" I can relax. It's not because I'm dumb that I don't understand, it's because I'm a man.

Most of the myths about women that float among the boys in high school are so dead wrong that I'm amazed they still persist. In high school, when most males are going batshit with hormones and trying to get laid, women are going through something different. Not only are they dealing with hormones, but they are going through emotional development. Your average high-school girl has a higher priority than sex: emotional bonding and closeness. Girls want to explore intimacy and relationships, while the other team is barking and drooling about getting their dicks wet. Women deal with something in their teens that most males don't explore until they're in their twenties. God damn, no wonder they damage each other.[1]

I cannot overstress how important it is to pay attention to the feminine side of the operating system you're in. It has a hell of an impact on how the whole game works. (I'll go into women and how your behavior around them affects your probabililty of encountering violent situations in greater detail in Chapter 13.)

I've got to admit that I just pulled a sneaky. By going through that little diatribe I pointed out how different someone that you snuggle up with on the couch is different than you. That is not news. Anyone over the age of fourteen spends a good deal of time trying to figure out his equivalent in the opposite sex. That's how different someone from the *same* culture can be. You want to guess what the differences are of someone from a *different* culture? You got it. That person standing next to you in the Stop and Rob store is literally from another planet. You've got to pretend you're from the *Enterprise* dealing with someone who has funny ridges on his nose and eats "gaghk."

Earlier I said that an operating system is designed to keep the group going. This is true. There are, however, three different types of operating systems: cultural, family or group, and personal. Basically, an operating system is a group of people who have gotten together and agreed that certain things have this meaning or that meaning. Other things are not allowed into the system and are therefore not noticed or seen. Certain courses of behavior are acceptable and others aren't. By everyone agreeing to play by these rules, a group identity is formed. Players from other groups are not allowed unless they take on these definitions and rules. Different ages and levels are expected to act differently. There exists set rules and systems for dealing with this.

In fact, to keep the balance and channel the young's energy, an ongoing antagonism may be agreed upon with another group. Depending on the group's standards, individuals who fail to conform are either expelled from the group or killed. This is all done with the consent of the larger group. Surprise! If you keep two subgroups fighting each other, they won't go ballistic on other groups. Ah ha!

Now this may sound like it was a conscious decision to do all of this stuff. Ugnh-ugnh. It wasn't. It sort of evolved. Initially, the people had to adapt to the environment, and this had a whole lot to do with how the people turned out, both physically and mentally. That's why the Nazi master race theory is such a crock. Every group evolved to survive in its own environment. This means not only body type, size, coloration, and skin thickness but also what foods they can digest best.[2] Don't think that coming from different environmental situations doesn't affect the way that these people look at the world; it does, big time. An Eskimo has forty-two different words for snow—not forty-two different ways of saying the same thing, but differentiation between forty-two types of snows and ices. They'd better if they want to make it out there.

One of the biggest shocks to anthropologists was when they discovered that the so-called Stone Age people of New Guinea didn't see things far off. These people live in some thick-assed jungle in which you can't ever see further than fifty yards. They're more likely to see only twenty yards before the bush cuts the view off. Yet, these people who can't see past a mile when they first come out of the jungle, see *everything* that's close to them. We're talking how many caterpillars there are in an area at any given moment.

The nastier the environment, the nastier fighters the people are. This does not mean that the people themselves are necessarily hostile. I have been shown some of the best hospitality and kindness in my life from these people—*once I had been accepted into their operating systems.* People from severe environments have to be tough, not in the sense of being badasses, but down-to-the-core rock hard. Otherwise, they'd just shrivel up and die.

We're talking surviving against the environment. Weather doesn't care how bad you think you are. It'll kill you just as fast if you're a would-be tough guy or a wimp. It's stone-cold-too-stubborn-to-die-type of people who make it in those areas. Take a hint about these people's fighting abilities. If they're not afraid of drought, famine, blizzards, tornados, scorpions, and snakes, why should they be afraid of you? Believe me, that has a whole lot to do with the development of a culture.

Another factor that affects how tough a people are is the number of times they have gotten their asses kicked. The so-called suppressed people have survived years of getting stomped on. The fact that the smaller number ethnic groups haven't been wiped out by superior numbers should indicate that they are some tough cookies. Look at the Jews. They've outlasted the Egyptians, Babylonians, Romans, and the Nazis. They've survived Muslim and Christian purges throughout history. Now the Israeli army is the top fighting force in the world today. We hoot and holler about *Top Gun*, yet every one of the Israeli pilots is that well trained.

Look also at the Koreans. The ROK soldiers are some of the toughest motherfuckers you'll ever meet. They were the ones who started ear collecting in Vietnam. They'd cut off the left ear of people they killed. Instead of confiscating rice caches, they'd slit some fucker wide open and let him bleed all over it. They'd leave the body and the contaminated food just to let the VC know where it's at. Koreans have been getting invaded since day one by the Chinese, Japanese, Mongols, and Manchurians. They've survived. I don't even have to tell you about the Filipinos. Once again, I'm talking about a down-deep core toughness.

These situations lead to operating systems that are a unique blend between rock-hard and ruthless. Anyone not of the tribe/people is looked upon as a potential unfriendly. In short, these operating systems often look at outsiders as targets. Whether it's to hustle you or kill you, they size you up right quick.[3] Anybody raised in this cultural system will have this characteristic.

So here you have a group of people who have survived the nastiness of the environment, as well as continuous incursions from other groups. Each of these has left a distinct mark on how these people operate and view the world. Now let's add religion.

This is probably one of the biggest double-edged swords you can get. The type and intensity of the religion determine how well you're going to get along with your neighbors.

There are seven major religions in this world: Christianity, Islam, Judaism, Buddhism, Taoism, Confucianism, and Hinduism. Each has its own particular flavor and mark that it will put on a people. Even if you have never set foot in a church, your parents were atheists, and you don't agree with religion, the prevailing religion will have left its mark on you. Religion has become so ingrained in our culture that it's impossible to escape.

The younger religions are usually the most violent, which means less tolerant of those who don't quack exactly as they do. Christianity and Islam are spin-offs from Judaism. Christianity didn't really pick up speed until the Roman Empire started rotting in the second century A.D., while Mohammed was kicking around in the late fifth and early sixth centuries A.D. Both of these religions were born of blood—Islam from the jihad and Christianity from the civil chaos of a dying empire. Islam is a warrior religion, while Christianity became bloody in its rise to power and subsequent power struggles.

Christianity did a complete about face when it came into power. Staying in power can be a brutal and bloody process. If you are of an ethnic descent that was Christianized, you've been getting double messages all your life. While it preaches, "Thou shalt not kill," the underlying message is "Thou shalt not kill anyone the powers that be haven't told you to off." Our military contains a huge number of good old Southern boys. Things may have mellowed somewhat in today's army, but there used to be an attitude of "Kill a Commie for Jesus." Western culture denounces the use of violence, yet we have the highest body count of any culture on this planet.

Religion changed over the centuries to stay in power. Unfortunately, many of the changes have been to gain or maintain secular power. As was to be expected, with power came corruption, greed, and violence. The U.S. system of government was set up to maintain a separation of church and state. For three hundred years prior, Europe had been washed in blood by religious wars. No amount of white washing can cover this fact. Don't think this doesn't affect what you were taught. American culture is deeply entrenched in this operating system.

Getting back to the present and how this affects behavior, one of the things that turned out to be real convenient for the elders was to label things that threatened the group's existence as being "against God's will." People's operating systems carry this stamp. A sizable chunk of the cultural operating systems that we have in America today come from the desert as it was two thousand years ago. In areas in which we have made significant technological advances to overcome these problems, we've blown off the restrictions.[4] In other areas, there has been little advancement. They may have dropped the "God says" part, but they kept the "it's wrong" part. The thing to ask yourself is, is something that would have threatened the continued existence of a small nomadic group in the desert applicable to you today?

Let's look at another cultural more that presses the buttons of young men in this culture: homosexuality. Eeek! Freak! Wig out! Guess what, folks, if you are living in a band of twenty people and dependent on producing a load of kids to keep the tribe going, it's not a good idea to have two breeders out of the program. The bottom line is that it threatens the group. What are operating systems for? Right, to protect the group. Since we now have something like four billion people on this planet, it's not likely that a few people deciding not to have children is going to hurt us any. There are a number of cultures where people just don't give a shit about whom you're sleeping with. Sorry, folks, no wrath of God, no burning hellfire; much of the stigma of homosexuality goes back to people being used by the group to keep going.

I purposely chose that example to hit your buttons. You have to look at what you were taught by the culture you grew up in. I'm talking about both the spoken and unspoken rules. Double check them. Do you agree with them? Disagree with them? Are they still applicable to the world you live in? Or are they antiquated and in the way? Or, worse yet, are you just carrying them around like extra baggage? The last case is worst because this crap was passed on to you by somebody who didn't want you to think about it. When you asked about it, you were told to shut up and take it. If you don't question now, you can pass it on to your kids, and the shit will never get weeded out.

In this wide world, very few things are across-the-board unacceptable. Things regarded as sacred by one operating system are totally irrelevant, of different value, or interpreted differently by another culture's system. In short, *social convention and beliefs are nothing but air.*

All of this relates to self-defense in that you have to be aware of cultural taboos and operating systems to survive. Even though these things are just air, like a tornado, they can kill you pretty fucking quick. It doesn't matter if you're blown off a cliff or a house lands on you, you're still dead. Air or not, people believe in these things. If you unwittingly cross one of the boundaries of an operating system, or fail to conform, it will not be the operating system itself that comes at you, but a person. Learn to make this differentiation.

Cultures deal with people who do not conform in three different ways: punishment, banishment, or death. Death can be attained through the other two, but it is still distinct enough to warrant its own category.

1) *Punishment.* Ah for the good old days—floggings, keelhaulings, the stocks, dunkings, and, my favorite, the gamut. These things were designed to induce pain and damage and to let you know that someone was not pleased with your behavior. Today, society has cut out most of the real exciting techniques and limited itself to things like fines and community service. (We'll talk about prison next.) For the most part, physical punishment toward adults is no longer culturally sanctioned. However, society still condones violence toward children. If a kid gets out of line, smack him one.[5]

Generally speaking, official American institutions have backed off punishment. However, punishment still exists in the subsystems on a social level. (Those of you in the military who've pulled shit detail for infractions know what I'm talking about.) This is the basis for a large section of violence in America. So even if punishment doesn't have the seal of approval from the Supreme Court, you're going to have to deal with it. Some guy busting your jaw is punishment for crossing some line.

2) *Banishment.* This is a real nasty one. In the old days it was damn near a guaranteed death sentence. You get kicked out of the tribe and not only are you dealing with losing your support system, but wild animals and other tribes do not have your best interest at heart. These days it can still kill you, but it takes longer. This really gets you in the heart and mind.

There are two ways this works. One is out-and-out banishing. You are not allowed here. Adios, good-bye, and get the fuck out of here. This can be forever or (more commonly) for a set period of time (prison) or until you shape up. Read: *Repent your evil ways and do what the fuck we tell you to do.*

Banishment is still sanctioned by formal American culture in the form of prison. The Catholic Church still practices excommunication. (I have a buddy who has been excommunicated three times. He's a little rambunctious.) Primitive people just declare you dead. They don't bother with too much brouhaha. They just ignore you. Nobody gives you food, drink, attention, or shelter because a dead man doesn't need these things. You have a choice: either straighten up or leave. Socially, this is what happens most often in America. The primitive people just do it formally. You can get banished from the operating system you're in real quick if you don't figure out the unspoken operating rules.

The second type of banishment is the "trash can" (yep, the same one we talked about earlier). When you are banished, you're automatically sent to the trash can, which means you have been written off by society. Yet, officially society hasn't kicked you out all the way. Banishment in the first sense is physical—you are thrown out of the territory of the old group. Cuba's response to America's telling it to allow its people to leave in the 1980s was to empty out all of their prisons and ship the people here. That is classical banishment. "Go and do not come back!"

The trash can is the most common form of social banishment. It's a real mind fuck. Being trash-canned means that, socially, you are being deemed a third-class person. Not only does it cut you off from society, but it literally brands you as trash. This is the proverbial scarlet letter for all good citizens to see and spit upon you.[6] For this to work, the culture must agree on what constitutes the trash can and then condemn it socially. At the same time, the culture must also support it as a dumping ground for its culls, which we'll look at later. The unfair aspect about this form of banishment is that you can be born to it. If you are born and raised in a trash-can operating system, you'll be branded as trash even if you haven't done anything wrong. It is in trash-can societies that violence flourishes. Most muggers were not born with silver spoons in their mouths.[7]

As you might have guessed there is a lot of overlap here between the two types of banishment. In order to understand them though, they have to be separated into two poles. After you get the idea, then you can begin to smudge them together.

3) *Death*. This is the final cut-and-dried version of the death sentence. This is not when somebody decides to teach you a lesson and hits you once too often. That's punishment that gets out of hand. This is the signed, sealed, and delivered hit, either an assassination or execution. Somebody has decided that you are a mad dog and need to be removed permanently. On the cultural level, this is the court-imposed death sentence.

There are only two levels of society that use death as an acceptable means, the very high and mighty and the trash can. At the upper reaches of society, political and industrial assassination is a very real thing, folks. One of the scariest things I've ever heard was when an old FBI friend of my dad's would say nothing about JFK's assassination except that: "First we did a cover up, then we covered up the cover up." Although most of the time the hits are on the individuals causing the problems, this is not always the case. The good news is that unless you are directly involved in big games, or closely related to someone who is, you're safe from punishment at this level.

The trash-can version of using death as punishment is pretty similar, with a few other twists. Ripping off somebody in a drug deal, breaking the code of silence, or any other host of operational violations will get you snuffed. The flip side is when somebody is looking for a promotion. You are a drug dealer, and you want to expand your territory. Unfortunately, the guy who occupies that space does not see the wisdom of working for you. Instead you do the trash-can version of a leveraged buy out (LBO). This comes in the form of a guy named Guido from Chicago. A personal version of this type of punishment is referred to as murder. In 1988 there were 20,096 reported homicides.[8] While there is no exact breakdown as to how many of them were planned versus spur-of-the-moment things, you can bet that a majority were done by someone who felt that the soon-to-be DOA had done something seriously wrong. In fact, a whole lot of them were done by people who did indeed mean to kill, not just hurt, when they moved. Depending on the situation, the courts will decide on the punishment for this little foray into natural selection. The first time I heard the "He needed killing" defense, my jaw hit the floor, and I nearly fainted when the jury understood what the guy meant. Generally speaking, though, the courts frown on this sort of behavior. Oddly enough, there is great deal of support from subgroups on a lot of killings. If the person was a real asshole, generally there's a sense of "good riddance to bad trash." Or to shorten it down to Texanese, "There ya go."[9]

These are the general operating systems of any culture. These are the professed and the not so loudly spoken rules that have shaped a culture or an operating system. I hope I have pointed out to you the serious impact these systems have on the way people think. They color the way people deal with you and how you should deal with them. Regardless of what you think of the validity of their system, when you are on their turf, you dance to their music. If you want to stay around, this is especially important. Understand that, like the basketball game from hell, the real operating rules are unspoken. The official rules seldom have anything to do with what is really going on.

Not only do you have to respect other people's rules, you also need to unplug any knee-jerk reactions from your head. If you adhere to a system and its rules, do it by choice, not from a belief that it is the only way to do things. It's amazing how deep this implanting goes. Most times it's like a land mine that lies there quietly for years, then one day you find yourself in that territory and boom! I have certain knee-jerk reactions that were instilled in me by the way I was raised. I've spent years getting rid of them. I've spent time in places where regardless of what I felt, acting on it would have caused a blood bath.[10]

To tell you the truth, it's most often a matter of degree. Most cultures are more or less tolerant of different things. What one culture tolerates with a shrug, another wigs out about. You have to be the judge of what you do and if it will get the taxpayers nervous.

Notes

[1] Guys, as a recommendation to get through this phase, I would highly suggest finding yourself an older woman. Someone in her teens or early twenties or so is great. She can take you by the hand (and other parts) and show you exactly where it's at. This was one of the best things that ever happened to me. I avoided the damage most people get in high school from the opposite sex. Instead of two kids groping around in the dark hurting each other, I was taught how to be considerate and caring about my partner's needs and feelings. In short, I was house-trained early, and I enjoyed the process. Any women reading this, consider it a chance to teach a man to do it right. It's a hell of a nice gesture to your sisters.

[2] While I admit that the Dairy Board has gone overboard with its advertising, people of Western European descent can digest cow's milk products better than other races. Nonherding people can't break down the lactate as well. Orientals handle rice a whole lot better than Caucasians. Their bodies grew accustomed to whatever was around. We're talking evolution here.

[3] Since many systems believe they've been fucked, they feel justified in hustling others. The system you're dealing with determines how likely you are to be hustled. Many groups have strict rules about doing business inside the community. They will remain honest and straightforward with anyone of their tribe, but, with outsiders, all rules are off. Other groups will rip off each other just as quickly as an outsider. It's every man for himself. When you deal with them, everybody is looking for the opportunity to screw everybody else. It's like playing poker, and everybody is cheating. However, certain groups play across-the-board with everybody, but they will also immediately drop you into the ground for fucking with them—without even *thinking* about it. It's routine business for them. Needless to say, it's important to know which one you're going to do business with.

[4] Refrigeration, science, medicine, and urbanization are the leading causes of old systems being dropped. As advancements were made in these areas, the reasons behind the rules became clear, and some changes could be made. For example, did you know that, technically, indoor plumbing is a sin? It is according to Deuteronomy 23: 12-14. If you camp out or have been in the military, where do you put your latrine?

[5] Oddly enough, I'm directly opposite. I believe in violence toward adults, but children are off limits. Hitting kids is no fun; they can't fight back. Hmmm, maybe that explains why kids are the targets of violence.

[6] In Puritan society, women found guilty of adultery (whether they did it or not) were forced to wear a large letter "A." This way everyone knew who they were and what they were accused of. The Nazis did the same thing with Jews and gays—not with an "A," of course, but with a recognizable symbol.

[7] This is why it is so important to look at the system you were brought up in. What may seem normal and right to you could very well be a trash can to the rest of society. You can spend your entire life beating your head against the wall trying to get out of there. But the truth of the matter is that, unless you drop the subsystem's operating procedures, you'll never get out. Race, creed, or color isn't what traps you; what will keep you down is failing to adopt new operating systems.

[8] *1988 Uniform Crime Report,* printed by the Government Printing Office. It's in the library.

[9] Texans amuse me. They are such a weird blend of rock-hard, friendly, kind, generous, down-to-earth people mixed in with the biggest egotists and most convoluted, crooked operating systems I've ever seen. God bless Texas; I think He's the only one who can understand 'em.

[10] Rapists and child molesters are the two groups for whom I'm going to hang onto my knee-jerk reactions. While I joke about the good old days, these people's heads should be put on stakes. Everything else I can tolerate, but not these guys.

CHAPTER THREE

Family/Group Operating Systems

> "A society founded on the family territories, innumerable peripheries, and an unholy complexity of inner antagonisms is a society of remarkable staying power. It is flexible. Lacking heart or head, it is difficult to kill. It may lose a portion of its body this century and get it back the next; in the meantime the absence of an arm or leg goes virtually unnoticed. It is healthy."
>
> —Robert Ardrey
> *The Territorial Imperative*

Here they are, boys and girls, the little beasties that cause more bloodbaths than any other thing in this world. These things define our identities, our rules, our morals, our loves and hates, our sexual standards—in short, everything about us.

I'm talking about the family/group operating systems that we grow up in, live in, and die in. They mold us, shape us, use us, and sometimes kill us, depending on their needs.

There are two aspects of an operating system: core (deep) and surface (temporary/outer). Most people never see past the surface systems.

Do you remember the story about the three blind men who had never encountered an elephant before? One grabs the trunk and says the elephant is like a snake. Another grabs a leg and says that the elephant is like a tree. The third muckles onto . . . what does the third guy grab? Shit, I forget. Anyway, he grabs onto some other part and makes a call as to what the elephant is like. Then the three blind men proceed to get into a fight as to what the elephant is really like. The version my lady and I remember is that their fighting scares the elephant, and he squishes all three of them. As kids, we used to giggle how dumb these guys were. Yet as I get older, I see where that story was coming from.

Most people make the same mistake that these three blind men made. They take the part that they know and deem the whole thing to be that way. Or to put it plainly, they think that their operating system is the whole world. This is what I meant when I said that most people mistake the model for the real thing. This can also happen with groups.

The longer a group holds onto believing that their models are reality, the more entrenched these systems become. This is how the cores of a group are formed. In time this results in filters that come between the group members and the larger whole. In short, entire groups begin to suffer selective blindness. They then search out others who will substantiate their blindness. Those who generally think along the same lines gather here, while groups of radically different ideas gather over there. All of them make judgments about the other groups (which are invariably wrong) and then proceed to teach their children these judgments and models.

This is like the blind men teaching their blind children what an elephant is, and why so-and-so over there is so stupid for saying otherwise. In the meantime, so-and-so is over there telling his kids the same thing about the other two guys. The various groups occasionally throw rocks and insults at each other. Since they're blind not much damage is really done. Of course, if they get too out of line or accidentally bean the elephant, it just tramples them until the next group of blind men come along.

Regardless of what you may have been taught, nothing is locked in concrete. Another one of those "if you get nothing else out of this book" is—even if you know that nothing is locked in concrete, remember that you are dealing with people who believe it is. The belief that it's locked is in itself a blinder. This blinder is protected by the never-question-the-system rule.

This has to do with self-defense because parts of these systems are designed so that you'll fight some other schmuck from another system. I'm talking hereditary enemies here: group, religious, and racial hatred. I grew up in a place that had race riots—blacks against the Mexicans, Mexicans against the whites, whites against blacks, etc. This legacy is dangerous if you don't unplug it. Understand, you've been set up by your system! You were taught to dislike—if not to out-and-out hate—other operating systems!

Until a person leaves the blinders of his system, he cannot see the reality of another. Each particular operating system holds on to that part of the truth that is applicable to it. No one is entirely right or, more importantly, entirely wrong. As with physical evolution, operating systems evolve to meet the needs and problems that confront them most immediately and threateningly. (To hell with it, from now on I'm just going to call them OS rather than spell out operating system.) They've worked for generations and are as dug in as an Alabama tick. We are talking core here.

Reread the opening quote of this chapter and then realize that none of the major cultural upheavals we've experienced in the last two hundred years lasted much longer than ten years. What came out of them may still be in existence, just in a milder form. That quote talks about centuries and rightly so. Rocks change faster than core operating systems.

The surface structures have been replaced consistently, but what's down deep remains amazingly similar. It's not whom you hate, but rather that the system is designed for you to hate someone. The groups hated by society change like the wind, but the fact that somebody is always hated is the important part. In the early 1800s, it was the Irish, then the North/South split, then the Indians, then the blacks, then the Jews, then the Mexicans—it doesn't matter, somebody gets spit on.

What I'm talking about here is the deep structure of a socioeconomic/family subgroup. This is the OS part of a cultural strata. The core OS is amazingly similar. If a drunk from 1800 were to meet a modern drunk, they'd spend a hell of a lot of time trying to figure each other out, but they'd both get bombed while doing it. Does this surprise you? If you were to take a person out of a culture and put him/her into another country, that person would gravitate to the equivalent social level that they were from back home. The surface structures change all the time; literally every decade, they are totally replaced.

Deep structural changes, however, occur over several generations. This is what is meant by the old saw, "If you want to make a lady out of someone, start with her grandmother." Core systems don't change unless there is an extreme emergency or something radically improved comes along. Radically improved systems take generations to implement. The only type of extreme changes that work over the long haul are emergencies, like the land becoming desert or big, strong invaders who aren't going to be leaving soon. Even then it is slow going to implement change.

In fact, the best analogy I can come up with is mushrooms. There are certain mushrooms that are like giant spiders turned upside down and buried. Instead of eight legs though, these things have thousands. The mushrooms are all part of a connected central underground net. The individual mushrooms poking out of the ground are nothing more than tips of this giant net's fingers. Some of these nets can extend over a square mile. With every change of the season, the surface mushrooms are wiped out, but the net remains. The core OS is like the net, while the surface OS is the mushrooms.

You may be operating in a group (one mushroom over there) that is part of a huge socioeconomic strata (or net). You can move from group to group ('shroom hopping) without too much trouble. Of course, you can get your head blown off while going between groups—nobody said it was entirely safe. It's when you try to leave the entire network to go to another one that it gets hairy. It can be done, but it's rough.

This brings us to an important concept called Sturgeon's Law. Old Ted Sturgeon was an anthropologist who came up with this maxim that has won the hearts and mind of many. Sturgeon's Law says, "Ninety percent of everything is crud." Well, I like that, except I'm going to amend it slightly. *"The remaining 10 percent is the core operating system of that network."* That is the stuff that does not change no matter what toadstool you are sitting on in a particular network—the network from which all like mushrooms spring. The 90-percent crud is the exact rules and regulations of the particular mushroom (group) you're perched on. (Again look back at the chapter quote.)

Most subgroups are surface-operating systems. They come and they go. Like the little mushroom that sprouts up, each subgroup is different. It has its own rules and acceptable behaviors. While it is there, it is valid. Next year it dies out, and another pops up to replace it. Now a number of subgroups can grow next to one another and appear interchangeable. They pretty much are, but they are still separate. The rules can change from cluster to cluster without your ever leaving the network.

Taking the mushroom analogy a little further, I want you to think of some little guy standing on a toadstool in the middle of a cluster, claiming that his particular cluster of mushrooms is the entire world. This is what most people do. They don't even get close to the network before they start claiming that they have a monopoly on reality. When the little SOB has a gun and starts using it on those who don't agree with him, you have a problem on your hands. If you're from another cluster—or worse yet, another network altogether— homeboy there might just get an attitude about you.

Remember, when you are dealing with other operating systems there is no such thing as right or wrong. But, more importantly, remember that not too many people know that. If they deem you out of line, they will react somehow— often violently. But if you know the core operating system of any large group, you can travel the smaller systems without too much trouble. Because I know the nine rules of the street discussed in the Introduction, I can survive in any subsystem that is based on them.

• • •

All right, I've bored the shit out of you by rambling about networks and operating systems. That still doesn't give you an idea of how this stuff works in reality and what it has to do with self-defense. It's time to bring it back to nuts and bolts that you can apply to not getting your ass kicked. So let's look at applied theory in the big bad world.

USING LOCAL CAMOUFLAGE
TO AVOID TROUBLE

The object is to get by. If you can do it without fighting every step of the way, it'll be easier in the long run. I used to be real far-out looking. I had my street identity, and I flaunted it wherever I went. Motherfuckers came out of the woodwork to fight me. I'd be walking along and some guy would have to try the hippie. I got into a lot of shit that way. At first, I knocked heads with every Tom, Dick, and Harry who came up against me. After a while, that shit got real old. I was trying to get laid, and they were trying to pick a fight. Go away, pal, I'm busy.

In time, I began to watch people and see what the ones who weren't getting into fights all the time were doing. There were two (actually three, but the third method applies to specific individuals and is discussed in Chapter 14) ways of avoiding shit.

The first way involved being a beta, or submissive, personality. The idea of going belly up all the time didn't really appeal to me. (Alpha, dominant, and beta behavior is discussed in more detail in Chapter 12.)

The second, and more attractive, way was to look and act like the locals until you were out of their territory. The idea was to not stand out too much. I began to watch what was involved in that little bit of camouflage.

To survive in a subsystem, you must know (and be able to do or imitate believably) the following:

1) **Language:** This is the key tipoff for many people. It consists of:

Dialect: Even though English doesn't have official dialects in the classic sense, there are enough differences in the way we speak to identify the locales and social levels we're from. Dialect includes accent and cadence.

Grammar: How are sentences constructed? Not what is good English, but how do people talk in certain areas? Cajuns, for example, have a habit of changing the sentence structure. "Middle, boat put de" means, "Put the boat in the middle." Not that you or I would understand it, but another Cajun would.

Slang: The casual shorthand that a group uses to communicate is slang. Words like "ya'll" and "ain't." are common slang words.

Bang words or slogans. These are different from slang in that they are more specifically applied to the operation of certain groups. They are also called "buzzwords." For example, anyone from Texas can use "ya'll," however only someone from a twelve-step program (Alcoholics Anonymous, Narcotics Anonymous, Gamblers Anonymous, etc.) will talk about "The Steps" or "one day at a time." Bikers talk about pans, shovels, knuckles, and evos (evolutions for you nonbikers).

2) **Level of Awareness:** This one is tricky. If everybody else is going, "Baa, baa, ba!" and you go, "Howl," there is going to be trouble. Then again, going, "Baa," when everyone else is howling ain't the sharpest idea either. Oddly enough, one of the most revealing points of how the white middle class operates is not in what they talk about, but rather what they don't talk about. If you show that you are too aware of certain things, they will get upset. On the other hand, lack of awareness means you're lunch in other circles. Street people are extremely aware and alert.

3) **Similar Ideas:** If you suddenly find yourself among members of a selected Crip gang, it is not the time to express your ideas of white supremacy. While that should

be obvious, you'd be amazed. Another thing is if you find yourself in rural Kentucky, you don't tell them that their ideas are holdovers from the Dark Ages. Generally speaking, you stick a toothpick in your mouth and grunt an affirmative at the right times, and most people will think you share their ideas. You do that until you can get the hell out of there.

4) **Similar Toughness:** This isn't exactly the same as awareness. It's more along the line of being able to turn the volume of how tough you are up or down. For example, when I hit the Indian reservations, I look like someone who would casually flip rattlesnakes out of my way. When I am sitting in a millionaire's mansion in Beverly Hills, I look so civilized that I would die of shock at the very idea that I wasn't house-broken. By the way, it's harder to become less tough once you have it than it is to become tough.

5) **Intelligence:** If you show too much intelligence, the natives will get restless. If you don't show enough, they'll get snotty. If you're around a pack of sadists, their snotty can get vicious. I should point out this also includes "foreign" ideas. If you have been traveling abroad, asking the real estate agent in Harrisburg, Pennsylvania, if the bathrooms have bidets is going to get you talked about on the local gossip circle. Then again, telling a bank president to go outside and pee in the bushes instead of waiting is going to get you looked at mighty funny as well.

6) **Food and Eating Habits:** In a greasy spoon in the middle of Kingman, Arizona, I order eggs, corned beef hash, and biscuits and gravy, while my lady orders eggs florentine. I suddenly develop a headache. Different operating systems look at food in different ways, including what is considered edible. (The banquet scene out of the

movie *Indiana Jones and the Temple of Doom* is priceless.) However, in many systems it is considered a mortal insult if you do not partake of offered food. If they offer you squid, you eat squid without a fuss. Then again, don't order sushi in Bay City, Michigan.

7) **Nonverbal and Other Body Language:** This includes eye contact, space between people, blind spots, how people move, and whether touching is allowed. If so, where and how much? How loud you can get, and how do people hold themselves and move? This is especially important in warrior societies and during drug deals where a wrong move can be interpreted as your going for a weapon. (Eye contact and the trouble it can lead to are discussed in detail in Chapter 12.)

8) **Sexual Roles and Interaction:** What is the status of the opposite sex? How are the different sexes supposed to behave? Can you approach the women, or are they off limits? Is the woman supposed to be kept on a leash, or is she an equal? Is the male responsible for keeping her in line? Is a woman supposed to be independent? If so, how and to what degree? Want to commit suicide? Take a New York Jewish American Princess into a sleazy honky tonk bar in west Texas on a Friday night. You won't get out of there alive. (I have already discussed this topic briefly in the Introduction and in Chapter 2, but it is so important that it will crop up again from time to time in other chapters. Also, Chapter 13 is devoted entirely to the relationship between women and violence.)

9) **Age Status.** Although virtually forgotten in white culture, a large number of societies and operating systems respect the elderly. You may be able to get away with knocking down an old lady in New York City, but you will be hunted down and killed if you try that on an Indian

reservation. What is the expected behavior for your age? Jumping on the barroom table and singing the "porcupine will never be buggered" is not acceptable behavior for a fifty-year-old.

10) **Etiquette:** How and in what order are things done? Do you insult someone by sitting down before he does? Does sitting there with your toes pointed at someone insult them? (It does in Vietnam. A friend of mine who is a district attorney in Long Beach told me about this murder case. Long Beach has a large Vietnamese population, and the Vietnamese have serious rules about feet. It's considered rude to point your feet at someone, and showing them the bottom of your feet is a mortal insult. Well, this guy walked into a Vietnamese nightclub in Long Beach and put his feet up on the table, with his toes pointed toward the musician on stage. The musician pulled a gun and wasted the guy. Charges were initially filed, but they were ultimately dropped on the grounds that the deceased had knowingly and intentionally instigated a fatal conflict.)

If someone bows, how low do you bow in return? (Depends on your status.) Is it healthy to flip someone the "Okay" sign in Italy? (Don't.) Is burping after a meal rude, or does it show the host how much you liked the meal? Do you hold the door open for women, or are they on their own? Is being polite an indicator of your knowing how to behave and the fact that you don't want trouble, or does it signal that you are a target?

11) **Local Talents and Jobs:** If you are in a place where knowing how to fix you car is expected of a man, you better learn something about automotive repair. If you live in an area where you're expected to go out and help the neighbors harvest the crop, you better learn how to pick. I've been places where the local talents were hot-wiring

and B&E (breaking & entering). What are the expected skills of the operating group? Stockbrokers are not expected to know how to fix plumbing, and a plumber isn't expected to know how to manage a portfolio. It's funny, I sit there minding my own business until suddenly somebody locks themselves out of house and/or car, and then everybody looks at me. *What?*

12) **Similar Belief System:** If you are a fundamental Baptist living in the middle of Jamaica, you might be in for some problems, especially if you go around calling everyone else devil worshippers. If you are an agnostic who has sworn off the church and you suddenly find yourself in the middle of a group of devout Christians, smile and start looking for the door, casually edge toward it, and make good your escape.

Basically, the only time you should tell people to go fuck themselves over religious beliefs is when they bang on your door at eight on a Saturday morning when you are hung over. Before reacting to behavior that seems strange to you, check out whether you are dealing with a lone nut or the entire area feels this way. In certain places, not being seen in church is social suicide. If you piss on somebody's beliefs, you can get hurt. Even if you are a devout Christian, do not go spitting on someone else's religion. Doing a "Jesus and the money lenders" routine on someone's relics is going to get you sliced from asshole to eyeball.

13) **Similar Energy:** This is like the "miscellaneous" category; it covers everything else. It is kind of subjective, but it is critical. All I'm going to say about it is that different areas have different "feels" to them. I sometimes call them smells. Music colors it. Songs like the Doors' "L.A. Woman" capture the feeling of the Hollywood that tourists never see. What are the batwaves of an area? What is the people's energy level? Are

the people charged or totally D-watt? If you go prancing around singing "Zippity Do Dah" in a low-energy operating system, you're going to stand out like a sore thumb. If you hit an area that just doesn't feel right, get the fuck out of there.

All of this may sound like hypothetical woo-woo, but let me assure you, it is not. If you go into a place and you do not match these operating systems, you can get torn up real bad. Realize that, as an outsider, you do not have the protection of the group, or as a group member who fails to conform to the OS, you run the risk of trouble.

It is critical to remember that most people have never even considered looking at operating systems and their rules and mores, much less done an in-depth study of them. Most folks just go toodling along in life, reacting to this operating system, never looking at what's really going on underneath. It's important to have a general idea of what is going on before you enter a territory. The details you can get as you go along.

Your family has instilled in you a deep structure. This is stuff that is imprinted in your psyche. It's so deep that it is the equivalent of body knowledge. You're mind can say one thing, but if your psyche is imprinted with another, it's going to drag you that way, like a dog by its dick.

Here is real ugly. Regardless of what parents/teachers/society said about not being violent, the imprinting that most people received contains violence. It is useless to hit a kid while telling him not to hit his siblings. That imprints violence. Generally speaking, people bring it out with them into the world. When you are dealing with people in a conflict situation, most of them think that intimidation and violence are the only ways to solve problems. This is not the best conditions under which to negotiate.

Now as you may have gathered, surface groups come and go. A particular cluster may remain, but the individual groups are ever changing. They change because of age, outside influences, migration, marriage, divorce, deep programing overwhelming participants, evolution, and, of course, death.

Look back at your own history and think of a group of friends you once had. What happened? Somebody moved, someone else met this girl and went off that away, other things started coming up that took more time away, a couple of the folks had a fight, one person died, or, more often, you just went separate ways. This is part of life.

Understand that even if you don't decide to go traveling like I did, you will be staying in a cluster. Different groups and cliques will come and go in that cluster. You'll find yourself in different places throughout life. The groups change as you change. You get older, and you'll find yourself doing other things. Getting married and having kids will do all sorts of things to the way you look at the world.

VIOLENCE-PRONE GROUPS

Let's begin to take this discussion back toward self-defense and examine the groups that use casual violence.

The Young

Generally speaking, most groups that use casual violence are young. They haven't caught on yet to the fact that they are mortal. The human body is an amazing thing when it's young. It can repair itself at an astounding rate. You can heap all sorts of abuse on it, and it just bounces back. So hey, hey, hey, let's go for it. This is one of the things that makes being young such a pain in the ass. There are people out there who don't think twice about starting a fight. In short, they haven't caught on that violence is not a game yet. And they really aren't that precise about the violence that they start.

What generally slows down these groups are that they get older, they heal less quickly, mornings begin to hurt, they get fired from some jobs because they were too torn up to go to work, they get an old lady, maybe have a kid or two, they end up taking friends to the hospital, they get tired of hassling with cops and getting thrown in jail, and—the biggie—they start burying friends. All of these things slow down violence-prone youngin's.

(What I have said here about youth-oriented groups is generally applicable to a great many groups. However, it is not specifically applicable to formalized gangs. I'll talk in detail about some characteristics that are specifically applicable in Chapter 10.)

Warrior Societies

Now we get to the part of the map that reads, "Here Be Monsters." The second group that uses violence is the warrior society. These are people who may be beaten by superior numbers and firepower but are pure hell in a one-on-one. For example, your average Apache won't try anything if he thinks the odds aren't in his favor. On the other hand, an Apache's idea of good odds is around twenty to one—that's twenty of you to one of him.

In short, when dealing with warrior societies, throw them some raw meat and leave them alone. An important safety tip: *Every culture has a warrior segment.* You can meet white, black, Mexican, or Oriental warriors. They're easy to spot and usually easy to avoid. Generally speaking, they don't mix outside of their own. It is a comforting thought to realize that the only way to get hurt by these people is to mess in their territory. But if you piss in their territory, you will disappear.

A less-organized version of the formal warrior society exists in certain communities. These groups attract a select group of people and are not organized or localized, but they definitely must be considered. Their members are generally older and much more efficient with violence, e.g., the biker community.

Bikers have formal clubs, but they also leave room for independent warriors within their midsts. They are not in clubs or cliques to show you how tough they are. They're tough, and they know it. It's not a game to them. They will hurt you bad—no fluffing, puffing, or bluffing. Stompings, chain-whippings, stabbings, and shootings—they use them all. If you annoy them, they'll stomp you. If you piss them off, they'll stab you. If you get them really angry, they'll kill you.

Drug Dealers

We now get to the third group that uses violence: drug dealers. In my opinion, there are four general types of drug dealers:

1) the addict who is supporting his habit
2) the person or couple who is supplementing his/their income
3) the gonzos who like the flash and style of "The Life"
4) the professional who is doing it for a living and is no-nonsense about it all

The addict who is peddling can be dangerous if you deal with him. You're never sure if he's going to sell you drugs or rob (and maybe kill) you. Not only is he spooky, you never know what he's selling. He is addicted to the product and is basically a corkscrew with legs. This also applies to the manager of a rockhouse or a storefront. If this type is not an independent, he works for the fourth type of drug dealer, the professional.

The second type of dealer is probably the safest. This is the person who has a regular job and may also supply the office with drugs. Of all the dealers, this type is the least violent and has the most established location. This is the kind of person that you go over to his house after work to buy some product and then party with him. A deal still can—and often does—get out of hand, but it does not occur as often with this type as with the first, third, or fourth types.

The third type is a real pain in the ass. This is the guy you see being shot by TV cops all the time. He really loves "The Life"; he's addicted to the bigshot aspect. He's the dude you see zipping around town in his Lamborghini, talking drug deals over his car phone. (This is really fucking stupid because car-phone conversations are broadcast, and, therefore, the cops don't need a warrant to monitor them like they do with a tap.) Guys in this category are dangerous; they use the product and think violence is their exclusive domain. They're the ones who do rip-offs and get in shootouts with the Drug Enforcement Agency (DEA). They eventually get taken out either by others like them or law enforcement.

The last group, the professionals, are the people who never touch drugs. They don't import, move, distribute, or use them. They operate through middle men and phony business fronts. Raid their houses, and you find nothing. Cross them, and you end up in a trash bin in an alley. In short, these guys are the prototype mob.

Police Officers

Another group that uses violence is the police. If you get lippy with a cop, you are in shit. You seem to develop problems getting in to the police car. You try to get in several times, and it doesn't seem to work. (Maybe the door still being closed had something to do with it.) Once you are in custody, your rights cease to exist. The most dangerous time is when the cops just get fed up. If the cops have been after someone for a while whom they can't catch, they'll set him up. Generally, they'll just plant something; however, I have encountered extreme situations in which people were killed and then written off with "they had a gun." Oddly enough, an unregistered gun somehow always shows up at times like these. Criminals scream and cry about how unfair this is, but I just laugh at them.

Of course, there are other groups that sometimes use violence, which we'll look at in the second half of the book. Right now, I want you to understand that there are certain groups that are inherently violent. It comes with the territory. If you choose to live in one of these group—or in a system that is in conflict with one of them—you have to accept the fact that violence will come your way on a regular basis. In summary, shit happens.

In the next chapter, we'll see how violence can emanate from a personal level, as well as from a group system. But just be aware that often when a person acts out violence, he is acting as the group's enforcer. He may be throwing the punch, but the rest of the group agrees with what he's doing. This is one way that the group deals with those it doesn't approve of.

However, by understanding how systems work and the operating rules of these systems, and by recognizing the rules when you see them, you can avoid a huge amount of trouble by not crossing certain lines. The object of the exercise is to get through, not to convince the world that you have a dick that can drive a six-inch spike through a wooden plank. I hate to say this, but sometimes you have to fight. There is no other way. It has been my experience, however, that you don't have to fight nearly as often as many people think they do.

.

CHAPTER FOUR

Personal Operating Systems

> "Rules are meant to be broken, a dictum much loved by liberal arts professors, psychiatrists, and would-be swingers but quite apt to get you killed if you try applying it in a serious poker game."
>
> —Kelly Frieas
> Science fiction artist

If you happen to run into me somewhere and I am in the presence of two other longhairs, beware—they are my clan brothers. One is named Tim; he's about an inch taller than I am (somewhere around 5'9") with dark hair and a beard. The other is Richard, who has regal features and gray hair and stands about 6'2". You may get the impression that you have been invaded by the three stooges. The truth of the matter is that they are both just as dangerous as, if not more so than, I am.

Recently, we were sitting around playing penny-ante poker. Richard pulled out a copy of *American Survival Guide* and opened it to a knife review. He commented, "It's a really nice throwaway." We agreed, and I looked back at my cards for a moment. I looked up at them and said, "Ya know, the deep structure of that sentence is really scary."

Both of these guys are teachers of psychological systems and trained in neurolinguistic psychology (NLP). We looked at each other for a moment and started laughing our heads off.

Deep structure consists of the ideals transmitted by a sentence, or in other words, its underlying meaning. The surface sentence is actually rather vague. "The cat jumped onto the table" tells you that an undefined feline jumped (either up or down or across) onto an undefined table. What kind of cat? Think of a cat, and then ask someone else to do so. Odds are your ideal cats are totally different. We all fill in the details with our own experiences and concepts.

The deep structure of that good throwaway sentence is this: it is a good, cheap knife, whose sole use after you assassinate someone with it and wipe off the fingerprints is to be thrown away, preferably somewhere away from the homicide scene. The casualness of the reference and the fact that we all understood what Richard meant are what's most important. We're all from places where violence is not only common, but normal. We've all come through more than our share of murder, mayhem, and destruction. The casual reference to competently killing another human being was less important than trying to figure out if anyone could beat two pair, ten high for a thirty-six-cent pot.

Unlike many people, I still have a little bell that goes off inside my head from time to time that points out when something is just a little too psycho.

Most people never see the information you're getting here, much less critically examine it for what it means to them. Few people inspect their underlying assumptions and the ideals that drive them. They are so unaware of their operating system's programming that they are damn near robots. Actually, cyborgs is a better term, half-human, half-machine. The human part often screams in protest, while the machine just keeps on doing whatever it was programmed to do.

I loved the comeback by one fellow, who—when asked, "Off to drown your sorrows?"—responded, "If I could drown my sorrows, I wouldn't have to drink!" It is this programming, this version of reality, that really is in control. Most people are no more in control of what's going on than a passenger is in control of a bus.

CASUAL VIOLENCE

A major part of this programming is what I call "casual violence." Most people don't think about violence any more than they pay attention to how their cars operate. I'm talking about the "I dunno; I put gas in it and go" crowd. If you ask if they are violent, they'll stop hitting each other long enough to tell you no.

While sitting in a parking lot one day, I saw a kid walk over to his little brother, who was wandering away. Their mother had told him to fetch the younger one. The older kid casually grabbed little brother's arm and twisted it. When it comes down to it, I know a little more about what hurts and what doesn't than the average person. This kid glommed onto his brother's arm with such intensity that a few more pounds of pressure would have dislocated the shoulder. I watched the older kid's face for any sign of sadism or anger. Nada, zippo, zero . . . the kid just did something on autopilot that I used to do to collect money. He had no emotion or conscious thought invested in his action. He wasn't some kind of sociopath; he was a normal kid. He wasn't aware of the amount of pain he was inflicting. He was just acting out a program that someone else had done to him.

People are incredibly violent and inflict tremendous pain without even thinking about it. What's really scary is that, to them, violence has no meaning. They aren't being cruel; they are being machines.

One thing that makes people nervous about me is they can see that, once I decide to do it, I'll plant a knife in your chest without a moment's hesitation. Once that decision is made, it's about as predictable as nightfall. *It is gonna happen.* They see me as someone who is "violent." What that really means is someone who is *capable of violence* and would use it, they fear, as casually on them as they use it on children. They recognize the difference in our types of violence; mine is on a more severe level. If they push me far enough, they know they will be lying on the floor.

Most people don't consider themselves violent, yet at a drop of a hat they'll whale on their kids. Yet, they deem someone who does that to another adult as violent. They are afraid that someone will lash out without hesitation at them as they would on children. That kid, without paying attention, did something to his brother that professional muscle does.

The difference between an amateur and a pro is that the latter does not use casual violence. Violence is not a power trip to a pro; it is a tool. A pro never uses violence without planning for it, whereas casual violence is not consciously thought of or planned. It's like a line that people, while throwing a hissy fit, somehow find themselves past and in the middle of a fight. What this means to you is that the guy who is facing off with you may not be thinking about the results and ramifications of his actions. He's so wrapped up in something else that he doesn't realize that somebody is very likely to get hurt. That is, until he gets older; then violence becomes more serious, and he begins to catch on.

Remember, eighty times out of one hundred, fights among adults are for keeps. Teenagers and young bucks are the ones who usually fight for show and position. Look at the murder statistics of the *1989 UCR*. Fifteen- to eighteen-year-old victims numbered 2,001, that includes a shitload of gangbangers. In fact, it is probably a safe guess that most of those homicides were gang-related. Twenty- to twenty-four-year-olds numbered 3,159, including gangbangers, but the body count is rising even excluding gang-related deaths. Twenty-five to thirty-year-olds were the worst with 3,300 bodies showing up in that range. It begins to taper off after thirty; only 2,641 bought it. This down slope occurs because the older a person gets, the less likely he is to think he's immortal; therefore, the less likely he is to get in a fight for no good reason.

These are serious numbers. As you go along, understand if you don't cool your jets, you're more likely to run into someone who will plant you rather than risk getting hurt himself.

Back to the poker players I mentioned at the beginning of this chapter. Mr. Richard, aside from being damn good at kali/sulate, worked his way through college by being an orderly at a mental hospital for the criminally insane. He used to have to deal with 51-50s (police code for dangerous to self and others) all the time. Like I did when I was running the correctional center, he saw more felons and wackos in one day than your average cop sees in a month. Every now and then, one of these guys' rubber bands would snap, and Richard would have to drop the cracker case onto the floor. So here is this hippie orderly, who is working his way toward a Ph.D. in psychology, dealing with criminal looney toons. During this time, Richard came up with a theory about violence, which I'm going to share with you. I had a nice theory all set up, but I took one look at his and tossed mine aside.

His theory is that there are four bases of violence: fear, frenzy, tantrum, and criminal. I sat there and looked at his theory and said, "Yeah, but what about . . ." three or four times until he explained where each type went.

Fear: For some reason, real or imagined, the guy is afraid of you or something you represent. His motivation for attacking you is based in his fear. The guy thinks you're going to take something away from him, displace him, or hurt him or something he cares about. He gets scared and goes ballistic on you. I've seen shit start because too many big bouncers surround a guy. Shit, I've seen little guys go batshit when just one big guy starts telling him what to do in a threatening manner.

Frenzy: This is the person who doesn't perceive any limits. All of his apparent resources are gone. In short, this person feels helpless and out of control. Violence is the most obvious and easiest way to deal with the situation. He whips himself up into a frenzy and then goes berserk. The dude who pulled the Big Mac attack in San Diego years ago was a frenzy-type. Many gangbangers fall into this category as well. Often, unlike with a tantrum, the "whipping into a frenzy" part is internal. This is the guy who pops a cork and goes 51-50 on whoever is around him. Now, oddly enough, frenzy-type violence is often based in a real and rational event or cause. Some guy's wife dies, he and 19,999 other guys get laid off from the factory, he comes from a totally dysfunctional background— all of these can lead to frenzied violence.

Tantrum: This is the bully who wants his way, regardless of how irrational that way is. If you tell him no, he basically pitches a hissy fit. His fit, however, includes pounding the shit out of you. Tantrum violence is totally irrational and involves escalating demands. The person who is trying to pull this is *never satisfied.* The demands keep going up until they are impossible to fulfill. He'll walk up and say, "Give me a cigarette"; if you concede, he'll demand a certain type (usually not the type you have). The best way to tell if you are dealing with a tantrum type is a sense of "What the fuck?" that you'll experience when faced with his escalating demands. The basis of this type of violence is to get attention. A lot of alpha and beta behavior falls into this category. By proving that he is the top dick, he gets all the attention. The person who gets his ya-ya's by hitting people also is a tantrum-type. He gets ego gratification out of hitting someone, which translates into internal attention.

Criminal: This is contract violence. Either it is coercion or professional violence. It basically consists of: do this or I'll hurt you. Somewhere, there is a contract. Either you face the likelihood of pain for failing to comply with someone's wishes, or someone has contracted a bonebreaker to hurt you. The guy who sticks a gun in your face and says, "Gimme yo' money," is offering you a contract: pay or die.

It is extremely easy for criminal violence to slip into frenzy violence. Just as it is easy for fear violence to slip into tantrum violence. Violence has a habit of bouncing back and forth from one type to another. While occasionally it will bounce in other ways, it is more normal for it to go in the order I just described. This is often what happens when a robbery or burglary gets out of control and results in rape or assault.

Do you want some sexy news? Just as there are types of violence, there are effective ways of dealing with each type. This is what made me go, "Holy shit!" when Richard explained this system to me. Unconsciously, I and damn near every good bouncer I've ever known use these techniques. See, as a bouncer, your actual job is to prevent violence and protect the interests of the owner. If word gets out that the place is bad-assed, the civilians (who have the real money) will shy away from the establishment.

This is why the really good bouncers, orderlies, etc., seldom throw blows. They handle the situation before it turns violent.

The way that you deal with one type will cause another type to go apeshit on you, so you have to be able to identify each type of violent person. Also, another important safety tip: *This stuff works until the first blow is thrown.* Once it turns violent, all bets are off, and the game goes to whoever is still standing after it is over. Fortunately, after a while it becomes easy to spot the point at which a situation will turn violent or not.

When you're dealing with a fear type, you approach obliquely in a nonthreatening manner. You are talking this person down, just like he was freaking out on drugs. You soothe his fears and get him to trust you. Then, you don't do anything to betray that trust. When you face these types, your body language is open and nonthreatening, like you're dealing with a scared animal. Your voice is soft but high-pitched and breathy. You're scared, too, but it's all right. Try a "Hey man, I understand. I've been there too" approach. I used to crouch down to make myself look less threatening, while making petting gestures with my hands when I'd face these kind of people.

You deal with a frenzy type in exactly the opposite way. You draw the line and set the limits immediately. You get right up in his face in classic alpha pose and tell him where it's at. You are the commander, and these are the limits, does he understand? Your gestures and body language are those of someone ordering a dog to sit. You point down sharply and use a commanding power voice. You're the general and he's the private—there is no question that he will obey. You draw the line, and if he moves across it, you nail his ass immediately. When he wakes up, he can reconsider the wisdom of messing with you.

I used to have people swear that they were sure I was 6'4" when I roared. I can get real big when necessary. I had one guy, who after knowing me for three months, looked at me in amazement when he realized something. "Damn Animal, you're short!" he said.[1]

A tantrum is dealt with exactly 180 degrees from what most people expect. This is why it blows up in their faces. The way to deal with tantrum is, as any parent of a two-year-old will tell you, withdrawal of attention. This means ignoring it. This does not mean acting as if nothing is happening; rather, you'll pay attention to him when he starts to behave. This often includes leaving. "I'll be back when you start behaving yourself." No matter what happens, you become calmer and more rational. Your body language expresses disapproval: crossed arms and legs and body turned away.[2] Your voice is rational and shows no emotion. You're simply stating facts, "Excuse me, I don't have to put up with this. When you feel you can talk rationally about this, we'll proceed."

This person is looking for an excuse to swing, so you don't give him any feedback. I used to deal with some people in a stone-cold robot manner. I was a loop tape. No matter what they did, it didn't bother me They'd scream and bluster, and I'd calmly tell them that they were leaving over and over again. I had a few move on me, but most chilled out.

Criminal violence is easy to deal with—you just renegotiate the contract. Instead of it being "Do what I want, or I will hurt you," it becomes "If you try violence, I will defend." Perhaps defend isn't the best term; retaliate is better. The more nebulous the defense, the better. Instead of saying, "If you try, I'll pull out my gun and shoot you," say something like, "Feeling lucky, huh?" The better you can convey that he no longer holds the best hand, the more likely he is to reconsider. He has to face the fact that you are just as likely (if not more so) to leave a knife in him as he is in you.

Do not make this a threat; make it a statement of fact and not a particularly exciting one either. Your voice is even more neutral and calm than the one you used with tantrums. Your body language shows a neutral fighting pose. This is not a fighting stance, but it flows into one real nicely. My preferred one is hands held loosely together at my crotch with subtle body shifts that protect my groin from a kick. If you go into an actual fighting stance, it's going to show that you're afraid of him. A neutral stance is nonthreatening but not particularly attackable either. I used to drop into my Iceman voice and tell people things like, "Go for it." They seldom did.

When you walk into a place, you have to be able to identify the fighters, the spectators, the hustlers, the workers, and, of course, the instigators. It's like different roles in a movie. Not everyone is going to be a violent bad guy. It is critical to be able to determine what roles various people are in instantly. You walk into a situation, and you had better be able to pick out the potential trouble before your ass is too far in.

The role a person plays depends on temperament, situation, who's around, what OS the guy is coming from, and if he is in the middle of rebellion. These key factors determine what will happen if a troublesome situation arises. Understand that there are people who will not move without the go ahead from a higher up or unless someone else moves first. There are also people who will not move at all; they just sit there and glower. Other people will move only in a pack. Certain people will move independently with very little provocation. A large number of folks will move only because they feel they have to. A few will ignore you until you get in their faces, and then they'll drop you right quick. The ones to watch for are the out-and-out loose cannons. They will do things contrary to common sense just to prove something. Start watching people and try to figure out what category they fall into.

By the way, with all this information, go out and see that it works *before* using it. If you've watched it work beforehand, it will operate better when you apply it to a self-defense situation. If you drag it out of the closet for the first time when you're heading for trouble, it won't fly. Crashing and burning is not fun.

The various roles people play generally determine whom you're going to have trouble with. The personal operating system of a person will let you know exactly which lily pad he's going to jump to when he's feeling froggish. His cultural and group operating systems will let you know which pond and what part of the pond he's in, but his personal operating system lets you know his state of mind.

NONVIOLENT TYPES

Not everyone who is in a cultural, family, or group operating system is going to be violent. What's more, the more nonviolent someone is, the less likely he will be any good at it when and if he decides to be violent. This is how most murders get solved—someone does somebody in the heat of the moment and leaves a trail a mile wide. He leaves witnesses, he threatens the guy earlier, he kills someone in his home, or, my favorite, he shoots someone with a gun that is registered to him. Of course, wasting someone in your own home or screaming, "You asshole!" in a crowded bar before shooting them also ranks up there in the stupid move category. Figuring out most murders is about as hard as tracking a muddy dog across a kitchen floor.

This same tendency to be nonviolent also stands out as a beacon to would-be muggers and attackers. "Gee, who doesn't look like he can fight back too good?" Peyton Quinn came up with the term "interview" in his book, *A Bouncer's Guide to Barroom Brawling.*[3] It's a damn good concept about a guy who is looking for a fight—999,999 people out of a million will walk up and conduct a verbal interview of the guy they are thinking of fighting to see if they can get away with it. The same is true with most muggers.

It is critically important to be able to spot which person is likely to take on a violent role in any situation, the one interviewing for a victim. Once you get this down, then you can begin to add in the scale of competency. Just because someone is prone to be violent does not mean that he's good at it. In time you will discover that those who are exceedingly good at violence are the least prone to do it. Here's a secret: *The reason most people are effective with violence is that they are the ones who do it first.* They move before anyone else decides violence is the way to go. In short, they catch most people with their dicks hanging out in the breeze. Moving first is not the same thing as being technically proficient, even though it looks like it to the untrained eye.

The three most likely troublemakers are the guy in rebellion, the guy in pain, and the guy with the weak ego. There is a period in life where people are expected to rebel. Psychologists say it's a period of separating and establishing an independent identity. Most people simply call it a pain in the ass. It usually ranges from age fifteen to twenty-five, or, more exactly, that's the accepted range. I've got some news for you: society expects you to go out and be an asshole. (Who was I to disappoint society?) It is part of the cultural operating system that, during this time you go out, get drunk, try drugs, get laid as often as possible, do stupid things, and generally raise some hell. This is referred to idiomatically as "sowing some wild oats." I call it my "Boomtown Days." (I'll talk about Boomtown in the next chapter.)

There are, however, boundaries set up by society. This is society's training and culling-out process. First of all, it's set up so you dent your nose a few times. If someone tells you not to go through a door in the house you live in but never tells you why, you're going to wonder about it. Well, one day when you are feeling adventurous, you're going to try that door. Surprise, it's not locked, but, unfortunately, there's no light in there, either. Since you're not supposed to go through that door, nobody told you where the light switch is located. Well hell, you're bold and brash, so in you go. It's a hallway. Further and further in you go, saying, "Hey this is okay." Well, guess what? There's a short flight of stairs in there, too. You have no light to see the steps, and suddenly you go, "Ouch!" Once they pick themselves off the floor, most people limp back to the starting point and say, "Ya know, they were right about not going through this door."

This is an accepted boundary of society. Hell, everybody is going to go through that door at least once. *They* know that. *They* also know that you are going to bump yourself a good one when you find those fucking stairs. Once you've done your recon by nose, you're going to be coming back to the fold asking for a Band-Aid. That's why no one tells you where the light switch is. If they told you about the light, you wouldn't fall down. If you didn't knock your snot locker loose, they couldn't say, "I told you so." This and choreographed violence with other groups are how society lets its young blow off steam—all the time while keeping them in the system. Not only is the hallway prebuilt, but society knows most of the kids will be coming back after the first flight of stairs.

However, let us imagine someone else who doesn't come back after the first flight of stairs. The guy keeps going. He's got so much juice that he doesn't care that he fell down a flight of stairs. He goes deeper. The lights are still off. If he's feeling his way, he's going to encounter doors. Since it's dark, he doesn't stop to see how they're secured, which is a bad mistake. Instead he keeps going full tilt. This is the culling process; beyond a certain point, there are pits. With no light and his going too fast, sooner or later he is going to find one of these fuckers. Welcome to the trash can. This is the guy who went too far and was shit-canned.

In the meantime, the people back at the homestead smile at the people who have come back and say things like, "I hope you've learned your lesson," or grin conspiratorially with the now "wiser" young members of society. For those who bit it in the trash cans, they shake their heads and cluck about how terrible it is that these young people should go so wrong. This is the "safe" channel that society sends its young down. Remember that I told you the idea is to keep the group going? The group writes off a certain number to losses. The military calls it acceptable losses or casualties. Fun, fucking fun, when they're talking about you and your friends.

In short, the rebellion period is usually about as predictable as a politician's becoming corrupt. When the person is in it, he thinks that he is "boldly going where no man has gone before!" Wrong. Cultural, group, family, and personal operating systems determine which hallway a person is going to go down.

This ties in with self-defense in that violence is one of the major stairways you can choose. If you go hanging out in a place where you aren't supposed to be and somebody busts your nose, you're going to think twice about going back there.

You get a pack of kids—like dogs who got free from the yard— and you are guaranteed to have violence. Clubs that cater to the young come and go almost every week because of fights and trouble. Young bucks full of juice think it's a game. Therefore, they run amuck. Someone who is programmed for casual violence in a place where the stops are kicked out is going to be pure hell to deal with. He's operating purely on testosterone, ignorance, and programming—in short, he's a loose cannon on deck. This is either the frenzy or tantrum mode of violence. The first involves the guy who doesn't have any limits and is just running hog wild, while the other is the guy who is flexing his newfound muscles and trying to be a major alpha.

For everyone else, these assholes act as the stairway. You're there having a good time and all of a sudden this guy decides to impress you with the awesomeness of his scrotum. Without knowing the four types of violence, you try what you think is the right response and *blamo*! Next thing you know your girlfriend is trying to stop the blood. It's insult to injury. Not only are you hurt, but you've just gotten shown up. All in all it's an ugly scene.

These pyrotechnical rectums will continue on until someone whacks their pee pees. As I mentioned earlier, casual violence is a scary thing. Fortunately, most people are not that good at violence. If they by some knack or the amount of experience do manage to become good at violence, they will meet up with their nemeses much quicker if they do not become less casual about it. A great number of these people will end up either dead or seriously maimed if they don't cool it. The bigger their caliber, the more in control they need to be. Sooner or later, they will meet up with someone who is not amused by their childish exuberance. They are going too fast to make the shift to purposeful violence. I once quoted a man as saying, "Violence is the first option, and the last choice, of the competent." People who make it their first choice don't last long out there among the big leaguers.

When you are dealing with someone, you have to judge how far he is down the corridor and how juiced he is. Just because someone is raising hell doesn't mean he is looking for a fight. If you go roaring at someone who is simply having a good time and maybe getting a little out of line, you're going to end up in some shit. This is the major mistake most amateurs make when dealing with a situation. It's the fear or frenzy response to a perceived threat. I've seen people blow it to the point of almost criminal response. Do this or I'll kick your ass. Gee that's effective, do you need help picking up your teeth?

It's often best to walk among them cool, confident, and easy going: sharing their good time. You're a hellraiser yourself, so you know what is going on. Everybody becomes a "pardner." Then, from one hellraiser to another, you suggest that they ease off on the throttle on this one. You're not exactly ordering, just recommending. Oddly enough, most people know when they're being out of line. If they aren't violence prone, they will generally cool off then and there. Most people aren't looking for trouble, just to have a good time. Also, knowing there are others around who could meet them in a head-to-head if they don't take your advice usually will mellow out those who are prone to violence.

The topless bar scene from *Roadhouse* with Sam Elliot is a perfect example of what I mean by this. Elliot's character handles the drunk soldier so smoothly that everyone has fun while staying in bounds. On a personal note, I was walking with my partner doing major event security[4] when I spotted about ten bikers passing a pipe. My partner declared me brain damaged and suicidal, and he hung back to make radio contact before he committed suicide by trying to bail me out. As I walked up, the leader palmed the pipe and said, "We ain't doing nothing."

I responded, "Yeah, I know, but could you do me a favor?" I pointed to the far reaches and said, "Could you do nothing up there?" The guy looked at me blankly; this was not what he expected. I continued, "See, someone sees you blowing dope with all these kids running around, and they're going to come running to security. Then we're going to have to go . . . (I mimed doing a line of cocaine) What?! Someone doing *drugs*! We'll put a stop to that!" I looked at the guy staring at me in amazement. "Just do it where we don't have to notice it," I said.

The biker looked at me for a second and then he got a big ol' grin on his face and said, "All right!" and handed me the pipe. I took a hit, croaked, "Thanks," and walked down to my partner and blew it in his face. "It's cool," I said. He just stood there saying, "You're out of your fucking mind." In that particular situation, had I roared we would have had a full-scale brawl on our hands, and yours truly would have had his ass in a meat grinder.

I should point out that I had to learn this lesson the hard way. In fact, this was why I got into as many fights as I did. I used to sit there not saying anything until I just couldn't stand what was going on anymore. At that point, my patience would run out, and I'd start conversations with, "You asshole, you fucked up!" Not too many people respond positively to this approach. In fact, if you use this approach, you can bet your milk allowance that people are going to get defensive. From that point, I had the option of arguing with them for a half hour or decking them. Since I was already at the end of my rope, guess which one won?

A great many situations turn ugly because the person approaching the troublemaker A) has waited too long and, consequently, gotten too angry to be rational when he talks to him, B) is so caught up in being righteous that he is a total asshole when he comes at the other person, C) has forgotten that "your enemy is not a bad guy in his own eyes" and does not leave avenues open for negotiation or deescalation.

If I am totally flamed at someone, I will not talk to him at all until I calm down. I will walk away rather than confront the person because, in the heat of anger, I'm prone to say the first thing that comes to mind. Often the first thing is designed to hurt, belittle, or intimidate. Upon being verbally attacked, the other person will respond negatively. This is how it works with people, bottom line. I spent a lot of years learning how to approach people in potentially hot situations in ways so it wouldn't blow up in my face. Eventually, I got to the point where I was doing it professionally.

If something is bothering you, the secret is to mention it before you get to your boiling point. This is the difference between being assertive and being aggressive. Most people who are trying to be assertive actually end up being aggressive. It doesn't matter who was "right" after the first punch is thrown.

Having a nonviolent person, who feels he has to stand up for his rights or someone else's, confront the aggressor is the worst possible scenario. Violent people eat those kind of people for lunch. I'll go into more detail about body language in Chapter 9 and explain how to avoid tipping your hand when dealing with potentially violent people, but overall, the best way is to ignore them. Unless they actually get into your territory, don't bother staring at them or giving them hard looks. Don't ask them, "Would you please be quiet?" Keep their positions pegged out of the side of your eye and just keep on with whatever you're doing.

The thing to remember is, these kind usually run in packs. If you are at a party and one of these guys gets out of line, it's not because he's having too much fun. It's a trap, he's looking for someone to say something so he can stomp him. The person who feels he "has" to stand up to this guy is going to get nailed hard. He doesn't have the commitment necessary to deal with this kind of person.

It may ruin the fun but, if necessary, leave. The party may be spoiled, you might not be able to see the end of the movie, etc. So what? It's better than getting your head knocked in or being around to watch the stomping that is about to happen. Somebody is going to get seriously hurt. That means hospitals and police—not fun, folks. Oddly enough, when you are really tough, it's easier to walk away from this sort of thing. It's when you are not sure how tough you are that you end up on the short end of the stick with these people.

If, however, you find yourself dealing with these kind of people, there are a few things you can do. One is call reinforcements. Do not go at these people alone. You have to be an absolute wolverine to get away with that sort of thing.[5] Then surround them with your reinforcements. Let them know that they will be fighting on several fronts at once. This usually takes the wind out of people's sails.

Two, do not expect these people to leave quietly or stay gone. If you and five buddies toss three troublemakers from a party, expect them to be back. "That's it folks, party's over. Everyone go home." That way, if they show back up, there's nobody there for them to harm. My brother-in-law had a friend get blown away because they didn't do this. He was with a group called "Westside Posers." They'd won a fight with a rival gang called "Korean Killers" and were still hanging around after it was over. A car pulled up and—bang! bang!—one dead friend.

Unless you want to explain to the cops, everybody leaves. Violent people often aren't choosey as to whom they hurt.

They'll nail an innocent bystander just as fast as the guy who made them look bad. Then you fade into the shadows yourself. The problem is if you prepare for a siege, it's called first-degree murder. Setting up an ambush for when your attackers return is frowned upon by the law. Oddly enough, the fact that they returned and started shooting up your house seems to slip the DA's mind. Fun, that. If you want, you could call the cops and tell them that you are in fear for your life. They'll just tell you to leave everything behind for the glee club. Yep, that's our judicial system for you.

The guy whose violence is predicated on inner pain is a real cocksucker to deal with. I've met people who were so tweaked that they were looking for someone to cancel their ticket for them. They won't suck the bullet themselves, but they'll use someone else to check them out. I'll talk about "freaks" later; they are a real and horrible aspect. More often than not, though, these people are not so far gone as that. Mostly, it's the guy who is in pain who wants to share the wealth with you. This is usually a minor form of frenzy violence. The guy has just gotten his dick chewed by his old lady and is looking to take it out on someone else. Oh boy, just what I always wanted, the proverbial looking-for-a-fight guy. This usually happens before someone has realized that fighting is not a game, often in and around the young buck and rebellion stage. He doesn't have to be drinking, snorting, or toking when he decides to punch someone, but it usually happens then. The chemicals remove the normal resistance to this sort of behavior. If he's prone to violence, there isn't that much to take away and recreational chemicals seriously speed up the process.

There's a certain feeling, a certain tenseness, about these people. They're turned in and stewing. They won't willingly let go of anger, but it's leaking out like radiation. Actually radar might be a better analogy. Usually they aren't in the center of the situation; they are off in a corner sucking down a good deal of whatever substance is around. Unlike someone who's nonviolent and trying to kill the pain with intoxicants, troublemakers are watching what is going on around them. If a shark had active radar, this is what it would feel like. When these people do a radar sweep, they are looking for a victim.

I use the term victim intentionally. These people aren't really looking for anyone who is hard-core. They want someone they think they can beat. They're looking for someone to blow a little steam off with. Now if they find another person with the same thing going on, hot damn! They're going to have some fun together. It's always best if there is another bozo with the same thing going on, so they can go off and play with themselves. If not, old stud muffins might just cast his eye your way.

Believe it or not, these guys are actually one of the easiest type of situation to handle. Unfortunately, they are as common as cockroaches. The first way is to be so totally hard-core that they decide they'd rather kiss a rattler. This, unfortunately, will usually result in your not getting laid that night. Also, being in that mind-set will seriously ruin your fun for the evening.

The other way is to spot him and then ignore him. Keep a bead on him out of the side of your eye, but other than that don't look at him. If he moves toward you, turn terminator until he wises up and leaves you alone. I have a signal that my lady knows when I have spotted someone who is potential trouble. I say, "Click . . ." in a flat tone. Anytime she hears that she knows I'm going to be sitting with my back to the wall and at Code Yellow status. From then on, I don't officially pay attention to the person. If I were to spend time looking at him, it would indicate that I was nervous about him. And if I appear nervous, he thinks it's obviously because I'm not sure I could take him. This puts the ball in his court if he wants to move. It is important to realize that fights and interviews are two-way energy exchanges. He's looking for someone who will interact with his pattern in the way he wants. If I give off victim vibes, he's going to look closely at me. On the other hand if I look like a lion who is idly ignoring the jackal at the edge of my territory, the jackal knows that I know it's there. I am, however, the one who chooses not to act, and as long as it behaves, I will continue to ignore it. If he does act up, he's buzzard bait.

With bucks who are too juiced up, a good way to avoid a fight is to go up and introduce yourself. It sounds weird, I know, but it works. If you have a guy thinking about jamming with you, cruise right up to him and say, "How's it going?" The first thing is that it brings up another program in him. You're not meeting him with confrontational energy. This is another way of ignoring what he's about. If he's got a hard-on and you are relaxed enough to be friendly, it's going to spin his optics. This especially works when you've entered an area and he starts getting nervous. He looks down into his pants and then looks over toward you and gets insecure as to who is going to get the blue ribbon. What this does is telegraph to him the fact that you are aware of his awesome butchness and you're not in the market to challenge it. You're cool, he's cool, it's cool. This is what a lot of bouncers do when they see would-be trouble-makers come in. A good bouncer will cruise over and shoot the shit with the people for a minute or two. Without verbalizing it, the message of "Keep it cool" is slid into the conversation. Unless the guy is too far gone or totally stupid, this works.

Another good way of avoiding a fight is to have an excuse not to fight ready. This includes lying if necessary. For example, I have never been to prison, but I have enough experience with convicts and parolees that I am often mistaken for one. If someone gets in my face, I tell them that I'm on parole, and if I get in a fight, I'm going to be "violated" and sent back. I'm not afraid of him—I'm afraid that if I eat his face, I'll go bye-bye. If he keeps on pushing it, I'm really going to hurt him bad for making me go back to prison.

Another way not to fight is to have promised someone you won't. Never mind if you actually didn't, it sounds great. You promised your old lady no more fights. Most guys understand this sort of blackmail—you quit doing something or she'll make your life hell. It's pretty cut-and-dried. Ignore the calls of pussy-whipped and mamma's boy. It's much more important to keep the relationship with the fine lady on good ground than it is to embed your fist in his face. Even if you aren't with a lady, pretend you've gotten out of the yard. If you go back with a black eye, you're going to catch hell. I'll tell you the truth—I'm more nervous about tangling with the women in my life than I am about most punks out there. Most people around will go, "That's valid," and back off. Often you will find someone else will interrupt the trouble.

These techniques usually work on someone who is not too far gone. These are the young bucks who are out blowing off steam, not the mentally disabled. An interesting subdivision of this is the "friendly fight." In one sense, they aren't really out to cause much damage, but settling for a fight instead of getting laid is not the sign of someone who has his plating rivetted on tight. If these people cross you, they can hurt you. They don't really mean to cause that much damage, but these things often get out of hand. There are a lot of guys in prison for friendly fights that got ugly.

There is a particular character between the two categories I'm talking about here, those just blowing off steam and the freaks. (I'm going to get to the freaks in a bit). These in-between characters are not as ineffective as the young buck looking to blow off steam, yet they aren't quite walking corkscrews either. Peyton Quinn called the ball perfectly in his book *A Bouncer's Guide to Barroom Brawling: Dealing with the Sucker Puncher, Streetfighter, and Ambusher* (available from Paladin Press) on this one. It isn't too often that I sit up and say, "No shit!" because someone brings up an aspect of fighting that I hadn't consciously noticed before. Well, Monsieur Quinn rattled my cage on this one. I had always known that I had gotten into more than my share of fights because I was raising hell and calling attention to myself. I had always written it off as my either being too weird or too far out of line. Peyton called it on the nose when he pointed out that he (like me) had gotten into so many fights because he was having *too much fun!*

There you are having a good time and out of nowhere somebody comes up and jumps in your face. What the fuck? Who are you, what did I do to you, and why the hell are you in my face? If you've ever asked someone those questions, you've likely been visited by the fun patrol, those charming people who show up when you are having too much fun.

This guy has mental and emotional pain. He's in misery. Well, guess what? Misery no longer loves company—it demands it. So he sees you having fun and gets pissed that you're having fun while he's suffering. So what does he do? He decides to come over and show you what pain is about. He wants to drag you down to his level rather than come up to yours. This is a form of frenzy violence. Watch for these people because to the average person it seems like they come out of the blue. Truth is, they've been sitting in the corner stewing for a while. They often start conversations with such friendly comments as, "I don't like you, asshole!" As you might have guessed, he's not going to invite you to his place for hot toddies later on. There are entire establishments with patrons like this. Go into a dive bar and start having too much fun, and you'll get into shit immediately. This is what I mean when I say you have to have the same energy level as the people in a particular place.

Let's move on to the other category, people who are so twisted that a sidewinder can give them lessons on being straight. Thank God, we are talking about a small section of the population. Police know them as "freaks" although other terms may be used locally. These are people who are so damaged that they are beyond all fear and are damn near unpredictable. When they start rolling, they are the 51-50s. Most of these people are killing themselves with drugs, but that takes too long. I've seen a shitload of crackheads who fall into this category. Regardless of who you are, they can go ballistic on you. I've had them wig out on me, and I've seen them go berserk on people I wouldn't want to mess with. They just don't care. They are so screwed up that they don't care how tough you are.

The dangerous thing about these people is that they aren't totally nuts. They haven't lost it enough to be the mumblers/screamers who live in boxes downtown. Nor have they blown it in tandem with a crime to get locked up in a mental ward. So instead they are walking the streets. Fortunately, they restrict most of their damage to the strata of society that accepts them.

Freaks come in one of two packages: those on all the time and those who turn on and off. In my life, I have met about twenty "on all the time" freaks. That's from someone who spent a great deal of time in the borderlands and trash-can societies. These are the serial killers, the Charlie Mansons of the world. They are no longer human beings. I don't know any other way to describe them. There is something about them that causes an instinctive reaction of "Wrong!" in normal people—not wrong in the sense of moral right and wrong, but wrong against nature and evolution, like someone has intentionally bred rabid dingos.

Anthony Vachss writes about these sort of characters in his "Burke" books.[6] It is really important to realize that these people do exist. They are not just movie characters. Fortunately, because of what they are, they remain mostly in the trash-can societies. However, also because of what they are, they are very transient. Your average serial killer is always on the move, either in his location or his stalking.

The on/off variety occasionally goes batshit. When they flame on, they're dangerous. They can go from whiny, broken dogs to berserk werewolves at a moment's notice. The most common example is the crackhead or PCP freak. Although drugs are not always involved, they often are. But something peculiar to those people's own horror stories will trigger them, and they go AWOL on you. If they snap while in the process of doing a robbery or a burglary, rape/torture, homicide, or other such pleasantries usually occur. You've seen this in the newspaper or on the news: the guy snaps and wastes twelve people before blowing out his own brains.

You can't reason with these people. They are so deeply damaged that hardly any will ever make it back. The best way to deal with them is not to be around them. Being a total badass is very little help here. No matter how tough you are, these people are so fucked up that they don't care. They'll do lemming suicides on you if you make a stand. And like lemmings, more will keep on coming. By the time you've killed enough to let everyone know to leave you alone, the cops will have enough to convict you for a few thousand years. Even if you manage to get away with it, a year later, an entirely new batch will have replaced the old, and you'll have to start over again.

The closest thing I've ever figured out as a way to deal with these people is to draw a line and post "No Trespassing" signs. Then, you stay in your yard. If any of them come into your territory, you bust them up a good one and tell them that if they talk you'll come back and finish the job. Then get a cast-iron alibi because they will run to the cops. That technique only works about 20 percent of the time. Face it, these people are beyond all boundaries of normalcy. It's easier not to go places where they are. If you are in an area where there are a lot of addicts, get the hell out. It's easier.

The thing to remember about freaks is that they don't come from nowhere. It takes long years of nursing on poison and rot to turn out someone like that. They have been shaped into what they are by very specific types of energy, abuse, and experiences. One of the great horror writers of all time, H.P. Lovecraft, wrote of places of evil and filth, of places where slimy things crawled away from the light to nurse on poison and scum. This is the type of place that breed these people. You have to learn how to spot this sort of area. Because this is where these maggots go, you don't want to be there. You can find these areas anywhere but generally in backwater areas or nearly abandoned pits in the city. These are places in the city where beggars in Bangladesh have a higher life expectancy. Entire families of junkies and dopeheads live in their own shit. Areas back in the byways where it is normal for the father to beat and rape his daughters until the son kicks his ass and takes over. I highly recommend you stay way clear of areas where life means absolutely nothing.

You know, I was talking to a guy in Colorado about self-defense recently. Now, this guy is no slouch; he's been through a whole shitload of violence. He told me that I was being a little too melodramatic about self-defense being a life-and-death situation. I looked at the rolling plains and the groves of quaking aspen, and I realized something. I was in Colorado. The streets that had bred me were more than a thousand miles away; they were light years away. Out there people still fought with fists. In the city, the first thing you do when trouble starts is grab a weapon. The systems are radically different.

To tell you the truth, I don't know which one is harder to make the transition to—going up or going down on the system ladder. Each has its problems. My other clan bro Tim used to love to fight. He had been in all sorts of scraps when he was younger. It was the Midwest, and by the Midwest rules of the time, people did punchouts. Naturally he joined the military. He joined the navy because they would take him first. He shipped out to Japan, where after a few days, he saw some marines. He made a comment about sea-going bellhops, which quite naturally went over like a turd in a punch bowl. The jarheads casually took off their belts and proceeded to give him the most thorough stomping in his life by systematically working him over with their belts.[7]

As he was recuperating, he realized that it was an entirely new ball game over there. He learned the new rules and became a real nasty motherfucker. He got the point that, when he moved on you, you wouldn't get up anytime soon. He found himself in a group of like-minded, hard-core guys. This man, in his time, racked up a body count of more than two hundred kills. Before you get too impressed, he's the only one left alive. Of all his old running buddies, every single one of them died violently.

If at times I sound too far out of line and overly melodramatic, remember, we're passing in the borderlands. I'm coming in, and you're heading out. There are places nastier than most people can imagine. I've been through them and survived. What's more, I've buried a lot of friends along the way. Remember, where I'm from it was a slow Saturday night if there were only three separate exchanges of gun fire—and it's gotten worse since then. L.A. has more murders every weekend than most places have in a year. I'm telling you what it's like out in the extremes. Take what I say and tone it down to where you are and what situation you're in. Everything is adjustable.

There are many different reasons that violence may occur. In the scope of things, what is considered by most people as "fighting" is actually a very small portion of the violence that occurs. There is much more going on that people have no real concept about. Learning about these other operating systems will keep you from being blindsided by them. Too many people wake up in hospitals asking, "What happened?" because they didn't know what to look for.

If you learn how to read the different operating systems and how they affect what people will do, you will be much safer. Remember, a large cultural system consists of smaller networks and stratas. Each network consists of different communities or clusters that are based on the network's core assumptions, while individuals act out certain roles in each particular group. The trick to surviving anywhere you go is to be able to read the deep structure laws and the surface structure rules. Once you understand this technique, you can mimic any operating system that you find yourself in. It is always important to realize that people attack what is unfamiliar to them. This knowledge allows you to hot wire, short out, or D-watt a situation rather than having to fight your way out.

You are not expendable. The John Wayne macho attitude is the best way to get yourself killed. Yet it is what we are taught. It is also the fastest way to the trash can. To keep from becoming a statistic, you have to use more than just your testosterone. If you use your wits, knowledge, and awareness, as well as your right hook, you will be more likely to live long enough to celebrate your old age.

Notes

[1] I picked him up and threw him down a hill for that comment. I know I'm short; everybody else doesn't need to know that though.

[2] Of course, you watch the son of a bitch like a hawk out of the side of your eye until you are safely away.

[3] I highly recommend this book. Peyton knows his shit.

[4] Thirty thousand people a day and six beer stands, each bigger than my house, is too much fun.

[5] You have to go into that one knowing that you are a dead man. In fact, what you're doing there is avenging your death. As they are killing you, you're going to be killing their leader. He has to know this. Truth be told, it's easier to go in with reinforcements.

[6] Anthony Vachss is a writer who I highly recommend if you want to know what deep street feels like. I have never encountered a writer who has captured the feel of the street so well. The guy who turned me onto these books said, "When I read this book, I thought of you. The main character could be your brother. He thinks just like you." Gee, thanks a lot.

[7] Fortunately, they weren't sharpened. Marines have a habit of sharpening the edges of their belt buckles. This makes a sort of a whip knife that can get rather ugly.

CHAPTER FIVE

Welcome to Boomtown

> "Uh, she's getting a little wild there.
> Hey, Cean, go stand between her and the
> Jacob's ladder. If she gets too close,
> she'll arc out on her nipple rings and
> electrocute herself."
> —A safety conversation about the
> topless dancer at the *Road Warrior* party

All right, for some twisted reason, you've decided that you want to hang out in Boomtown. Just because music pulses in the sultry night air like some giant, throbbing heartbeat. Drugs and booze flow freely, gently caressing the senses. Exotic, sexy women wantonly and willingly do things to your body that previously only filled your midnight fantasies. Sparkling lights cut the darkness, casting a luminosity over the dreams of the world. Warriors on gleaming machines of steel and chrome roar through the neon-sliced darkness. Money flows like champagne. Sleek, shiny muscle cars snake their way through the night traffic. Warlords with names and reputations well earned roam the ways. Leather-clad panthers haunt the jungles of man. The place is a sensuous orgy of the senses that draws the bold to it and spurns civilians and the timid. Cool is the way of life.

Okay . . . I can understand that. I had a hell of a good time while I was there. So it makes sense to me why you'd want to give it a shot. However, as someone who made it there, let me explain a couple of things. Boomtown is actually a mind-set. It's an undefined area, the crack between different worlds where no operating system rules. From Boomtown you can cut into any territory that you want. Some of those territories are very sweet indeed, while others are sheer nightmares.

Imagine a world floating in space. It's not exactly a planet, though. It's like a plate of spaghetti, but instead of noodles, it's made up of plants. Interwoven roots and mushroom networks all exist in a symbiotic relationship, all interwoven with each other like a living ball of spaghetti. No one plant is more important than the any other. All the different mushroom clusters from different networks pop up next to each other in a giant patchwork design, all aiding each other but each separate and often never touching. Even though they exist next to one another, they're from different networks. Got that in your mind?

Now, Boomtown is all the spaces between the different networks. Each network needs a little space around it to breathe and allow necessary light and fluids to travel to it. If a network is not allowed this space, it will eventually suffocate, wilt, and die. Its rot will be felt throughout the entire system. Also, certain networks are detrimental to one another. If they actually touch, trouble is guaranteed. Each network produces something the other needs, but the bartered items are passed through these buffer zones. These exchanges often come in the form of services, but not all services are what you might consider positive. Sometimes the service is in the form of an established enemy—someone to point your youngin's against their youngin's to keep them out of the old folks' hair.

Boomtown serves as a neutral territory, and sometimes it takes on the appearance of a demilitarized zone (DMZ). Regardless of the rules of the different networks in the area, no one system rules in Boomtown. *Everybody* is a guest, and tolerance is extended to other systems. This is why it so attractive: your system's rules are put on hold there. People often mistakenly think that there are no rules in Boomtown, but I'll go into that later. While there, you see all sorts of travelers from other places. This is the ultimate cantina scene from *Star Wars*. People from other systems mingle freely here, and some of them look pretty far out.

There are a variety of Boomtowns, but the ones most people are familiar with are the service-oriented ones, i.e., areas or services that, like it or not, must be shared. Believe it or not, schools and hospitals are the most common. Think about it—where do you *have* to go? Often, members of rival gangs have to attend the same high school. If the school exists in one gang's territory, the other gang has to enter into the other side's turf. The factions deal with this by establishing acceptable corridors and times. You can travel along these streets during school time, but God help the fool who veers off the established course or enters after hours.

Another biggie is hospitals. I know of one hospital that sits at the four corners of four different gang territories. Theoretically, it is possible to lie down spread-eagle somewhere in the hospital and be in four different turfs at once. You can take your pregnant girlfriend there without much of a problem. You may get a few hard looks, but nobody is going to start shooting until after you leave. Its services make it off limits for trouble. Another interesting aspect is when a guy goes down, he's pretty much off limits when he's in the hospital as well. We'll look at the concept of off-limits people in Chapter 14, but right now it's enough to know that there are necessary areas that operate under special Boomtown conditions.

The key thing to remember about Boomtown is that it is not permanent. It is a border town. You stop off there for supplies, entertainment, or rest, or you use it as your starting point if you are a traveler. You go there for education, entertainment, and a good time (a vacation) if you are going to stay in a particular territory. You cannot set up permanent camp there. From Boomtown, you have one of four options:

1) Go back to your network operating system
2) Go into other systems as a new resident
3) Slip into one of the trash-can systems
4) Become a traveler

If you try to stay there, you will eventually get pulled into a trash cans by one of Boomtown's currents, which are necessary for circulation and transportation between the different networks. There are two ways to travel in Boomtown: active, in which you decide where you want to go, and passive, whereby if you do not make up your mind, the borderlands will do it for you. The latter explains how people wake up after ten years and say, "How the fuck did I slip this far?" If someone is kicked out of his community and thinks he'll just hang out in Boomtown, the current will eventually take him to the closest trash-can system.

Boomtown is ever-fluctuating. It has to be. The networks shift constantly, and the communities or clusters rise up and die out regularly. This alters the layout of the borders in between. Remember, the mushroom groups that are part of a network also spring up in these in-between spaces, not just on the outside of the ball, and line the corridors.

Mostly it is the young people of a network who make up the particular clusters lining the corridors. These younger groups act as receivers and buffers for things that come floating down the corridors. The young usually have a more open outlook and are willing to try new thing. If it's good, the young assimilate it faster. Look at computers; show me a kid who's computerphobic. Hell, kids were raised on video games. On the other hand, I've met fifty-year-old secretaries who wouldn't give up their typewriters if you held a gun to their heads. They're afraid to learn computers. In time, as the young grow older, the new items are integrated into the system. That's on the bennie side. On the negative side, if something ugly comes down the pikeway, it nails the fringe groups first. That means the young and the nearly expelled get clobbered first. Racial violence is an example. It usually happens that young groups of an operating system clash long before the elders get involved. In other words, it is the young of a network that bears the brunt first; this way the core elements of the branch are spared.

If the violence continues, the branch itself will become involved. The entire network will begin to channel extra soldiers and support in to the branch, while accepting the refugees. If it loses, the network will abandon the branch and continue on. The best example of this is the underground railroad that the Jews set up to get their people and money out of Nazi Germany. After a certain point, they had to let nations settle it, but they still kicked some ass from behind the scenes. After the war, they were able to reclaim that branch.

So understand that the group you run with is probably the buffer for your network. You have one foot in the network and another in Boomtown. Network rules still apply, and you work with them. This is different from being entirely in Boomtown. You're probably all the way in Boomtown if you find yourself in a place where you—and apparently everyone else—is unsure of the operating system. Several groups are there, but no one has control. Just remember that there *are* rules.

In areas where it acts as a DMZ, Boomtown isn't that big. You can easily go through its neutral zone and end up in another operating system. Make sure that you and your buddies aren't the only people who do not know the rules. For example, a bar that is the haunt of a particular group (or ethnic persuasion) is not Boomtown. It is the buffer of a particular network.

Remember the corridor that has the stairs and pits, the one they told you not to go down, knowing full well that you were going to take your wobbly ass down it? This is the same thing. But instead of going down a corridor, you've crept out onto a rock that sticks out in a river. Here you're watching all sorts of things and people go by—big fun, really interesting. You and your friends sit there drinking beer and hooting and hollering. Unfortunately, while jumping up and down, you fall off the rock, or someone from another group gets pissed at you and knocks you off. Just like with the stairs, back you go to get fixed and tsk-tsked at.

Here's another one of my famous important safety tips: *When you first come down to the river, ain't no one ever taught you to swim.* As you may have guessed, this seriously impedes your chances of surviving if you fall into the river. While there is traffic on the river, down river is a big-assed waterfall. The current leads to the trash can. This is the pit I was talking about. You fall in, everyone cries and beats their chests, and you achieve a form of immortality. You become the example given to children to explain why they shouldn't go down to the river—at least until the next kid doesn't make it back, then he gets the title.

As you're standing there watching all the people on the river, you wonder, "If it's so dangerous, why are they all able not only to survive there but also apparently to flourish?" Some are swimming, some are kyaking, some are working big old barges and bringing up supplies. (By the way, the wacko zippy doing around in the flame-painted Zodiac is me.) In short, there are all sorts of people existing on the currents of Boomtown. As with a real river, there are dangers out there, but people who know what they're doing survive in spite of these dangers. Boomtown is really only dangerous if you drop into autopilot. It's not the guy working a supply barge who is going to buy it in the falls; it's the party dude with his shades and a drink drifting on an inner tube.

The real danger is laziness. If you were to climb down off the rock to the shore of the river, you'd find two booths. One guy is selling swimming lessons, while the other is selling inner tubes. With the first option, you end up spending a lot of time working and learning, while with the other you get to party immediately. They hand you an inner tube, a drink, some cool shades, and a Hawaiian hat and shirt. Cowabunga dude, let's party! Off you go, partying and having a good time.

The river is filled with people on inner tubes, drinking, snorting, dropping, fucking, and having a great time. Some get tired after a while and manage to paddle their way over to shore. Then they merrily go back to where they're from. Others party hardy, until someone tips over and either drowns or nearly drowns. Suddenly, the revellers realize that they don't know how to swim. They haul ass over to the side and stand there shaking, realizing that it could have been them.

Some hang on, however, partying and having a good time. They don't realize that, after a certain point, they don't see any more boats or barges. They're still partying away with others like them. By the time they realize that they've picked up speed, they're fucked. They're caught in the current of the falls, and since they don't know how to swim, they're stuck. Sooner or later, viiiip! Over they go.

This is why you've been told all your life that Boomtown is dangerous. If you walk in and immediately stick your dick in your ear, it is fucking dangerous! Most people walk out there and simply drop every rule and bit of common sense that they have. They do not learn the skills to survive. Boomtown is not black or white; it's thousands of shades of gray. I cannot tell you the numbers of times that I've seen the shit go down because someone said, "Hey, there ain't no rules here. I can do what I want, and I don't have to worry about it."

A critical thing for you to know, folks, is that *under stress people will return to the operating system they know best.* So even as you're raising hell and having a good time, someone who gets his little duck feelings hurt is going to revert to what he learned in his operating system. If what he learned was violence, you're about to get punched. That is part of why Boomtown is considered so dangerous. You're standing next to something from an entirely different operating system, and, if you do something to piss him off, he may turn violent.

Systems that discourage violent behavior usually have someone around guarding the outer perimeter so those inside can be nonviolent. This is supposedly what the police and army are for: to protect the populace. Actually, the police have turned in to a buffer to protect the upper classes from the rest of the world. The fastest way I know to talk to a cop is to drive an old beat-up car in a rich area. You *will* get stopped.

Boomtown doesn't have protectors. You are responsible for your own protection. The cops aren't going to bother if you get your face pushed in. This is why it is important to master the basic skills of survival in Boomtown. The hard part is differentiating between someone floating and someone working the system. Both will willingly teach you, but one's teachings will wipe you out in the long run.

Generally it isn't the first people that you run into in a situation who are the professionals. That's like going to a new school; it's the losers who usually approach you first. In Boomtown, this kind of person either says don't worry about it because there aren't any rules, or he doesn't practice what he preaches. But there are people out there who can and will teach you how to survive in Boomtown. The trick is to never stop learning.

I have gotten more good information and ideas from just sitting around shooting the shit with major leaguers than I can begin to tell you about. You never finish learning about how to survive. After a time, you're no longer a student. You may not be a "master," but you have the hang of it. It's like driving; once you have the basic skills, when a pro mentions a trick, you go, "Yeah, that makes sense."

The major leaguers in Boomtown look at most people as FNGs (remember the fucking new guys from the Introduction?) and figure that many of them will get wasted in the not-too-distant future. In Boomtown, FNGs outnumber the major leaguers about five to one. They're not squared off against each other, but if they were, the major leaguers would walk through the FNGs like the U.S. military went through the Iraqi army during Desert Storm.

Most of the time, they just ignore the FNGs. They just sit there and watch the bozos on the inner tubes with a bored expression. They also watch every other fucking thing that goes on. If you bop up to them, wearing a Hawaiian shirt, straw hat, and cool shades and say, "Dude! Teach me what it takes to make in party town!", you ain't going to get shit. You come to someone with your shit wired tight, and you're more likely to learn something from the guy.

Most people who come out of an operating system really don't want to leave the assumptions they grew up with behind. They are content with the way they view the world, and that's it. This is not how you survive in Boomtown or in the networks. You have to drop your belief in the God-given righteousness of whatever system you were brought up in. If you can't do that you'll never make it. Most of what you will be changing are the definitions and parameters of what you have been taught. For example instead of "Thou shall not kill," try "Thou shall not murder." There's a big difference between those two, and you had better learn it. If you believe in the not-kill part, you're fucked if you meet someone who doesn't. If you adhere to the not-murder view, however, you can, if necessary, kill someone. It is much more functional in the networks and Boomtown.

This is the sort of definition changing that you must do to survive out there. It's one hell of a tough job. I'm not going to tell you it's easy because we're talking about deep learning here. I know one system that calls it "sculpting and armoring." That's pretty accurate.

If all you want to do is hang out on the rock and watch the show on the river, that's okay. Really it is. Cutting territories is an exciting adventure, but it is also as dangerous as fuck. I do not, in any way, think less of the man who decides that he really doesn't want to risk getting his ass shot off. I mean that sincerely. I have buried too many people who really weren't cut out for being out in the bush but had some damn idea that they had to prove something. The only thing I ask is you tell those with a hankering to go yonderin' to watch their asses. There are some rough spots out there, and a little bit of warning can save a lot of asses.

Let's say that you've found yourself in an operating group that sticks out into Boomtown, or you have found yourself in Boomtown proper. Hot diggity damn! It's Friday night! You've got some pistolas in your pockets. You got some juice in your pecker! It's time to go have a good time! Yeee ha! When most people set out under these conditions, they don't really pay much attention to what they should be doing to avoid getting into violent situations. This is probably why, sooner of later, they get in to one. So how do you keep your dick out of the microwave when you are in Boomtown and adjoining suburbs?

The first thing you have to understand is that having a good time does not mean you should let your awareness lapse. Please note, I did not say, "You should not let your defenses down." Contrary to popular opinion, being tough is only a small part of surviving in Boomtown. If you are so busy being a tough guy, the likelihood of you meeting that exotic woman from the midnight hand flexing sessions is going to pretty damn thin.[1]

The other thing is that while you are sitting there telling yourself how tough you are, a real hardass is sitting next to you trying to keep from cracking up. I have run into some of the toughest people I have ever met in Boomtown. Some were good guys, some were bad guys, some didn't give a shit about definitions—they just did what it took to survive. This may sound weird, but your defenses should be like those on the USS *Enterprise*. You should have long-range sensors, short-range sensors, and shields. At a moment's notice, you can snap your shields up. What's more, there are degrees of shields. Maximum protection should be applied only when you are going in to battle. Keeping your shields on minimum scares most of Boomtown's flotsam and jetsam away.

You keep your long-range scanners going at all times. They let you know what's in the area. Your short-range scanners are much more intense. They can scan for particulars, like the exact location of life forms on the planet. On a self-defense level, this translates into "Where does this guy have his concealed weapons?"

You should be scanning your surroundings subconsciously at all times. Take a break now and then for a casual glance around the place you're in. Check to make sure that everything is kosher. Does anyone in the place have an attitude? Is anyone getting too rambunctious? Figure out the overall energy level of the place and look for pockets of energy that don't gel. You'll know immediately if anyone is getting too far out of line.

For example, at the party mentioned in the quotation at the beginning of this chapter, a topless dancer with pierced nipples and dressed in leather and chains was not too far out of line. In fact, it was right on par. (It was one hell of a party.) However, the guy on acid who started chain-whipping another guy was a little much. He realized his mistake when I landed on him. I should point out that everyone at that party was heavily armed, and we knew how to use them. The only weapons rule was that you checked your ammo at the door. I and a few more like me were bouncing. This was not the kind of place where you wanted to cross the few existing rules.

In this situation, you learn to be rock-hard, not just tough. Remember, I was talking earlier about hard-core types who've battled the elements and survived? In Boomtown, you really have to watch where you are and who's around you. Warriors, warlords, dog soldiers, and borderlords all move in Boomtown channels. These are the heavy hitters who eat tough guys for breakfast.

If you're just stepping onto the circuit, be advised that there are people out there who will chew up and spit out people a whole lot harder than you. In fact, one such hardass could be sitting right next to you. Generally speaking, they'll ignore any posturing coming from youngins, but if pushed too far, they will move. I have seen a whole shitload of kids who thought they were tough get mauled by one of these grizzled old fucks.

Even if a punk looking for trouble gazes your way, check out what's going on elsewhere before you go countertough— especially if there are pros around. A body count is a very real thing in Boomtown. Usually it consists of people who got too cocky at the wrong time and in the wrong place.

Before I go further, I should explain something here. Let's

look at you average predator, the ones that appear in nature. We're talking lions, tigers, and bears, not the mythological goofball that you see in the movies or high schools. You will notice that a lone predator does not stand up on a hilltop and yell, "Yo hoo, everybody! I'm here, and looking for lunch!" If animals are smart enough not to do that, why aren't people? The only predators who announce their presence are certain members of the "top-line" club—such as the cheetah—who are doing it to recon an area and only then when special conditions are met. Every other predator has to rely on cunning, camouflage, trickiness, blindshots, selective targeting, stealth, and, most importantly, its prey's lack of awareness.

What's more, your average predator has to worry about those higher up on the food chain. While they're looking to volunteer someone for lunch, somebody else is looking to volunteer them. They are both the hunter and the hunted. They have to sneak up on, bushwhack, or somehow trap their lunch, while at the same time keeping the same from happening to them. This is the existence of about 95 percent of all so-called predators. Generally speaking, all predators are also scavengers. Real romantic, huh?

The top-of-the-line predators are different in that nobody is actively hunting them. Other than that, the rules are about the same. If a lioness sneaks up on a herd, when she pops up and goes, "Boo," she's already in their faces. There is no choice left for the hunted except to get the fuck out of there. Prior to the attack, there was a shitload of skulking and sneaking from downwind and behind bushes.

It is the surprise attack that is successful in nature, even with the big guys. Learn this and live it. If the lioness tips her hand too soon (or another lion accidentally hits the car horn), the buffet will object—either in the form of a bugout or a defensive circle. If the prey bugs out quickly enough, the lioness can't catch them. If they form a defensive circle, the lioness has a problem. A gnu with an attitude and a pointy end aimed at you is not something you want to tangle with. This is why surprise is so critical to a predator's survival. If they do it wrong, they'll get fucked up. The safest way for any predator to attack normal prey is from behind. The sharp parts are usually up front. When running, the back is what you see. Ah, how nice, no points. The only predators who do anything like an announcement are those who hunt in packs or want their prey to run. If they've spooked them earlier, they've already picked out the weak, sick, and lame. Those are the ones that they'll go for. Then they'll sneak up and go boo. That way the rest of the herd won't get defensive.

A cheetah, on the other hand, has a nasty trick. It lets its prey get going at top speed and then trips the fucker. The cheetah's jaws are actually too weak to kill like a lion's, so it trips a gazelle at forty miles an hour and falling at that speed breaks its neck. No run—no lunch for spots. A wolf pack will chase down its prey and wear it out first. Even then, they go for the hamstrings. Which would you rather fuck with, a fresh moose or a tired moose who can't cover his ass? You will notice, even these top-line tactics still conform to the predator's little blue rule book: hit from behind and with trickery. Boom, pass the ketchup.

Face it, if you don't sneak up on your prey, you ain't going to get lunch. Not only that, if it decides to fight rather than run, you're going to get hurt. If your prey decides to fight instead of run, you can get torn up real bad. I once saw photos of a rat that had battled a rattlesnake. The rat eventually died but not before jacking up that rattler so bad that it could not eat the rat; it could only limp away. I suspect the snake died later, too. I don't think that snake would have attacked if it had known that the rat would turn on it instead of trying to run. Keep this in mind about the bad guys on the street. I'm making a real big circle here because 99 percent of all the predators you meet are not top-line.

The other way to sneak up on your prey is to let them come to you. You pick an area, pull some leaves over your head, and wait silently in the cracks and for lunch to amble by. You pop out and say, "Bon appétit!"

The next most common way is to trap your lunch. The old spider web relies on lunch just happening to drop in and not getting out. There is the old ant-lion trick: get them in the hole and keep pulling the ground out from under them until they're in too deep to get out. Then there is the old wiggler-fish trick, which is to put out bait and then eat anyone who comes for it. But my all-time favorite is cornering. The prey enters an area where there is only one way out, which unfortunately, is blocked by the hunter. The predator may chase its prey into a cul de sac, or, like the badger, dig out anything that goes down an end tunnel.

Of course, there is also poison, an advanced form of trap. You wait for the sucker to get too close, and then you zing it. The poison keeps it from fighting back. Generally because the zappee tries to run rather than fight, the poison works its way into the bloodstream quickly. By the time the poisoner catches up to the victim, the job's done. The photos of the rat and snake were in a cage. Ordinarily the rat would have tried to book rather than fight. This is a good defense against poisoners. You may be able to survive the poison, but you won't make it if they're still standing while you're wrestling with the poison.

The reason that I mention this little biology lesson about predators is that you will see the same things in Boomtown. Instead of coyotes and rabbits, you're going to see muggers and civilians. You will see these same techniques among the hunted and hunters out there. The bad guys know these.

Fortunately, very few of them really have more than one form down. If you're dealing with dangerous snakes, you're either dealing with poison or constriction. It's not likely that you'll meet up with someone who has perfected both. Your average street scum doesn't have enough imagination to perfect more than one, maybe two, approaches. However, you still have to watch yourself because if each scumbag perfects just one approach, you still have enough to cover all the possibilities.

Generally speaking, though, all avenues of attack are through some blindspot. If you don't know I'm there until I jump out of the bushes, you're going to get fucked. To varying degrees, all of these techniques rely on the prey not being aware of the danger. Most people don't realize that it isn't smart to put themselves in an area with no exit. Some techniques rely on the prey being so blinded by its desire to get something that it forgets everything else. They end up getting nailed instead. This is real common on the streets.

Now for the good news. Not all predators are successful. They often snake out and grab hold of the wrong item, like a coyote accidentally pouncing on a bobcat instead of a house cat. Whoops! Or they may tip their hand too soon and get nailed by something that fights rather than runs, such as the tiger that gets gored and stomped by a water buffalo. Damn, that looked real painful.

Some things you just do not fuck with, regardless of who you are. I don't care if you are a lion, you don't fuck with a rhino. A cougar doesn't fuck with a wolf and vice versa. Nothing plays with a puffer fish—not only will it be like swallowing a ball of razor blades, it's poisonous to boot. It's not worth it.

When I say you must have your awareness up, I am talking about scanning behavior that most people don't even know exists outside the animal kingdom. Regardless of what our moral high-horse factions say, we are animals. The rules that apply there also apply to us. When I talk about blind-spots, I'm talking about areas that most people not only don't see, but don't know that they don't see them. You have to be aware of your own blindspots.

The biggest blindspot is that there are people out there who think like predators. If you know that most attacks come from behind, you can spend time looking back. Not in fear, but so as you can turn the pointy end around at anyone trying to sneak up on you. Learn how these people attack and you can set up alarms for anyone coming at you that way. Someone comes at you from that angle and you are aware of it immediately. Suddenly he is looking at the pointed end of an attitude. If you know cul de sacs are a trap, don't go in there. Find the box canyons from the ridge line, not by wandering into them.[2] Don't walk by shadows and cracks without looking into them for possible skulkers. Remember, some folks pull leaves over their heads and wait. When you enter a new area, step to the side and scope out the layout and what's going on before diving in.

Be aware of other predators' habits and smells. Learn to identify their dens, haunts, and traps. When you walk into a place, look for the strategically superior places to sit. Then check out who has already claimed them. It may be an accident, but generally if they know enough to be there, they're worth watching.

One thing that I am going to say across-the-board is that white middle-class culture has lost its primitive edge. It has become totally dissociated with the natural flow and systems. To make it in Boomtown, you have to become like a mountain man: wily as a fox, harder than a badger, cautious as a wolf, and as aware as a mountain lion. Just as the Indians lived in awareness of the wilds around them, you have to become aware of the new wilds you'll find yourself in. If you were a mountain man back then, you had to be aware of everything. Indians, while they could kill you, could also trade with you, teach you, and share with you. You had to understand their ways when you were in their territory. Each tribe was different in ways and temperament, and you had to know these things to keep from crossing lines.

But that was only a small part of what you had to know. You had to know the seasons and forest. If you wanted to live, you needed to know where to find food, when to start digging in for the winter, where you didn't want to go for no good reason, what you had to do to survive if you decided to go there anyway. In short, you needed not only to know what was going on around you, but also how to do all sorts of things. An avalanche could kill you just as fast as a hostile Indian. So your awareness needed to cover a whole lot more than just how to shoot.

Now, I got a problem here. Ordinarily, when I want to make a point, I just pull up a movie reference. Describing something and then saying it's like in so-and-so movie is a really good way to get ideas across. That way, you've already seen what I'm talking about, or you are just a quick trip to the video joint away. What's put my dick in the mud about this one is that I know no movie that even comes close to representing the kind of awareness I'm talking about. I mean zippo, zero, none!

This is a real bitch. First off, most people have no idea what I'm really talking about. When they begin to understand, it makes it look like it's some sort of mystical, unattainable power that only a chosen few can ever dream of attaining. What I'm talking about is a state of awareness that any junkie in America has. If a junkie can do it, I know most people can.

What I'm talking about is knowing things that people who don't know get their asses shot off for. In short, awareness can be broken down into two categories: how things really work and what's going on around you.

How Things Really Work

I'm not talking about the bullshit about how it's supposed to be. The only thing a bucket of shit is worth is the price of the bucket. I'm talking about the way that things really are. Like in the first business class scene in Rodney Dangerfield's *Back to School*, the professor is talking all this hypothetical bullshit, while Dangerfield's character is talking hard-line operating reality. The professor goes on about the way business is supposed to work, while the self-made millionaire is talking about bribes, kickbacks, graft, and corruption. (Whew! I needed that quick movie reference. I feel better now.)

This is knowing how things are supposed to work and how they really get along. This is, of course, the hypocrisy about which kids get bent out of shape. You have to know both sides of the fence. What's spoken and what's unspoken.

I've given you the tools to analyze whatever system you find yourself in so you have a head start on this one. Most people get about three steps out of the gate before they get knocked on their asses by this stuff.

Another aspect of knowing how things work involves a basic understanding how physics apply to self-defense. A moving car takes a certain amount of time and space to stop. That's if the driver is on the ball. Without awareness, the time necessary extends a whole lot. Keeping this in mind, you don't want to put yourself in any place where the propelling person or object can't stop in time or that you can't get out of the way. If the guy behind you doesn't realize you've stopped, he's going to give you an enema, no ands, ifs, or buts about it. This is the way it works. Getting smashed affects your reflexes. This is one of the laws of nature.

Booze also affects your central nervous system. Knowing beforehand how it affects yours can save your ass when the shit hits the fan. That way you can give yourself runway, in case it does get ugly.

What's Going On around You

Most people wrap themselves up inside their heads, listening to the internal conversations, and have no idea what is actually going on around them. This is really no shit here, folks. The reason they do this has little to do with self-defense and more with creating enough white noise to jam certain internal signals. The effect that it has on self-defense, though, is that it makes 90 percent of the population dinner on the hoof for would-be predators. When it comes to self-defense this is the biggest fatal flaw people make in this field. This includes most so-called martial artists.

Instead of sitting there waiting for your girlfriend or so wrapped up in thinking about what you want to say to your boss, pay attention to what is happening around you. I'll deal with awareness building techniques in Chapter 15, but what I'm talking about here is being where you are, not 50,000 miles away inside your head.

Being aware is not some mysterious occult power. Essentially, it is being consciously aware of who and what is around you at all times. It means being where you are attentionwise, not off in space-cadet land! It's incredibly simple conceptwise and a real pain in the ass to achieve in reality. The good news is that the hardest part of it isn't something you have to start doing. Rather it is what you have to stop doing: talking to yourself all the time. Most people are too busy yakking their mental jaws to see that either someone is sneaking up on them, or that they're about to get punched for pissing someone off. So, once again, as if we haven't heard it before, the first key to surviving in Boomtown is awareness. That is the stone-cold, plain and simple root of the matter. You can cut it any way you want, and it will still keep on coming back to this booger.

The next key to surviving in Boomtown also sounds simple: *Keep your shit wired tight.* If you ain't looking to catch a fish named trouble, make sure that your hook isn't in the water. You have to take responsibility for your actions and how they affect others. This is not to say that you are to blame for the world's feelings. Most people confuse blame with responsibility; there is one hell of a big difference. What I am saying is that you cannot expect to do or say certain things and not have someone react to them. I'm sorry, "It all started when he hit me back" does not fly here folks.

While in a very real sense, you should not let other people's feelings determine your actions, there are points beyond which this doesn't fly. Join me in a little reality break here. I cannot tell you the number of times I have broken up fights that, when I asked what happened, some guy with his lip quivering in indignation about the other guy hitting him replies with something like, "All I said was his mother sucks horse cocks . . . "

Jesus H. Christ! Let's get real here. You cannot do shit like that and not expect someone to swing at you! What is ha-ha funny to you could be a mortal insult to someone else. This is knowing what operating system you are in at all times and not crossing the boundaries without good cause. If you say something like that, there had better be an express purpose for it. If there isn't, don't piss on someone's shoes.

I admit that I have said things that were designed to get a fight going. Once when I was living in a co-op in the worst part of Hollywood, I got in a jam with some low-class Armenian bucks. One of them had violated our territory and then copped an attitude when one of my roomies retaliated for the infraction. I was in the back barbecuing when the troublemaker came back with reinforcements. A West Texan, a 6'3" guy from the south side of Chicago, a fella from Oregon, and a Sheffield Brit beat me out the door. The young bucks were confused about running into such resistance. But instead of backing off, they woofed their way up, making a move. I tried to talk them down, but they kept going. Finally I said, "Fuck it," to myself and looked at them and said, "Ya know what? The Turks should have finished the job!"[3]

This was a guaranteed "either you fucking move now or you get off my land" action. (It also in no way reflects my personal feelings about Armenians.) If we were going to fight, it was going to happen right then and there. I forced the issue. Now when I said that I fully expected him to go ballistic on me, and I was ready, willing, and able to pay the price. I also had a knife palmed out of sight in my hand. He would have been ambulance bait a split second after he moved. They figured anyone crazy enough to say something like that to their faces was too far gone to fuck with.

If I had not meant for it to end—one way or the other—at that exact moment, I *never* would have said anything like that. When I said it, I was willing to kill and/or be killed for my actions. This was the duelist mentality in action. Those bucks came looking for a rumble and met up with people who were ready for a firefight.

If you are not willing to pay that sort of price, be careful with what you say. I have never again said that to an Armenian, nor do I intend to. This also includes watching someone very closely who does this sort of move. Either they are totally out of touch with the reality of repercussions, or they've done it on purpose and it's a trap.

One of the things you have to look at is your sense of humor. Some people come from places that consider humor really insulting. I'm not talking about the put-down artist that I opened this book with; I'm talking about a group of guys who commonly call each other "asshole" and "dork." Usually, they don't really mean anything by it. Mike, the guy I opened this book up with, was counting coup with his verbal slashes. You may be running with a group of guys who communicate this way. However, what's appropriate in one place isn't in another. This can cause a whole lot of problems.

I knew a guy who was home for a visit from the navy. He was having a nice Jewish family dinner to welcome him home when suddenly the conversation stopped dead. He checked back on his conversation tape and discovered that his request for food to be passed to him was phrased as, "Pass the fuckin' potatoes." That was polite for the destroyer he was on but didn't do so well at the family dinner. I've been cussed out so many times that it doesn't bother me anymore. Say, "Fuck you," to me and I'll blow you a kiss, but there are other people to whom "them is fightin' words!"

Saying something that is perfectly acceptable in one area but not in another leads to a shitload of fights. Remember, even if you are unconscious of it, you are broadcasting signals to others. How your words are interpreted depends on who receives them.

One of the most common mistakes made in Boomtown is people relaxing too soon. Remember what I said about people resorting to the operating system that they know best under stress? The same can be said about relaxing. People have a habit of saying, "Hey, it's cool," and then putting it on autopilot. When you're on autopilot, who knows what signals you're sending out? It's all unconscious.

What's worse, when you're on autopilot, your radar gets turned off. Since it's cool, you don't bother with sweeps—bad move, really bad move, that one. Next thing you know, you're in a fight, wondering what the fuck is wrong with this guy. You were hanging out, joking, and having a good time, and the next thing you knew, he copped an attitude. The fact that you mentioned his sister having sexual relationships with a German shepherd had nothing to do with it. He was just being an asshole. Yeah, right. Remember, you're not going to win all your fights so you better be careful what you fight over.

Another aspect of keeping your shit wired tight is never putting yourself in a place that you can't get out of immediately. This refers to situation, location, and, most especially, mental state.

Let's look at the mental part first. If you know that the shit can get ugly, *never* get so fucked up that you can't come back immediately. Bottom line: if you are entering an unfamiliar area, do not proceed to get smashed immediately. Sit back and watch what and whom you are dealing with. Or if you are in a tough-assed place, don't get too bombed.

Years ago in Venice, California, I was at a primarily Japanese party, but since it was an open party officially, there was a pretty good mix. All of the valuables had been taken down and stored in a particular room. The word had gone out to keep away from that room. No problem—we were all drinking, toking, and having a good time. All of a sudden, there was a scream. A guy had gotten into the room and filled his fatigue pockets with goodies. When he was leaving, the girl who owned the house ran into him coming out of the room. He then made a real serious mistake—he hit her.

Everyone with experience at that party snapped into awareness when she screamed. They caught him about twenty yards from the front door. Then they proceeded to tear him up. I tell you people I have seen stompings by the Hell's Angels that weren't as thorough as this one. After they had whipped him around, they told him to finish emptying his pockets. There was a problem, though; they had broken all of his fingers. Instead they frisked him and shook out all of the stolen items. While they were sorting the stuff, someone began to drag him away. Another person looked up and said, "Hey, he can still walk. Let's break his legs." They did. Now I did not participate in this particular soiree. None of my family was out there. However, you can bet I was pretty alert when it went down. At least twenty people did an immediate come to when it got ugly.

For all the times I have gotten blasted, I never got a drunk-driving rap. The reason is simple. I never got toasted anyplace I wasn't invited to spend the night. The places that I got smashed were safe havens for me. I knew that the shit was highly unlikely to happen there. So I could relax and party down. I rarely got so polluted that I couldn't snap back. The main reason is that I used to practice self-defense when ripped. Going after me when I was buzzed did no good; I was trained to fight when stoned, drunk, high, wired, or frying.

The other aspect of drinking and self-defense is knowing what's inside of you. I am a happy drunk. When I get ripped, I want to have fun. I get loud, and I play. When I decide to let go I romp around like a tiger playing with a beer keg.[4] I can handle my high and keep from getting nasty. All too often, though, what happens with chemicals is that they lower people's inhibitions enough to bring out behavior people generally keep suppressed. Way too often, this isn't real nice. This is why so many fights break out around booze and drugs. If you are a mean drunk or an obnoxious drunk, keep away from booze.

Generally, speed freaks are mean, vicious people, and crackheads are on another planet altogether. If you find a substance that brings out the asshole in you, keep away from it. Only the traditional Japanese think that a man is not accountable when drunk. Everyone else will bust your jaw for misbehaving when ripped.

Watch what people do when they are smashed. Set up a little video camera inside your head to record what people are like. There are stages of intoxication. Different substances affect people differently. Even parties have cycles. The time that I most dread is the three o'clock vampire party. Almost everyone has gone home, except a hard-core, seriously ripped small group. For the most part, these are the pro drinkers who are nonviolent, but every now and then you get the amateurs out for the night. They're too fucked up for common sense, and, at the drop of a hat, they can turn nasty. A full 60 percent of the drunk, screaming arguments happen with this 10 percent of the party-goers. Make it a habit to bow out before this part of the cycle. If you're not there, nobody can pick a fight with you; it's a physical impossibility.

Practice keeping your shit wired tight when you are snockered. I know that it sounds like it takes all the fun out of partying, and I must admit that it diminishes spontaneity. It also seriously reduces your chances of a busted nose. The guy you don't want to tangle with is not the guy with the leather jacket and the Billy Idol sneer; rather it is the guy whose movements are measured and controlled, even when he is drunk or stoned. If he has that much self-control, you definitely don't want to play with him for no good reason. If you take this self-control over drunkenness and apply it to your mouth, you greatly improve the chances of having all your teeth there when you sober up.

The other way of keeping your shit wired tight is not to put yourself into locations you can't get out of in uncool situations. Never put yourself in a place where you can be cornered or bushwhacked, especially if the shit is hot. Normal operations is Code 1, but if you're involved in trouble it goes up a notch. If you do have to go into these sort of places, when you go in you are Code 2 status. (Code 1, possible problem; Code 2, problem with some hair on its chest; Code 3, serious shit storm). Most importantly, get your ass out of there fast! Do not stop to wag your dick at the locals. You go in and get out fast and tight. Watch your back and don't let anyone get close to you. While you are doing this, you are on guard and ready for any shit that may come down the pike.

When you park your car, turn it in the direction in which you'll be leaving. That way, if you need to leave in a hurry, you don't have to turn your car around. Also, if you park on the street, park so your front bumper is looking at someone's driveway or an open zone. In a parking lot, choose a site away from the door and all the way through to the other side of the parking spaces. Also, back into the space. That way it's not likely that you'll be accidentally blocked in. If you have to rabbit, you just go, no backing up or getting out of parking spaces. Just straight out. *Hasta la vista, baby!*

The fastest way to learn this stuff is under fire. However, that has a habit of seriously cutting down the number of alumni. CIA has a habit of recruiting kids from school, but I wouldn't recommend that as a way to learn this stuff. I've met former operatives of the "Company." It's not a way you want to go.The next best way is to simply sit down and use your imagination. Think about what can go wrong—both intentionally and by sheer coincidence. Ask what it would take to fuck up a situation. If this went wrong, what would you do? Keep it simple.

To show how this works, let's look at the car again. Something has happened, you have to get out quick. There are pursuers behind you. How many times have you been parked in? How often do you have to jockey your car out of a parking space? If you were being chased, would you have time to get the keys out and unlock the door, relock the door, start the car, and then spend all this time trying to get out of the parking spot? Not fucking likely, pal. Either you have a driver there with the motor running and the doors unlocked (if you're involved in criminal activities), or you leave your vehicle in a position where you can bug out immediately. I have my keys on a clip that hangs off my belt, and my door key is also my ignition key. It's on the outside of my key ring. As I run, I grab; when I hit the car, I'm gone with no delays. Ever notice bikers line their bikes up with the back tires against the curb, front pointing out into the street? Ah ha!

The next thing about keeping your shit wired tight is knowing whom you're dealing with. This includes not only the caliber of the person, but to whom he is connected. Is he an independent or a member of a group? The group doesn't have to be formally organized to be dangerous. And just because someone is alone doesn't mean that he's not dangerous. I have met certain professionals who were more dangerous than entire gangs. Not only were they willing to kill, but these guys were what Rambo was based on.

The more powerful a group/person is, the more dangerous it/he is. There are people that you just do not cross and leave standing. That is the most common mistake that hustlers, grifters, and rip-off artists make. In the beginning, they are careful. After a time they get used to crossing people who do not come looking for them. Going to the cops to complain doesn't count as coming after them. They know that a cop isn't going to chase them out of his district. So they go cruising along, laughing at the suckers they've ripped off. These people get cocky and go after the wrong person/group. This is where they are reminded that there are two parts to a hustle: doing it and getting away with it.

Paybacks are a bitch. This not only includes scams and rip-offs, but squealing and setting people up. A lot of people go down for talking about someone's activities. I know of one couple who were found in a Florida hotel room with small caliber bullet wounds in their skulls, lying next to a large amount of money. The hitters just capped them and left the money untouched as a warning to others. If the money had been taken, it would have been written off as another drug deal gone sour. But this was a professional hit, and everyone knew it. They also knew who these people had crossed. 2 + 2 = 4. When you are dealing with heavyweights, you do not get out of line. If you do, you had better be prepared for war. You can sometimes cross some of the big boys and get away with it if you are seriously hard-core and have heavy backing. Also it's a one-time deal. After it's over you leave for good. In fact, you were just backing toward the door anyway. All in all it's just not worth crossing certain people. "If you can't run with the big dogs, stay on the porch." The big dogs have rules, and, unless you are willing to play by them, you will either not get close to them, or you will get taken out.

The next basic of existing in Boomtown is cover your ass (CYA). This involves radar, spies, espionage, disinformation, debts, loyalties, backup, and insurance. You set up a safety net that protects you on at least three different levels, and you don't go waltzing into another person's safety net.

Let's start with the basics. What I am talking about here is that you do not leave any doors open for someone to sneak in through. You sit with your back against the wall or to a group that you've scoped out already. You sit in a place where you can see anyone coming in or going out of your area. You don't sit with your back turned toward a major thoroughfare. You don't walk close to places where people can jump out at you. You look both ways as you step through a door.[5] When you turn a corner, you swing wide in case someone is hiding there, and you look back where you came from. Before you approach a situation, you circle around it and see it from all sides. You always scope out locations where someone could hide and watch. You develop a sliding scale of how close you let people get to you before you turn the pointy end at them. During the day in New York City, it's wall-to-wall people, and there's not much you can do about it. At night in an unpopulated area, don't let anyone get within five feet of you. At fifteen feet, you have them spotted; at ten, you're turning toward them; at five, you're telling them to back off. If they keep coming, they fall down hard.

As you may have guessed, you do not go waddling into nasty places with your dick flapping in the wind. Nor do you spin over to the opposite extreme and go in with a big red "S" on your chest and an attitude to match. When you are in a dangerous location, you do not do anything that could be interpreted as an attack or the preliminary to one. You watch for similar actions on the part of those around you. If anyone gets fidgety, you call them on it ASAP.

With this awareness, you do not go into other heavy hitters' blindspots. I cannot tell you the number of civilians I have almost taken out because they came waltzing into my blindspot. What amazes me is the attitude they display about it. I scared the shit out of them by reacting when they scared the shit out of me. As far as they're concerned, they haven't done anything wrong, and I have no right to react that way. Bullshit, but I don't have time to explain it to them. Know that civilians will cross these lines and that heavy hitters are supposed to know better.

Remember, going into someone's blindspot or moving suddenly in certain ways is interpreted as the preamble to an attack. A civilian may be able to get away with it, but once you know about it, you won't.

Another aspect of CYA is being realistic. You must think both offensively and defensively. Often the winner is he who moves first. (This is short run; long run is he who gets away with it.) In some situations, a gun will not protect you. All a gun will allow you to do is shoot back. If the bad guys opens fire first, the odds are that you are dog meat. There are a lot of bodies in the morgue that bear me out on this one.

So offensively, you've got a gun. What about defense? Do you have a bulletproof vest in case you get bushwhacked and can't get out of the way in time? That's how it really goes down most times when you are running in Boomtown and the borderlands. Have you changed your patterns? Are you predictable as to where you'll be or which route you're going to use? While you are in a danger zone or def-con status, you don't get drunk or stoned. Always think strategically.

I've already talked about scanning and putting your back against the wall (especially at those fucking money machines). If you practice it consciously for a while, in time it will become an unconscious action. If your ass is covered even when you aren't thinking about it, it will show to anyone who is looking for trouble. Nine times out of ten, he'll decide it isn't worth it and leave you alone. This is the first line of CYA.

The second calls for a little more creativity. It also includes using your imagination. How can it go wrong and what can you do to counter that? Figure out rabbit holes and escapes. If the shit got ugly, where would you disappear to? Lying low in the same neighborhood in which the trouble occurred is not the best idea, nor is running to mommy and daddy's house. That's the second place police look, and the bad guys might waste your whole family if they think you're hiding there. Depending on whom you're up against, getting out of state or sometimes out of country may be better. Traveling on your credit cards isn't the best idea either. ATMs are also traceable As long as you're moving, you're fine; but once you settle down, the bad guys can find you.

Most of your disappearance aids are moles that you plant long before you have to disappear, and you only activate them in emergencies. How do you get new ID? Remember, the people who would be chasing you might know these tricks too. They pay a visit to the local ID man, who drops a dime if you show up. That's why it's best to get the stuff beforehand. (Paladin Press has a full library of new ID and personal freedom titles. Check these out long before you need them.)

When I was running a community correctional center, I had a guy who was given to me to be stashed away. He had pulled a Code Stupid and had the Shotgun Crips looking for him. Ripping off these kind of people in a drug deal is not the smartest idea that ever came down the river, but again and again, people try it. Also real common are lowlifes who have relatives who are on the other side of the fence. This guy had a sister who was a parole agent, weird but true. As a favor to the parole department, we squirreled him away in my place with a gag order, while "upstairs" was trying to get his case transferred out of state. He was strutting around playing it big, until word came by that his partner had been blown away on his sister's front porch.

She had also been involved in this little indiscretion, and the homeboys found her. He started chaffing under the ball gag. He came to me and wanted out. I told him what he was doing was suicide. He looked at me and told me he had people in Long Beach who would take care of him. (Long Beach is only ten or so miles away from the Shotgun's territory.) Furthermore, he proudly told me that he knew the "street," and he could take care of himself. I told him that the people who were hunting him also knew the street and there were more of them than him. We finally let him go, and he rabbited down to Long Beach. There he started running the same shit. About two months later, I heard that his fan club had found him. End of conversation.

This is the kind of stupidity that most people do when they

think they have it covered. Not only do you get out of the area, but you get out of the same network. The reason that the federal witness relocation plan doesn't work too often is the fuckers go back to doing the same shit that they were doing before. The circles are small: same network, same type of cluster. It's only a matter of time before someone is traveling though and IDs the bozo. Word gets back and blamo!

The third way to CYA is to create a network around you. Get people you trust and who trust you to take care of each other. Recruit some neighborhood kids to watch out for your stuff. Get to know the liquor-store guy, your neighbors, the guy at the newsstand, the mailman, etc.

There was a period of ten years when, if anything was going to be coming at me, I'd know about it immediately. I'd hit the area, and I'd hear from about eight sources that something was up. One place in Hollywood, I'd come home and the neighborhood kids would tell me who had been around my house. Machiavelli wrote, "The best fortress is to be found in the love of the people, for although you have fortresses, they will not save you if you are hated by the people." You can get a lot of good info from the old guy who runs the corner shoeshine booth. If he's on your side, he can also throw the hounds off. Get the locals on your side.

The other aspect is get an extended family. There are certain people who I trust with my life. I rely on these people to watch my back, and they rely on me to watch theirs. The tab is always balanced; they don't owe me too much, and I don't owe them too much. I know these people would not do things like rip-offs and drunken shootings. Because of that, I would avenge their deaths. Knowing I would not get out of line, they would do the same to anyone who got me.

"Avenge" is not the same as "revenge." The network is really critical for long-term survival. It is insurance. Before someone decides to make a move on you, he has to consider not only how to get you, but your people as well and, in some cases, your people's people on top of that. It can get ugly real fast. The downside of this is that you have to make sure the people you are floating your stick with are honorable. I'm talking about people who believe in "Carry out your own dead." If you're hit and hurting, someone comes for you. You would do the same for them.

Don't tie your boat to someone who has a habit of doing unwise things, especially when it comes to this tight of a bond. Even being a drinking buddy with someone who gets mean when he gets drunk isn't the best recipe for long-term survival. In some circles, you can be held accountable for your friend's actions if the aggrieved can't find him. It often happens that killing you will avenge their honor for his misconduct. In most places, though, if they see you are with him, they will bring reinforcements to balance the tab. You can get involved in a lot of shit that isn't yours this way. If your friend doesn't have the common sense not to mess in some territories, you can get blown away or end up paying his tab.

The way to figure this one out is to ask yourself, "Do I agree with what my friend did? Was he being out of line? Is he pushing it?" (Revenge is not applicable here.) If you think it's right, but someone thinks differently, then you should back him up. However, if your friend was being an asshole, and you're there because you feel that you have to back him up regardless, you are in the wrong place. If you and your buddies are having fun and someone comes over and threatens to kick your asses, that's one thing. If you were creating a ruckus and someone came over and asked you to cool it down and your buddy told him to go fuck off, that's quite another. There are places where past a certain point, backing up a buddy is not really applicable.

Revenge is the best example. Anytime someone crosses the line with revenge it opens a huge can of worms. Regardless of how justified someone felt when he moved in revenge, it's open season after that point. Right or wrong doesn't count after that because it's going to lead to trouble. Guaranteed. Let's say that your buddy jams with someone and backs down. Instead of letting it go, your buddy flattens the guy's tires. You may sit there and go, "Yeah, the guy was being an asshole and deserved it." Bullshit! That is a move that *will* escalate violence. The other guy *will* retaliate. Regardless of what happened before, all he will remember is that your buddy (and maybe you, too) flattened his tires. That's how a lot of shit starts. Someone's ego won't let it go, and he tries to even the score. The next thing you know, the other side is coming back at you harder than the first time. Voilà—instant escalation.

Don't let your buddies do this shit, or anything else that leads to retaliation. When I was younger, I was riding in this guy's van; his name was Mike or something. I didn't know him too well; we had met in class or something. He had a different group of friends than I did, but for some reason, we were together. Anyway, we turned down this street where there were ten or so guys playing street football. One of the guys looked at the van and said something to this monster of a guy. Instead of getting out of the road, they stayed there. Mike stopped the van, and they surrounded us. I was getting nervous, so I reached down and grabbed a tire iron from under the seat. Well , the monster walked up to the driver's side window and asked, "Is this your van?"

Mike answered, "Yes."

The monster asked, "Have you owned it long?"

Mike responded, "A while," whereupon the monster cocked back and punched him through the window. (That shows how big the dude was. It was a straight shot off the shoulder). I mean this beast rocked Mike a good one—if he hadn't been hanging onto the steering wheel he would have been knocked into my lap.

In the meantime, I'm sitting there thinking, "Shit! There's nine of them and Godzilla! Mike isn't a fighter; if they charge the van, we're fucked!" I wasn't about to get out of the van; if they wanted us, they'd have to come in and get us. Mike squeals, "Whaddya do that for?"

The monster said, "That's for nailing my friend with a fire extinguisher last week!"

I looked at Mike with a "You did what?" look and thought to myself, "You are on your own, motherfucker." It suddenly went from a "we" to an "I" as to whom yours truly was going to watch out for.

Mike whined, "It wasn't me! It was my friends who did it!"

The monster looked at him and said, "You were driving, weren't you?"

Mike said, "Yeah, but I told them not to do it!"

Mr. Monster told him, "Get the fuck out of here and tell your friends I'm looking for them."

Mike did, and we went over to the house of his friend of fire-extinguisher fame. A lot of other guys were hanging out getting stoned. When they heard what happened, we all gathered up clubs, bats, and knives and piled into the van for revenge. Note the equation: revenge for revenge because someone else was being an asshole. Fortunately, the game had broken up by the time we got there, and we were spared the joys of a rumble.

This is what I mean when I say you will be held accountable for the actions of the people you are with. This is how a thunderin' herd of shit starts. I really didn't know Mike, I definitely didn't know the rest of these guys, and yet there I was heading out for a gangfight over something one of them had started by being a complete prick. Not good. Keep away from situations like this. If you do, you'll prove that you are a whole lot smarter than I was.

The next rule of survival in Boomtown is: *Don't play games.* Not only should you not do shit like fire extinguishing pedestrians, but you should avoid messing with someone just to prove something to yourself. This is a particular game young bucks like to play; unfortunately it bears an uncanny resemblance to someone who wants to jump you by testing the water. You will occasionally, or maybe often, find yourself in a place with a whole shitload of badasses. Sometimes it will be their turf (a club hangout or group haunt), but often it will be in neutral territory (coffee shop, phone company, etc.). The mistake made by most youngins and civilians is to puff their feathers. *Wrong!* Whether it is to show that you are not afraid or to show how tough you are, this is exactly the wrong thing to do.

The difference is the same as that between a dog's hackles rising versus a cat's fluffing its fur when the same dog shows up. A small animal fluffs its fur to make it look bigger and supposedly more dangerous to mess with. However, to people on the street, anyone who is scared is a target. Someone puffing up shows that he's scared just by reacting to the street person's presence. That isn't a warning; it's advertising a free lunch. On the other hand, when Rover's hackles go up, he's definitely getting ready to go into it, whereas Fluffy will run like hell if charged.

Get used to it; you're going to have to allow that there are a lot of other tough-assed people out there—many of whom are tougher than you. This is okay as long as you don't fluff and bluster. Unfortunately, there are a lot of yo-yos who haven't learned this. The good news is that the ones who cause most of the ruckus generally aren't that good. The bad news is those very same people are the ones who get most of the press, which just inspires them to do more.

Out on the street, you'll probably encounter a real annoying game called "buzzing." If you achieve a certain amount of *cajones,* you're going to run into it. You'll be minding your own business, doing something as exciting as waiting in line at a MacDonald's, and in walks some whipdick little punk. He looks around and see's you. He then looks into his pants and can't decide if his dick is enough bigger than yours to make him feel comfortable. He has to prove that his genitalia are grander than yours, but since he is not that confident, he's going to test the waters first. Suddenly, like a fly, zoom! This guy cuts past you, usually within three feet and behind you. Since his probes are on, you're going to feel his intent. You shift slightly, while he circles around and warms up for another run. This is much like a bird buzzing a cat.

What I am talking about is people doing something that officially isn't happening (sort of like Air America, the CIA-funded airline that never existed in Southeast Asia). If you were to remark to a civilian that someone was messing with you, he'd look at you and go, "Huh?" Don't worry, these are the same people who were surprised when the government officially disclosed that cigarettes were addictive. What did they think a nicotine fit was for all these years?

Realistically, this guy's buzzing or managing to be in your blindspot is a game. While nothing overt has happened, it makes you real surly. If someone were to ask you what was going on, all you could tell him as to why you were getting uptight is that someone is walking or standing around. This is why I coined the term buzzing. It lets people know that something is going on, the connotations of which they are unaware of. Often, just giving this phenomenon a name makes people realize that something is going on outside of their notice.

Buzzing people is a bad game to run. If you're not sure whether you could take someone in a toe-to-toe, figure out how you would take him and let it go. Upon first meeting, my clan brother Tim and I both did a check on the other. He says he decided I was not someone he wanted to fuck with. I decided the only way to safely do him was through cross hairs. It boiled down to the same thing: neither of us wanted to start anything.

I still get buzzed by young bucks and street people. Generally, it starts when I do something that puts me in their blindspots. They come for a buzz run, and I shift to a place from where I could take them out or in such a way that it puts me behind them—sort of like Maverick hitting the air brakes in *Top Gun*. Since my action is not overt, they can't get upset. Since they're not doing anything, neither am I when I stop and look into a mirrored store front window until they go by. Then I fall in behind them. My attitude is usually, "Whatcha gonna do now, Stud?" If they try to shift, I countershift so as to retain position. If they look at me, I am either stonefaced or I have a "Want to try that one again?" smile on my face. This is referred to as "double-clutching" and is one hell of a good technique. It generally works on the lightweights, who get the message and go away.

Another form of double-clutching is innocently stepping in the way of someone going after a third party long enough for the latter to get lost. This only works in low-grade situations. Since the guy going for the other person is unofficial, he can't do anything about getting foiled. If the guy is serious, he'll just try to knock you on your ass and get to his target. That's why I say it's for low-grade situations.

It's an entirely different ball game for those buzzers who aren't real bright (and believe me they are out there). If I have double-clutched one of them and he still hasn't got the message (or seems incapable of getting the message), I go a little more hard-core. I wait until he starts a run and then smoothly move, not a jerky zip, more like water flowing out on fast forward. The next thing the guy knows, he's nose-to-nose with a wolverine, which, incidentally, is sexually excited about the concept of cracking his bones.

Here is the icing on the cake: while my energy is that of someone who would gladly gouge out his eye and skull fuck him to death, my voice is flat, and my words are polite. I'm talking about "Yes?", "Can I help you?", and "Excuse me?" The reason I control my moves like this has a lot to do with these people's heads. They think they are in control until the last moment. By moving smoothly, I don't alert their danger signals that something is way wrong until it's too late. By that time, they are nose-to-nose with the big bad wolf. My polite words, or silence, do not justify aggressive attitudes or responses on their part. Unless they swing right away, they've been outmaneuvered. They'd have to really work to hype themselves up to swing. It can be done, but it takes even fruitcakes a while to do it. In actuality, they just got double-clutched by the terminator, who has got them scoped and targeted.

If someone is waiting for you to make the first move so he can pounce, avoid making that move. This works ninety-nine times out of a hundred, but during that one-hundredth time, you better be ready to rock-and-roll. A lot of people find this hard to understand. It's not that difficult, but most people screw the pooch on this one.

Plain and simple, if you have to operate around hard-core individuals, either make friends with them or ignore them. I've already talked about this. You know to ignore the guy by not looking at or saying anything to him, while keeping a bead on him and what he's doing. If he moves, you glance over at him, nothing more. You don't say boo to him, and you expect the same treatment. A nod of the head is often all you need. In fact, a nod often precedes the ignoring part. That nod establishes the "I'm cool, you're cool, it's cool" environment. Both of you know that if you mixed it up, you'd both get hurt, and it is just not worth it. You both know when two tigers fight, one dies and the other is seriously injured. This is why petty shit is less likely to happen around hard-core folks, but when it does go down, it is usually major.

Two hard-core guys showing up at a coffee shop at the same time is real common. This is why the system developed. That way they can eat their toast in peace. How friendly you act depends on the situation. It can range from a "How ya doing?" to "Brothers." If you're new in a place and see someone getting uptight about the fact that you have testicles, you can walk up to the guy and say, "How's it going, guy?" Start shooting the shit with the guy for a moment or two to allow him to relax. Then move on back to what you were doing. You can save yourself all sorts of shit this way. If the guy isn't someone you really want to know, just hang around long enough to let him know that you're cool and not after his crown.

My bro' Tim has a perfect example of what I'm talking about here. When he was in Vietnam, there were certain "killers" on each team. On his team there were himself and a man named "Cajun." He and Cajun were tight. They relied on each other to cover their backs. On another team in the unit was a big black guy named Johnson. This guy was so bad that when he decided that he didn't want a nickname, nobody gave him one. (Tim's handle was "Craz.") Cajun, Johnson, and Tim were the lead killers in the unit. Tim was friends with Johnson, but Cajun and Johnson ignored each other. They were in the same platoon and same base, but they just didn't interact. It wasn't a matter of who was better; it was a matter of if they went at it, they'd both get hurt.

Realize that the people who come looking for trouble are usually the ones who aren't especially good at it. There is an old World War II cartoon with two grizzled old vets sitting there watching a young, fiesty, spit-shined buck swagger by. One of them says, "Yah can tell he hasn't been in combat. He wants to fight!" That's the attitude you need to have if you want to make it for the long haul in Boomtown.

Another factor in making it in Boomtown is knowing how to act. I don't mean act as in how to behave, but rather as in being an actor. In one sense, you need to learn how to have the ultimate poker face and not display what is really going on inside. This could give your opponent or would-be opponent vital information that could be used against you. This generally occurs when there are good players involved, but even the losers get it right sometimes.

It is scary what some people can read off faces, pronunciations, pauses, hesitations, eye movements, and other communications. Neurolinguistic programing (NLP) is a field of behavioral science that has done some serious studies in reading body language cues. I have had NLP training, and I can bug the shit out of people when I second guess them. All these researchers did was organize information that was out there already. Remember 80 percent of all communications is nonverbal. When I was a kid, I never understood how my mother knew I was lying until one day she told me that when I lied my eyes got big. Ah ha! I dropped that particular eye reaction like a hot rock. People who know you can read your facial signals and tone of voice, and they don't always use this in the positive sense.

The other side of that coin is that you show only what you want to show, or what the other person understands. If someone is coming from a place where they yell and shout when they're mad, the odds are against them seeing the danger signs of a quiet mad. Unless you show them the signs they're used to, they're going to keep pushing. It's sort of like learning how to speak their language. I once had an Italian lover. When she was yelling and screaming, everything was still okay. However, when she lowered her voice, narrowed her eyes, and said, "Que fatz," I knew that was the sound of a bomb being triggered, and I was in deep shit. Yet, I also know people who yell and scream for hours on end but never get past that point. These people think nothing of it. It's literally like a gale that passes quickly. It took me a long time to get used to these people. At the drop of a hat, they'll bellow about anything, but then they wonder why everyone thinks they're bullies and tyrants.

Some people who are slow to anger are also extremely slow to forgive. There can be either hot or cold mads. I'm a quiet mad. I don't say much when I'm mad. If someone asks me what's going on, I say, "I'm angry." My "angry" is equivalent to "furious" in most people's books. Quiet-mad people are the ones you really have to be careful around. They have a habit of suddenly exploding. Over and over, I have heard people say, "All of a sudden, he just up and nailed me out of nowhere." No, the attack didn't come out of nowhere; they didn't know how to read the warning signs.

In dealing with confrontations, you'll need to know how to use your acting skills. You have to be able to spot the various roles people are in and slip into the most effective counterrole. Do it right and you'll defuse the whole situation. Choose the wrong role and it will blow up in your face like a faulty grenade. Since learning this, I've gone off on some people, yelling and gesturing like I was furious. Later when a friend mentions how angry I was, I often tell him that I was not actually that mad; I was communicating to the person in the only way he would truly understand.

Another facet of acting is being able to pass as a local. If they are shuffling, you shuffle. If they are bouncing, you bounce. You can avoid all sorts of shit by knowing when to blend into the crowd. I learned this when I was being hunted by the Bay Street Boys. They were looking for me, and, presto, I changed the way I walked and put on a hat (back then I didn't wear hats), and I could walk right by them. No shit, it works.

The last thing to know about about making it in Boomtown is a corollary to awareness. You have to look at the cracks, gaps, shadows, and reflections. It's not only what is being presented, but what's next to it, around it, what isn't being presented, what isn't there, and who's behind it.

If you can't see a certain angle on something, figure out a way to get a peek at what's back there. Anytime someone tells you something, figure out what they aren't telling you, what they don't want you to find out. There is a major difference. If they have pointers saying, "Look here," take a look at what's in the other direction. I may not be able to see around the corner yet, but if the light's right, I can see the shadow of anyone who is standing behind that same corner. I don't mind sitting with my back to the door if I'm facing a mirror. Look around; you can watch street scum in the reflection of a store window without ever looking directly at them. What does someone coming down a hallway sound like? Close your eyes and listen. It's all out there.

Most people's eyes work by focusing on one thing, moving, and then focusing on another. These points of focus are actually predictable. Not only that, but people don't clearly see the things in between the points of focus. You can literally disappear by stepping into the areas between them and staying still. Learn to look into these cracks between the points of focus. Our world has more than four dimensions, contrary to what school wants you to believe.

There's a lot more out there than you were taught to look at. As the Apaches say, "Everything in between belongs to the shadow warriors."

As I said earlier, we have no real model that I can point to and say, "That's what I mean." A lot of this stuff was dropped out of our culture because it's "uncivilized." Remember about being civilized: the only guy who considers the wolf a bad guy is the shepherd. That's because the wolf is in competition with the shepherd.

To tell you the truth, the shepherd is a glorified parasite. He's like the guy at the auto dealer repair shop who gets a cut off every work order he writes up. That being the case, you know he isn't on your side when it comes to the bill. Domesticated sheep are not natural; they're specifically bred for stupidity and passivity. In short, they're civilized. Look at the bighorn sheep; that's one critter that does not need a shepherd. The Eskimos have it right. The only time they herd animals is to slaughter them. They got real bent when someone came by claiming to be their shepherd. They like the wolf; he's on their side. But like I said earlier, "Them with the biggest media coverage . . ." and the shepherds definitely have the media in their pockets.

All of this "uncivilized" stuff is what you need to make it out in Boomtown and in the various networks. All of these things are really hard to define, but they are the mortar that keeps it together out there. It's almost as if you pass a certain point and this clicks on. You become in tune with your environment. Once you have that going, 95 percent of the trouble will leave you way the fuck alone.

Notes

[1] This is bad news, guys. Most women do not want to be involved with Terminators. If they do, they've got

something wrong with their wiring. It takes one hell of a woman to be able to put up with this kind of person. Most women competent enough to do so are also smart enough to choose someone sane. In ninety-nine cases out of a hundred, women who are attracted to tough guys are missing a few sunflower seeds from their granola mix.

[2] Incidentally, if people think they have you trapped, they often get sloppy. If you've explored these canyons from the back, you know which ones you can get out of. They'd chase you in, and when they're getting ready to get you, you're wiggling out the back way. If you're going to explore, do it when no one is around to box you in. Before entering, look around real good. Never go into a place unless you know how to get out. When you go into a place, scope out the possible exits. This not only means seeing where the doors are, but if it's really a bad-news place, looking at what's outside.

[3] This refers to the Armenian Holocaust perpetrated by the Turks in 1915.

[4] I should point out that the development of an ulcer put an end to my serious drinking days. Mr. Animal had to take a serious chill pill.

[5] Look to your right first. Someone waiting in ambush will usually stand there so he can flatten against the wall, thereby reducing the chance of being seen and be able to strike without the wall impeding his swing. Of course, if the fucker is left-handed, it's an entirely different ball game.

CHAPTER SIX

Etiquette Basics

> "There is no substitute for good manners, except maybe fast reflexes."
> —Vlad Taltos, Assassin
> Steven Brust's Jerheg series

The trick to figuring out an operating system's key etiquette rules is to determine what is important to the people. For example, what is important to bikers? I'll give you a hint: it's not "Dear Abby."

If you said their motorcycles, you can pat yourself on the back. Now if a motorcycle is the symbol around which they organize their operating system, would it not make sense that there are some serious taboos about it? When you look at it that way, it sort of indicates where you should tread lightly, doesn't it? A serious gaff is to walk up and touch someone's bike. How you touch it determines if you are going to get a warning look or chain whipped. It's that serious.

Look around and figure out the important ideal of the people with whom you are dealing. Now the ideal may have changed or been polluted over the years from what it was originally, but it's still there. A great many Westerners feel that they have to fill the boots of the legendary cowboys. There exists a shitload of good ol' Southern boys who consider themselves "Rebels." Gangbangers are so wrapped up in respecting and disrespecting that they don't know the difference between their dicks and 9mms.

If a system is based on being cool, most of its rules will be based on what you have to do to be cool, what is considered uncool, and what you don't do to strip someone else of his cool. Now an extremely important thing to remember is that a majority of people really aren't comfortable with where they are. Most people are just out-and-out lost, scared, confused, and trying to get along as best as they can. They have no idea where they really belong. They watch what everyone else is doing and mimick their behavior. This can range anywhere from keeping up with the Joneses to wearing what everyone else is wearing.

You should understand that a whole lot of what is going on from an etiquette standpoint is that people basically fake it on the small stuff while drawing serious lines around major issues. Mostly this consists of etiquette fads that last a year or so. A lot of what people will tell you is bullshit or small-time local customs. For example, in a local pub where pools are held, local custom might dictate that you buy a round for the house if you win (doubtful, but possible). Or it could be nothing more than a sore loser trying to bullshit you into blowing your money. More often than not, the custom is for the winner to buy the next round for his friends and to hell with the rest of the bar. It really depends on who and where you are. If, for example, you aren't a regular in the tavern, the rules may not apply to you.

When it comes to local customs, most people generally don't expect outsiders to know and or abide by them. If it's a local celebration that hasn't been turned into a tourist attraction, generally people will just sort of ignore you and go their own way. The ones who most often have a problem with outsiders are the young bucks. If they decide to mess with you, you could be in for some trouble. Often, if you find an elder to talk with, the young will leave you alone.

Another etiquette consideration is how powerful these people are. What I mean is how likely are they to take matters in their own hands if you break their rules? In short, how likely are these people to push back when pushed? If I were to cross a yuppie, I really wouldn't have to worry about self-defense. If, on the other hand, I really messed up with a Navajo elder, I'd have to get my ass out of there. Now a yuppie may sabotage my career, but an Indian would end it. The reason being that there really isn't much you can do to yuppies that would consistently provoke them to violence, while that isn't so with Indians.

In addition to their probability of resorting to violence, you must consider how efficient they are when they push back, either individually or in a group. For example, most gangbangers I know really aren't that dangerous in a one-on-one. However when they get moving in a group, you better just dig a hole and hide. On the other hand, a single Sioux looking for vengeance will be able to do serious damage all by his lonesome.

Here is an issue that mixes the two aspects of group ideals and how powerful someone is. Any group that operates on being cool is likely to get your ass blown away from blatant stupidity. The biggest fuckups piss on someone's shoes and then don't take any precautions. They think it is cool to show no fear of repercussions, and this is the reason most people get blown away in these kind of systems.

It's not that these sort of people are really that good; it's that the targets make it incredibly easy for the guys hunting them. Nine times out of ten, being cool practically guarantees that you volunteer for being worm food when the shit gets ugly. These are the sort of idiots who get in a fight in a place and then hang around lapping up the oohs and ahhhs of the spectators. Then the loser shows back up again and blows holes in Joe Cool. Gosh, I'm impressed.

Another thing about basic etiquette is that there are certain universal issues in human culture: sex, violence, personal property, honor, public opinion, passing the responsibility on to the next generation, etc. These things occur anywhere you go. The only difference is how a particular society or group handles these things, which have a habit of getting hot. Etiquette is the oil that the machinery of society runs on. No oil equals friction, ergo heat. Too much heat, boom! No system. Etiquette allows us a way to deal with sticky situations. The real problem with it nowadays is that people don't take it deep enough to really work. We may think that our parents were really uptight, but their system was based on trying to find a balance between the reality of a situation and what the ideal was supposed to be. There is an actual term for this; it's called the finagle factor. The finagle factor is what is used to adjust the actual results to the desired results. If what you want is this, but what you are getting is that, you throw in the finagle factor to bridge the gap. A large part of true etiquette, the finagle factor is actually incredibly easy:

ACTUAL RESULTS X FINAGLE FACTOR
= IDEAL RESULTS

The finagle factor allows us all sorts of runway to deal with sticky situations. The most common aspect of the finagle factor in white middle-class society is the "Do Not Notice" mode (often referred to as "denial" by clinical psychologists).

Let's look at an example of the finagle factor in action. Daughter is coming home with boyfriend. Daughter and boyfriend live together in another city. Parents are not comfortable with the kids sharing a room in their home so they give them separate rooms. This is where most people stop with their so-called etiquette. However, if they take it to the next level, they bring in the finagle factor. That is, having given them separate rooms in a section of the house away from the parents' room, the parents ignore any nocturnal bumping around they hear. Also, they don't go in to wake up the kids in the morning.

In many areas this is what etiquette is about. *It is designed so people don't have to notice things that they would be obliged to kill you for!* That's pretty fucking simple, isn't it? In fighting societies it is designed so killers can exist in the same area without tearing each other apart. The next step is to ritualize the killing so it harms the fewest number of people. That is what dueling was about. Personally, I'm sort of pissed that dueling was outlawed. I think a great deal of our modern problems wouldn't exist if we dueled, or if they did, on a much smaller level. I get a lot of weird looks for saying this.

Etiquette evolves out of necessity. Unfortunately, in the 1830s, Queen Victoria ascended to the throne of England. This woman took etiquette and went totally bananas with it. This is what has left such a bad taste in people's mouths about etiquette. This is sort of like a reformed alcoholic setting the precedent for alcohol consumption. We're talking going seriously overboard with it.

During the Victorian period, people went so far into left field that the true reason for having rules of behavior was lost. The original reasons were pretty fucking good. Imagine, if you will, a group of guys all wearing giant straight razors; if you piss off someone, he's going to pull his straight razor and proceed to try to cut you up. The only thing you can do to prevent it is to pull your own straight razor and return the favor. Now this sort of behavior really fucked up everybody's fun at dinner parties. So what was invented was some sort of regulation where, if you decided to get a hard-on, you challenged the guy to fight later on. Then you both left the place. This was part of etiquette. You're pissed at him, he's pissed at you, but neither one of you is going to bleed on my pasta. That makes me a happy camper. You two get to try to kill each other, and I get to finish my fettuccine alfredo.

The other great thing about formal duels is if the other guy loses fairly, his buddies can't come after you. (That's officially; actually it did happen occasionally, or his buddies would sometimes challenge you afterward. But that's human nature.) What's more, there were certain places where everybody agreed to no violence, and breaking this rule would have everybody trying to make mince meat out of you.[1] Those were the formal days of violence. Even then there was the tavern brawls and scuffles.[2]

The only place that has total cultural okay for violence is the military. Does your kid like to fight? Ship him into the military. They'll take care of him. There they consider fighting to be good, and they know how to handle it. Eventually the kid will catch on that fighting hurts, and he'll slow down.

Oddly enough, there is no formal way of coping with the violence of people in this society. I'm not talking about dealing with it after it happens; I'm talking about everybody knows it's going to happen, so why not formalize it so innocents don't get hurt? Now what I just said is only applicable to white middle-class America. Know that in the subcultures there are places that have a network acceptance for violence. But you don't know how the violence is going to come at you.

Actually you have a pretty good idea depending on where you are. Without the formal boundaries to limit his behavior, the guy coming at you is going to do anything in his power to win. Bushwhacking, traps, or superior numbers are the norm. The guy that comes at you from the front alone is either very young, very stupid, or very good—sometimes all three. Remember since there is no widescale formal acceptance of violence, committing it will usually involve police, courts, jails, and prison. People who walk down the middle of the road gunning for someone leave a very wide trail of witnesses for the prosecution. By the way, that's another aspect of being "cool." You have to let everyone know you're hunting this guy. When he shows up in an alley, the DA has more than enough ammo to nail your ass to the wall. Being cool definitely has some serious drawbacks.

The concept of etiquette comes into play here in what you do so you don't have someone gunning for you. This also applies to the shit that you won't take either. Etiquette is designed as a buffer zone between people's actions and violence. It's what occurs so violence doesn't.

The fact that there is a shitload of violence means that there are a whole lot of people who don't know this little tidbit. If, however, you are going to run with the big dogs, you have to know it.

I amaze a lot of people. I come walking up, and people expect me to be a rude motherfucker. I have tough guys looking at me in total confusion when I say "Excuse me." This is not what they expect. Remember, the object of the exercise is to get by, not to fight every bozo that comes down the pikeway.

One of the things to remember is—once you've gotten to the point where you can kick ass, you don't have to prove it to yourself anymore. I found myself in a situation where I was with a friend in a store or something. Anyway, I walked up to another person and said something like, "Excuse me, may I get something?" The person moved out of my way, and

I got what I wanted. The guy I was with said something along the lines of, "I woulda told 'em to move." I looked at the guy and I remember saying, "I'm so tough, I can afford to be polite." The guy looked at me in confusion. To this day, I'm not sure that he ever got it.

I didn't realize it at the time, but that is true. A large number of serious, hard-core folks are not rude. It is really kind of interesting; in many ways, I'm more threatening when I'm polite. This has to do with real cool versus flash cool. If I am so calm about my abilities that I can be polite to some guy who's being an asshole, imagine what will happen when I get flamed. Most people do catch on to this message. There are the exceptions, but generally speaking this is true.

Imagine how you would feel if you're jumping up and down in someone's face and the guy is just sitting there calmly looking at you. You're ranting and raving, and he's not giving you any feedback to justify your swinging on him. It's not that he's meek. It's that he is just plain not scared of you. After a while, it's going to begin to sink in that maybe you're out of your league.

I have to admit something else. I used to be polite just to fuck with the civilians. I'd come shambling down the dairy aisle at a supermarket, and some stuck-up upper-middle-class broad would be looking down her nose at this filthy biker. (Actually, I hate being dirty.) So there I am in leathers, boots, and knives, looking like the kind of guy who, with her husband's entrails streaming from my teeth, would seize her innocent virginal daughter in one hand and steer a steel monster with the other. As I get closer to her, she stands there and quivers indignation that evolution should have gone so wrong! As I loom nearer, horrible fantasies of me stripping her of her diamonds and fur flash through her mind. Closer and closer I lumber. Suddenly a terrible thought flashes through her mind—what if I'm not after her daughter? Horrifying images of being thrown nude over a motorcycle tank and being dragged off and ravished by me and twenty of my heathen friends flash through her mind. Suddenly I am looming over her, and she steels herself for her impending fate. "Excuse me, can I get some milk?" I ask politely.

I cannot tell you how fun it is to watch people's heads do 180s this way. You can watch these movies run inside people's heads. When you walk up and are polite to them, it totally blows them out of the water. I've had people stare at me for a full two seconds trying to comprehend what it was that I just said. It's like their minds go "tilt." That I should be more interested in getting milk for my coffee, rather than looting, raping, robbing and pillaging is a serious mind-bender. I tell you, the personal entertainment value (PEV) is priceless. I never said I was above messing with the civilians' heads.

If you've read other books by me, you know that I have a habit of saying that violence doesn't usually come out of nowhere. Generally, it will take about ten steps to develop. Most people don't realize something is wrong until step eight or nine; by then, it's way too late. I often talk about the basis of self-defense being spotting trouble at step two, when it is still in the designing stage.

Here's a secret about most forms of etiquette and some of the operating system's rules. They are designed to function as a buffer. They draw a line long before you get into the actual danger zone. It's not that they are a fence around trouble, rather they are a "Closed, No Trespassing" sign on the path that leads to it.

Now if certain areas have more than their share of trouble spots, general society puts a "Keep Out" sign up for the entire sector. The kids usually look over at these things and say, "Gotta explore over there." They pass the first warning signs and wait for the bolt of lighting to zap them. Nothing happens, so off they go further into the area. This could be likened to the corridor that I talked about in the Introduction.

Step two here is that certain subgroup operating systems do not have general verboten signs for entire areas. In fact, they operate in areas that average America considers off limits to begin with. What they do have is those specific signs for trouble spots. This is no "stop it or you'll go blind" sort of thing; it's "cross this line and someone will blow your brains into a fine pink mist." Maybe you can get away with it once or twice, but keep doing it and your ticket will get punched.

The difference between these two items is that one is a static law and the other is an operating law. Static laws are found in the area that I bored you with earlier. These are the items that come down from a cultural level. They include prohibitions against homosexuality, racial hatreds, dietetic laws, etc. They really aren't that difficult to figure out. Someone decided a long time ago that this is the way it's going to be and that's all there is to say about it.

Operating laws, on the other hand, are ever changing, not only in development, but also in location. These things can change in fifty miles, or in the city, they can change in a few blocks. An obvious example is which football team you spit on, depending on which side of the city you live in. Home-team loyalty has led to many a brawl. What I mean, however, goes deeper than that. Cross onto a reservation and you are in a different world (same thing for entering Texas). Go into a different borough and you have the same thing. What's more, immigrants bring a slice of home with them. It then mutates into something else entirely. It may all be New York, but which part? Italian, Jewish, Irish, Puerto Rican, black, Jamaican, Chinese, Vietnamese, white? Shit, Chicago has hillbillies.

Operating laws came about so in the day-to-day inter-actions people don't step on their dicks or stomp someone else's. These come about through different ways of dealing with the predictable veins of human action that I mentioned. What is it that you can bet on about human behavior? (Other than someone is going to fuck up.) Well you can bet that there is going to be sex, violence, music, love/bonding, trade, social interaction, and emotions. That's on the light side; on the dark side, there're going to be betrayal, vice, hate, greed, divorce, corruption, crime, drug and alcohol addiction, power struggles, misplaced violence, insanity, high casualties, and walking wounded. Face it, it will all happen.

How people will deal with these things depends on whom you're dealing with. Overall, these things are determined by the particular operating system: how to approach a woman (if you can approach her at all or if you have to use inter-mediaries), how much space do you allow between people, how do you conduct yourself in business, how much protection do you carry (too little means you're dog meat, too much and they think you're gunning for them). What is the accepted way of blowing off steam and showing emotions?

I have to tell you something. Recently I went to Colorado on some business. I was wandering around shaking my head in amazement. I kept on repeating the phrase, "Look at all de white women!" It amazed me that so many blond-haired people could exist in one place. It was a very vanilla sort of place. In fact, I began to consciously look for brunettes. When I returned to Los Angeles, I was immediately plunged back into the melting pot of races and cultures: Oriental, Hispanic, Semitic, and Afro-American. Inwardly, I breathed a sigh of relief. In L.A., these sort of operating systems are more clearly defined. In places where one particular race is dominate, differentiation can be much more difficult because of subtlety. This is sort of like figuring out where a slice of white bread came from in the loaf. In places like L.A., you can get pumpernickel, sourdough, English muffin, rye, wheat, etc. Outside of Detroit, you have to differentiate between Midwestern Americanized Irish, German, and Slavic. Not what you might call glaringly different but different enough. You folks who exist outside of mixed cities have a harder job in figuring this stuff out. It's more difficult to distinguish subtle variations among a certain group than to spot the differences in a place where everybody is a minority.

Here is one of the most important keys about etiquette: *time spent*. Remember I told you about the dragon's lair and the people who have dragon-blocker sunglasses? Many people can get away with this because they don't spend enough time in the particular area to use up the slack that is granted outsiders. The locals kind of sit there in slack-jaw amazement that anyone can be that dumb while the social twinkle toes go dancing off out of firing range. This is explained in part by the phrase "Allah loves fools and children."

It actually consists of something so foreign to the natives' operating system that they go "tilt." Instead of attacking, they just sit there and stare, asking, "What the fuck is this?" Once they come up with a definition from their own system about the dancing bozo, ol' Bojangle's luck runs out.

What throws most people when they encounter a person wearing dragon-blockers is that the signals he is throwing out are totally wrong. If I'm a fierce gangbanger, I'm accustomed to various reactions, with fear, loathing, hate, and frustration being the most common. The key thing is everyone recognizes how dangerous I am. When there are nearly a thousand of us gathered, everyone from the same operating system clears out. Plain and simple: if you want to live, you leave. This is about as basic as the sun will rise in the morning.

I remember once, all of a sudden, this dumb motherfucker comes cutting through the group whistling "Zippity Do Da." Here I am, in my home turf, and cutting through it is a guy so white that he glows in the dark. Now I have survived in the streets all this time because I have not only eyes, but radar. Right then my eyes were telling me something that could not be true. I immediately dropped to radar and sent out a ping that would immediately send everyone from the same network diving for deep cover. What the fuck? The reading I got was like a stealth bomber—no signature on radar! Was it actually there? I still got a visual! Quick, shift frequencies! A fuzzy ghost of a reading, something to do with "Bluebirds on shoulders." Wait a minute! Suddenly, as quickly as it appeared, the apparition was gone from visual. I shook my head and decided that it was all a hallucination. I began to worry about what'd been used to cut the stuff I just smoked.

That fool walking through the gangbangers is the perfect example of what I mean. I could not have made up a better scenario. What's more, I can sit here and swear that I saw something that exemplifies my point. The reason that man did not get torn apart is that he was something so far out of the local OS that nobody knew what to do with him in the time that he was in range. By the time they could get a clear picture of what was going on, he was gone.

The only reasons that guy got away with what he did were A) he was not around long enough for the people to get a clear reading on him and B) he was totally unaware of what he was doing. He was so wrapped up in his own OS that he didn't see anything else. He was literally blind to the reality around him. Because he didn't see any of the signals coming from the gangbangers, he didn't react. This failure to react caused them to hesitate. This is how most people get away with things in territories that would get a local killed.

If you're wondering why, if violating OS rules is such a serious offense, you have seen people do it without repercussions, this is pretty much the reason. Street people will not act without radar confirmation. The signal can be (and often is) wrong, but they are still receiving a reading with which they are familiar. When they receive a null signal, they pause to run tests on the system.

This isn't a conscious act on their part. A street person uses this radar like you use your arm. What would you do if, suddenly, for a minute, your arm quit working? The first thing you'd do is stop and look at it in shocked amazement. It's always worked before. Then you'd begin to try and get it working again. This is why many people don't attack. Their OS has just been thrown a curve ball. Once they realize that the system is working, but they have something totally different on screen, the shit gets ugly.

An interesting variation of the radar-jamming aspect of this is the upper-class yuppie who is so wrapped up in the belief that he is superior to everyone else that the locals hesitate for a moment. To encounter such righteous arrogance stuns most people into inactivity for a moment. This is something like a bat accidentally flying into a rock concert and getting his sonar jammed by the sheer magnitude of the noise.

What stops the locals is that, where they're from, people with this kind of unmitigated arrogance have something to back it up. The only people who attempt this sort of behavior come from large powerful families that have people named Guido and Vinnie working for them. It's not that the natives are afraid of the guy, it's that they're busy looking for his backup.

This is the secret of how most people can step on their dicks and get away with it. To the locals, it's like in the movie *Time Bandits*. A doorway in space and time suddenly opens up for a moment, and a pack of weirdly dressed, bickering midgets go rushing through their reality. The visitors are so wrapped up in themselves that they aren't even aware of the natives. Before the onlookers can do anything, the visitors disappear, as does the doorway.

This is where the concept of "time spent" comes in. People have an amazing ability to adjust. If you stay around an area long enough, the people will tune their radar to get a reading off you. This may not be good news. It allows you time to adjust your radar and find out what the marching tune is around there, but there is a certain unspoken time limit that dictates how long the locals will cut you slack before you are expected to conform to their operating system. The closer your personal OS is to that system, the shorter the leeway.

Also, some systems have maps of outsiders already. These are people who have seen literally hundreds of others like you already. Often, they have developed set channels that you can pass through. These corridors are padded and simple: you come into this territory, and you go from point A to point B to point C to the exit. As long as you stay in these corridors, you're fine. You can waddle along, and nobody bothers you. However, if you get off the beaten track, you had better have been invited or be in the company of one of them. If you go wandering off one of the beaten paths, your ass is in some deep shit.

Often these sort of systems rely on the tourist trade. The people who work the tourists stations deal with outsiders regularly and write off most so-called bad behavior. The two most classic versions are on Indian reservations and in Chinatown. San Francisco's Chinatown has markings on the entrances of alleys that say whose allies they are. You do not go into these places if you want to come out alive. On the Hopi mesas, there are signs that read, "Private." If you go past these points, someone will materialize and tell you to go back.

Another version of "time spent" is the amount of time you have spent kicking around in the borderlands. If you have the look of someone who has spent a lot of time in Boomtown cutting networks, there ain't shit slack cut over your mistakes. You are expected to know better, flat-out and across-the-board. I'm not talking about "which fork you use" sort of stuff. I mean things like you don't approach a woman without checking out the situation.

This is something I should warn you about up front. Just by reading this book, you have expanded your awareness. You may not agree with the interpretations that I have come up with. That's fine and dandy. My dick ain't gonna get knocked out of joint if you think that I'm totally wrong on some issues. I know I've missed the mark on some of these calls. What's most important is to realize that these issues do exist. By knowing this, you will have to address them in your life—one way or the other. Know that this will happen; how you deal with them is up to you.

What I am trying to say is that because of who I am, and the awareness that I carry, I cannot plead ignorance. People look at me and expect me to be smart enough to research the local customs, whereas they just blow off your average unaware, yogurt-brained, nappy-headed granola eater as basically harmless. I walk in, they see what caliber of person I am, and they want me where they can see me. Nobody wants a cougar roaming around somewhere in the house.

All the stuff that I talk about here is what the real heavy hitters know and use to survive. I have never met any major leaguer who does not use this stuff in one form or another. They use different terms, organizations, and emphases, but it still is the same basic info. What truly differentiates the heavies from the lightweights is not how tough they are, but how aware they are. All that I have done is taken this awareness and sort of organized it in a manner that I hope people can understand.

Notes

[1] Even the most violent societies had areas where violence was verboten. Vikings had gatherings called the "Thing." The Irish had a similar situation. Sacred space is often off limits.

[2] Christopher Marlowe, a contemporary of Shakespeare, took a dagger in the eye in a bar brawl over the bill, although there is evidence that it was a "hit." He'd been a spy for the crown.

CHAPTER SEVEN

Names, Reps,
and Handles

> "Greatness is a transitory experience. It is never consistent. It depends on the myth-making imagination of humankind. The person who experiences greatness must have a feeling for the myth he is in. He must reflect what is projected upon him, and he must have a strong sense of the sardonic. This is what uncouples him from the belief in his own pretensions. The sardonic is all that allows him to move within himself. Without this quality, even occasional greatness will destroy a man."
>
> Paul "Muad'dib" Atreides
> Frank Herbert, *Dune*

Again and again it would happen. Some young person would look at me wide-eyed and, with awe in his voice, say what I had begun to dread: "You're Animal? I've heard of you!" Then he'd sit back and look at me expectantly.

Aww fuck, not again. Look, I'm sitting here, having a quiet cup of coffee with my friend. Nothing personal, but I'm not about to go into Animal mode just to entertain ya, kid. The wild man is not in at this time, capiche?

Yes, indeedy do, folks, reputations and nicknames are fine and dandy, and they can do wonders for your sex life. They also can become a pain in the ass if you don't spend a shitload of time in their care and feeding.

NICKNAMES

Before I go on here, I want to explain one of the biggest blunders you can do regarding nicknames. When you are introduced to someone with a nickname or handle, do not immediately ask where he got the name—especially if it implies violence. How do you fucking think I got the name Animal? I did not get it playing backgammon! I am a whole lot cooler about this than most people, but it still jerks my chain.[1]

The reason for this is twofold. One, unless you know how to do it, it immediately identifies you as a person who is not accustomed to being in an area where nicknames are common (read: you've just identified yourself as an outsider, hence, potential meat). Two is the way most people ask the question. Somehow, they manage to convey the impression that you have to perform for them on the spot. If you have a name that suggests wild behavior, they expect you to do something wild and crazy right then and there. It's probably not true, but that's how many people with nicknames interpret it. In part, it sounds as if they are asking if you if you really deserve that name or if you gave yourself it to yourself.

When it came to this situation, I eventually got to the point where I had a pat answer for these people. I'd simply answer their question: "By doing all the stupid and dangerous things that you have to do to get the name Animal."

My point is that you have to be careful how you ask. If it's a name like Creature, Animal, Red Dog, Snake, or One Punch, it's pretty obvious that you really may not want to be around when this person decides to exhibit the sort of behavior that earned him the name in the first place. On the other hand, some names really beg to be explored. My partner in the event security biz was known as Tup, shortened down from the Tupperware Kid. Generally speaking, there are three types of nicknames 1) those that you earn 2) those you give yourself 3) those that are given to you.

Earned Nicknames

The first type usually reflects a dominant characteristic of your personality. This is a name that causes people to look at you and go, "Yep, that fits." For many years, given certain stimuli, I would simply go berserk: biting beer cans in half, having sex on rooftops, riding collapsing buildings to the ground, jumping on top of a moving truck, or guzzling champagne from a bottle on the San Rafael bridge while leaning out the window of a speeding car. If it looked like the thing to do at the time, I'd do it. That's me. Thus, the nickname Animal.

The grizzled, red-haired biker named Red Dog was pretty obvious, too. Stick around long enough and you'd find out. The gorillas named The Mighty Ipock, One Punch, Big John, and Ajax didn't leave too much doubt either.

Self-Assigned Nicknames

The next type of name is the one that someone gives themselves. This can go one of two ways. One it reflects something the person does well. These are usually shortened down by those around as a sign of acceptance—Doctor D shortened to Doc. Another source of a nickname is an affiliation or strong emotional/image bonding with the source of the name. I can't tell you the number of "Cats" I've met. It is especially common for people who are involved with magic to hang names on themselves, like Yoni, Raven, Ishtar, or Star Dancer. Strange but true, in California, all you have to do is use the name all the time, and it's yours.

The second way is someone's attempt to puff up his own image. This is the skinny pimply-faced kid who calls himself Wolf or Cobra. The problem with this approach is that for a nickname to really work it has to reflect reality—not just three or four kids in a clique accepting it. The kid who tries to hang the name Wolf on himself had better reflect the energy of his namesake so when he meets someone from outside his group he will go, "Yep," as well.

The problem with most of these is that for anyone in the know these nicknames are obviously self-assigned. Nobody is going to go around allowing someone to call him Merc if he really is a mercenary. A skinny, acne-face "Dungeon and Dragons" player is not going to convince anyone that he is the big bad "Wolf" who preys on the sheep of humanity. (Why do they always pick the name Wolf? God knows.)

Assigned Nicknames

The third type of nickname is one that is given to you. These are names that people start calling you, whether you like it or not. You can get these in one of three ways:

1) As a variation of your name, either to identify you from another like-named person or to shorten your real name. An example is when two guys named Mike are in the same group; one is called Mike, the other is called Mikey. Or a guy is called "Carpy" instead of Carpetius.

2) As a recognition of who you are and/or an aspect or habit that you have. These include things like Professor, Silky (you'd never see him coming), or Moon (bald as a cue ball). Sometimes these can include your real name. For example,

Radio Dave, Little Chris, Steven the Heathen, Indian Mike, and Crazy Ruth. Other times, the name has to do with status or source of origin: Jersey, Sarge, Cajun, Oklahoma Ridge Runner, etc. Using nicknames can get a little nasty. The guy who got hung with the name Buzzard was a skinny, hunched-over biker with a huge nose. There's always a Short Round or Sawed-Off in a Company.

3) Based on some sort of particular or special incident in your past. These are the ones that get real interesting. Sometimes the person likes this kind of nickname; sometimes he doesn't. Examples are Tupperware Kid, Luaha Larry, Creature (of the Night), Trash Can, Amazing Eagle, Lucky, Elf (he's 6'5"). Generally these are based on something momentous, either good or bad, that people remember. These nicknames are the hardest ones to live down if they involve a blunder. I got hung with the handle T-90 when I was fifteen after getting drunk and sick in somebody's backyard. I never found out what it stood for. Everyone was ripped and was joking about my being passed out in the backyard, and somehow it came up. It took me a year to live that one down.

Overall, when it comes to nicknames you should understand that there are certain places where people just have several names. They have the names they were born with, street names, aliases, etc. When a street person hands you a name, you should figure that he has about three other aliases hanging in the background. It's funny, but there are a large number of people who, to this day, don't know my real name.

When you are operating in a place where handles and nicknames are common, it is generally advisable to call the person that name when you are in that group. Since people have several different aspects of their personalities, a nickname generally dwells on one particular trait, often one they feel comfortable projecting to the public. When you refer to a person in that term, you are honoring his desire for space.

You don't really have a choice with the name given to you at birth, but a nickname can help establish who you are in the world. The guy known as Priest is named Renato. Calling him by his real name is a good way to piss him off.

This works both ways. Sometimes a person wants to drop a nickname that he had at an earlier time. A common mistake is to refer to someone by a name he had in high school. If you know that some guy got the nickname of Cum Head because of an ugly incident five years ago in the boy's locker room, don't call him this when you run into him in his regular watering hole. Calling him that is going to get you into a punchout. Respecting someone's wish to be called or not called something is an important survival tip.

The best way to disengage from a nickname is not to associate with the crowd that hung it on you. The other way to do it takes time, patience, and calm endurance. If you got hung with a name that reflects badly on you, fail to respond to it. When someone calls you that, ignore him. I'm talking about being deaf as a post. If he forces it, calmly respond that your name is Bill or John or whatever. You do this for six months, and he'll get pretty bored with it. Since people are looking to get a rise out of you, consistently failing to respond will eventually wear them out. You will note that at no time did I say this was easy.

Generally speaking, once you have been around a person for a while, you can ask how he got his name. Of course, by being around him, you may have figured out why already. All someone had to do was to see me on one of my eating, drinking, fucking, and fighting sprees to have a pretty good idea where I got my name. If the reason for it is not immediately obvious, wait a while and then one day, in a casual manner, ask the story behind the name. If the person gives any resistance, let it go.

If, on the other hand, you have to know immediately on introduction and it really isn't obvious (like Tupperware Kid), mention—with a friendly smile—the name's uniqueness and ask the story behind it.

You will notice I did not once ask the dreaded "How'd you get your name" question. I asked for the tale behind the name, while never even coming close to challenging the person's right to carry it. This kind of faux pas can easily start the ball rolling toward a punchfest, with you as the star attraction. If you ask someone, do it as an equal, as someone who would be entertained by hearing a story as to how he got his name. If the guy shines you on or gives you a dirty look, pass on finding out.

Another way of finding out is asking someone else. This often gets you the glorified version of what happened, but whenever you're dealing with people, you should generally subtract about 25 to 50 percent as bullshit, anyway.

REPUTATIONS

Moving on to reputations, which are different than nicknames, you may have a nickname tied into your reputation, or you may just have a reputation alone. Andy Warhol once said that, with television, everyone could be famous for fifteen minutes. Although that may appear to be true with instant celebrities, it isn't for most of us. People have returned to the good, old-fashioned way of earning reputations.

The most common mistake people make is not to realize that a reputation is at best a two-edged sword. This error is what leads to many people cutting their dicks off with the second edge of a reputation.

When I was younger, my mom used to tell me that I didn't want a rep. Anytime some negative reference to a reputation was made on the TV, she'd use that as an object lesson. She'd use the sort of stuff like in *Support Your Local Sheriff* when one guy asks the other, "If you're so good how come I never heard of you?" The sheriff's response was, "A reputation will get you killed." She went apeshit: "See, that's what I mean."

Now being on the far side of a nationwide reputation, I have a different attitude about them. To this day, there are certain circles in which, even after five years, I get the "You're Animal?" routine. Bleech! However, having this experience, I have come to some conclusions about reputations. Most people who warn that you don't want a rep are simply parroting their operating system's guidelines about reputations.

This is the "Keep Out" sign around an entire area that I was talking about earlier. They got the idea from the so-called gunfighters of the Old West. They argue that, if you have a reputation, every whipdick young buck is going to come out and challenge you. They'd like you to believe that every time you turn around, there's going to be some youngin' snarling, "Draw!" Well truth be told, the high noon showdown in the middle of the town's road is mostly a Hollywood invention. The only real gun battle that bore any resemblance to that was the Okay Corral, which actually was closer to a gang fight than good guys versus bad guys. Both sides were seriously dirty. The same sort of fantasy also applies to reputations.

Another aspect of the double side of a reputation is the labeling of a young girl as a slut, often with no basis in fact. The reputation brands her and, whether earned or not, often cannot be easily removed.

A reputation in one way insulates you; it keeps the small fry from trying shit on you. On the other hand, it ensures that if someone is going to try to move on you, he's going to come at you full bore. I'm talking about the stuff that you don't get up from. Odds are, it's not going to come at you from the front, either. This may be what many people mean when they warn that you don't want a reputation; they're afraid of the intensity that someone will use to move on you. My response to this problem is simple: once you have a reputation, don't be an asshole.

A reputation actually is glorified gossip. People need to have someone to talk about. If you step into a reputation, people are going to be talking about you, for good or bad. In many ways people with reputations are the local heroes. Unlike movies stars these are people that the Average Joe can know. This isn't television; this is a live form of entertainment, right there, right now. It boils down to: "This guy is in some way famous, and I'm cool enough to know him or at least to hang out in the same place with him.

This is what is actually involved in most reputations, little people watching some guy's every move and blowing them out of proportion. When he's cool, he's everybody friend, but when he blows it and goes down in flames, everybody gets to see the wreckage. You don't go to the auto races just to see someone driving fast. While that is exciting, it's not nearly as much fun as watching the crashes.

This is where most people make the mistake about reps. They don't understand that the people are just as eager to see you go down in flames as they are to see you do a devastatingly hot move. In fact, they'll talk about the crash and burn more than everything else. A reputation is actually like an acting role. If it isn't you in the role, it's someone else. In short, a reputation is like being king. You get all the recognition (and bullshit) that goes with it, but once you're dead, it's immediately transferred to someone else. "The king is dead, long live the king!"

A rep actually is PEV (remember that from the last chapter) for the masses. They are the ones who will actually be carrying on your rep. Another hardass is not going to be spreading tales of how much of a hardass you are to the people around him. Don't get me wrong. It's not that people are intentionally waiting for you to blow it. Rather they are getting their yah yahs vicariously by watching your life. This is a living soap opera, right there in front of them. They watch you get all the glory and, more importantly, take all the risks. While you're hot, they can stand in awe of your courage to do things that they wouldn't. However, if you crash and burn, they won't get hurt. Just like watching a movie, they get the emotional roller-coaster effect without actually being involved.

What I'm talking about here is the myth-making imagination of humankind mentioned in the chapter quote. People need these kind of heroes. It is a role that certain people play. You may not intentionally set out to get a rep (I didn't), but one day you wake up and discover you have one. It starts out that a few people know you, then a few more get to know you, then you do something that enough people see that they start talking about you. Bammo! Now you have a rep. From then on, everything you do will be examined and talked about. Both good or bad, your actions will become like ripples in a pond.

The real drag is that, unless you lay some serious groundwork, people will expect you to behave according to your rep all the time. If you have a wildman rep, you will be expected to perform whenever you are in an area where your rep holds. I'd walk in, and everybody would turn their chairs my way and look at me in anticipation. Sorry, guys, my clown suit is at the cleaners.

The downside of a rep is if something ugly goes down, everybody looks to you. The rumor doesn't even have to be true. Once, after spending a quiet evening with my lady in a restaurant, I walked into a place and discovered I had been in a fight. I admit the curried beef was a little tough, but it wasn't an out-and-out brawl. After the third person asked me about the fight, I began to ask, "Did I win?" Eventually they figured out I had not been in a fight. I never did figure out how that rumor started.

More realistically, let's say you have a rep for being a demo man and something gets blown up. You know who the first person they're going to look toward is? Mmm-um. All I can say is you best have a better alibi than you were home alone watching *Homemade C-4*.

On a more serious level, though, a reputation can eat up all the slack that someone might give you in the event of trouble. This goes both for authorities and sparring partners. If something goes down and you have a reputation for being a badass with no other redeeming qualities, the authorities are going to shitcan you right quick. Even if the other guy started it, you are going to be the one they look at with the old hairy eyeball.

This can go seriously sour if you have a rep about being a tough-assed son of a bitch and you're having a bad day. Some bozo comes by and does a Code Stupid in front of you, and you go ballistic on him. Remember, the basis of a reputation is amplification of certain truths and the deletion of others. The story snowballs as it does laps around the track, and this guy is going to be talking to all of his friends, too. Do you think he's going to admit that he pissed on your shoes and deserved to get punched out? If you think so, then I got some property I want to sell you.

The next thing you know, this guy was just an innocent bystander who did absolutely nothing wrong, when without any provocation or warning, you turned into this berserk werewolf who ripped off both his arms and tried to cave in his skull with them. Fun, fun, fun—your rep has just turned sour. Instead of being a tough-assed son of a bitch, you now are a mean-assed motherfucker. You've just gone from being a guard dog to a rabid dog. In case you hadn't noticed, rabid dogs are not generally tolerated. This is the most common way that people with reputations crash and burn.

The second most common way that reputations go down the toilet is that the person begins to believe his own press releases. While you may want to reflect part of the image people put on you, you have to keep a certain amount of distance from it. Just because everybody says you're superman doesn't mean that you're bulletproof. Again, I point back to the quotation at the beginning of this chapter. By keeping it in mind, you can keep from taking a fall.

The closest analogy that I can think of is how most expert crooks get caught. They get too cocky and stop doing the things that they did to keep them from getting caught in the first place. Look at the antihero movies about bad guys rising to power. Somewhere in the plot, the guy gets too far out of line, thinks he's too powerful to be touched, and does something stupid. Shortly thereafter, he's taken down. In the movies, these critical mistakes are made obvious; in real life, they often aren't that clear-cut.

Often the person quit listening to information sources outside of his hangers-on. His yes men stood around going, "Yeah, yeah, the guy deserved to be dropped," while everyone else said, "Hey, that was out of line." As long as Mr. Rep is only listening to the yes men, he's not going to realize that he's crossed the line.

Now you know what's involved in dealing with a reputation, and you can probably guess that it isn't really all that it's cracked up to be. However, you can prevent many of these things from happening by simply enlarging your reputation beyond a single dimension. See, the problem with most people's reps is that they only focus on one aspect. If you have a reputation for being tough and you get in a fight, it's likely to be the one fight too many that catapults you into the shitcan. Think about it, what purpose does it serve to keep a tough guy around who indiscriminately gets in fights? If you are just as likely to go batshit on people around you as you are to go off on outsiders who are threatening the group, what's the purpose of keeping you around? Not much. If your rep is based on several aspects the group finds useful, you're more likely to survive. If you blow it in one area, they'll cut you slack that they wouldn't if your only contribution was in the area where you goofed.

I'll tell you the truth, if my reputation were based solely on being a wildman and a hardass, I wouldn't have made it. I saw lots of people with single-aspect reps like that come and go. This is what a one-dimensional reputation will do for you. Unfortunately, these are the easiest to get and build.

If you were to look at my old rep, you'd see that there were several aspects to it. Yes I was a hardass, but I was also a straight-up guy. If I gave my word, I kept it. I didn't rip people off; I played fair. The way to get nailed by me was to try and run a hustle on me or mine. I protected people. If someone was straight-up and not messing around, I'd protect him. I would also negotiate for the underdogs. If two people were having a problem, I'd come in and call a conference. I'd negotiate a settlement between the warring factions. And, if I called a council, you'd better fucking come, or I'd be on your ass.

Further, if there was a hard task to be done, I'd be there shoulder-to-shoulder with the crew working on it. If it was a nasty task, I'd tackle it. Part of being tough was that I worked my ass off. On the wildman side, no matter how wild it got, I was always keeping an eye open to make sure that it didn't get too far out of line. My eye was cast not only on me, but others. Also, when I did go over the line, I would make amends. If I broke it, I'd pay for it. If I slept with a woman, I didn't brag to my friends nor did I put attachments on her. When I ran into her later, I treated her as a human being, as someone I had done something special with. These things helped me with the wildman and hardass rep.

I also added on things like being a healer. If there wasn't a fully trained medic around. I did what I could. Or, I was the person talking to the victim while the medics did their work. If you had a problem and needed someone to listen to you and give you good advice, go see Animal.

No shit here, folks, this is what it takes to survive a reputation. You need to be able to do several different things. Maybe not the things I did, but you have to find your own talents to add to your rep. One of the biggest things that came out of all that is the group decided that I was too important to run the risk of losing to a minor altercation. When some young whipdick would come looking for a fight, as many as three people would stand between him and me and say, "You ain't going bother him."

This is when a reputation truly keeps you safe. This is what most people want when they dream about a rep, but unless they add these other aspects, they'll never get it. If you have a rep for just being tough and somebody comes looking for trouble, fuck it; you're tough, you can handle it alone.

When you encounter someone with a rep, take a moment to really look at where he is. Generally there are two kinds of people with reputations: the guy who got a rep and is going about his life anyway and the guy who is rolling in it. Depending on the guy's head space, he could be at either point or sort of bouncing somewhere between the two. Approaching the guy from the wrong point could be dangerous.

The guy who is rolling in it is the kind of guy who is actively trying to build a rep. This is the young hotshot with the poor self-image who thinks that a rep will replace self-esteem. These people are as touchy as an abscessed tooth and about as much fun as a game of Russian roulette. This is the sort of character who thinks that a rep of being cool or tough will make up for the fact that he doesn't think much of himself. Because he's not comfortable with who he is, he's going to be watching his image closer than a nun watching Catholic high-school girls. Any sort of slight to his rep, real or imagined, must be challenged immediately.

You will notice that I did not say might be, or could be, but *must be* challenged. These are the gangbangers who will shoot you for "dis'in" them (short for disrespecting). These sort of characters will blow you away for looking at them cross-eyed. Not that you actually did anything wrong, but according to their weak egos you have challenged their reputations. Remember earlier I spoke of three types of guy who are most likely to be violent? The guy in pain, the guy in rebellion, and the guy with a weak ego. Ha! I bet you thought I had forgotten about the egotistical equivalent of the weak-kneed! Well I didn't, here he is.

Understand that this kind of person will fixate on an incident. To you it might not have been a big deal, but all this person has is his reputation. He'll keep on chewing on this until he finally convinces himself that he has to come after you. This kind of person feels that if he doesn't have his reputation to protect him, the rest of the pack will turn on him and eat him alive. It is important to realize when dealing with these kind of people that is a true statement. The rest of the pack will turn on them.[2] In a sense, these people are always fighting for their lives. They cannot allow any incident to go by unchallenged. If they did, they would no longer be cool; therefore, they would not be accepted.

The flip side of this is that they end up fucking with the wrong person sooner or later. Their reputations force them to cross someone that they should have run from. This occurs when they cross a wolverine. When they start whipping themselves up into a frenzy over an incident, the other guy suddenly snakes out and rips their throats out. The real hardass recognized where the plot of the movie was heading and did some editing.

Another way it goes down is that the fool does beat someone to the draw. There he is, big and justified, hanging out, lapping up the applause over dusting this dude, when the other dude's people show up looking for revenge. He didn't have enough common sense to go into hiding and gets wasted for wanting to show everybody how big his dick was. Oddly enough, every now and then, the cops show up, sometimes with an independent witness, often with another guy who they got to roll over on the big bad dude for a lighter sentence. Remember the sixth rule of the street: If it will save your ass, squeal like a piggy!

It is in this place that a reputation can truly get you killed. If you are a gang's warlord or major hitter and one of your people does something that leads to war, the other side is going to target you. Not only are they going to take out the guy who did the original transgression, but they are going to knock off the heavies on your side. This ensures that you can't lead a counterstrike and makes the rest of the folks on your side hesitate. If the heavies they were relying on got taken down by the other side, do those that're left have enough juice in their cabooses to make the run? This buys the other side time.

Remember, heavies don't hesitate; once they've decided, that's it. Second stringers, however, hang around going, "Hommina, hommina, hommina!" while trying to work up courage. Remember, this isn't just like doing a regular drive-by shooting on civilians. If you're on war status, the other side is alert and looking for you. Gang members know each other. If you're spotted going into a 'hood, the other side is likely to return fire. The game changes when the other side is shooting back.

Dealing with someone who is actively trying to build a rep is a pain in the ass. It is almost a no-win situation. Since they want people to notice them, they go out of their way to get people's attention. Once you notice them being an asshole, they get in your face. There they stand, waving their dicks in your face, daring you to do something about it. If you try to back down, they'll often chase you. Backing down isn't good enough; you have to grovel. Often if you grovel, it's open season on you. If you try to stand up to them, they jump you. Once they move on you, your life will be pure hell until they find another target for their attention. They love people who stand up to them with quivering lips and shaky determination. We're talking free meal here.

Basically there are three ways to avoid trouble with these kind of people. One (and the best) is to not be in the same area that they are. If you end up there, ignore them. If they get on a roll, leave. Two is to be an untouchable (more on this in Chapter 14). There are rules to the game out there; one of the biggies is that you leave certain people alone. They are off limits. The third way is to hammer them.

You've been ignoring one of them, not giving him any feedback, but he decides to move on you anyway. You sit there, drinking your coffee and minding your own business, until he walks over and tries to stick his dick in your coffee. You give him one warning (not a threat, a warning). If he makes a move, you rip his dick off and show it to him. When he opens his mouth to scream, you stuff his cock and balls into his mouth and cut off his head. Then you take your little trophy outside and stick it on a pole. If the guy's an independent you go back to what you were doing before. If the guy was attached, you do a ghost. If you have no attachments, keep going. If you think you have to stay, stay low and watch from the shadows. Half the time the group will go, "Yipe!" and leave you alone. The other half, some mouth will start advocating going after you. If it's a half-hearted, one-night sweep, sort of like looking for land mines with a stick, let it go. If, however, they are doing a serious, ongoing sweep, the heads of the mouth and those leading the sweep suddenly end up on a pole with their genitals hanging out of their mouths. You go ninja on them until they decide it costs too much mess with you.

You get so ferocious when you do this to let the pack know that you're not fucking around. It takes one kind of person to kill someone and another to do the rest of the grizzly process. Collecting ears, gouging out an eye from a body then stuffing it into a knife wound in the body's back, castrating genitalia, chopping off fingers, tying hands together and putting a bullet in the head all are vicious signatures. All of these show would-be tough guys that you are not playing around. Of course all of these are also illegal as shit in America. However, since the judicial system has proven itself so effective in dealing with these sort of problems you don't have to worry about this. You just sit and wait for the nice system to take care of it for you. Ha!

As you may have guessed, it takes a special kind of psychotic personality to do these acts. It's not in most people to do them (or to be able to get away with doing them). Then again, what I just described, is how to deal with the extreme cases. I'm talking about gangs, psychos, and superstitious mad dogs, and these kind of people are out there. You have to go pretty far afield to find them, but they do exist. I, however, seriously advocate getting the hell out of there instead.

Most people are forced to deal with a little less severe form of rep hunter. But while your actions are less severe, your spirit has to be the same when the rep hunter shows up. When he walks up and unzips, your warning look has to show him that you will be willing to go as far out as I just talked about. This is not a message you can convey verbally; it's more of an energy thing. Something you broadcast in how you look at him. If you move, you don't have to go as far as castration, but you do have to hurt him badly enough to remove the idea of revenge from his likely responses. I once told one of these guys to back off, and when he didn't, after I beat him, I snapped his forearm. That's what I'm talking about here. You don't leave this sort of person standing. He will back up on you later if you do!

We are not talking about a normal person here. We are talking about someone who is frantically trying to fill a gaping hole in his self-esteem. He'll use anything to try and fill it. That's why he crosses you in the first place. If you show fear or he can beat you up, that's a sacrifice to the god of low self-esteem. He doesn't want to be swallowed so he throws in sacrifices. It's the old "When attacked by a shark use the buddy system—throw your buddy to the shark."

Anything that causes him to slip nearer the pit or further damages his self-image has to be attacked. Any time he loses or backs down, the hole gets bigger. If you fight and beat him, he has to come back at you. The only way to prevent that is either to hurt him so badly that he can't come back at you (because he's dead or spending all sorts of time recovering) or convince him that he doesn't have a chance, that even his best shot would fail. Let him know that you have him so scoped out that, if he even begins to make a move on you, his last living thought would be what his testicles taste like. He must know this to the very root of his being.

The problem is that few people have this kind of awareness or commitment. This is why I say dealing with a rep hunter is almost always a no-win situation. It can be done, but it has to be done right, or the guy will back up on you. It's easier to stay out of their way or to become an untouchable.

Also to be considered is the guy who already has the rep and is carrying on anyway. This can include the guy who has the rep and is still living the life, the guy who has the rep that he's trying to live down, or the guy who has a rep but is doing other things as well.

Most times these guys are a lot further down the trail than a rep hunter. While they will still smash someone for crossing lines, the lines will be more realistically based. With a rep hunter, if you look at him too long, he'll interpret that as an affront. With these guys you really have to be an asshole to get stomped. I'm talking, after you get stomped, bystanders walk up to you and say "Ya know, that was really stupid."

The best way to deal with someone with a reputation, if it's positive, is to respect it and the bearer. I'm not talking about your getting on your knees and giving this guy a blow job. I'm talking about calmly accepting that this person has a track record that indicates that you should not cross certain lines. People don't get real reputations without having some basis in reality. You respect his territory and expect him to respect yours. If your paths go the same way, great; you might be able to travel together. If not, you won't cross him, and you expect the same courtesy from him.

This is especially true if you're dealing with someone who is still active in his rep. If he is a wildman, you might end up partying together. If he's a hardass, you may be able to strike a deal in which you cover each other's back. If no, then you respect each other by ignoring each other.

There are all sorts of reputations that people do not want.

When you have a rep for something, people expect you to behave like that all the time, and it can become a real drag. All the rules of behavior just somehow go out the window. It's like a girl who sleeps with one too many guys for the local gossip mill. Suddenly, she's a slut, and every galoot with long horns is over there trying to get into her pants. This is not popularity; it's pestering her. What's worse, they are incredibly rude about it. They seem to think, "Well hell, she's a whore. You don't have to treat her with manners." Bullshit! Everybody you meet is a person and has feelings, emotions, and limits that he will not be pushed past. Even if she's a prostitute, you don't walk up and act like an asshole. If she is a girl who got hung with a rep because some asshole couldn't keep his mouth shut in the locker room, you especially don't behave like a jerk toward her.

Now if you think I'm joking, let me tell you a little story my blood brother saw. He was in a bar in Japan. One of the guys he was sitting near had a bar girl on his lap. This guy was getting out of line, and the girl was trying to exit gracefully. Well the guy pushed it too far, and the woman, who had a balisong in her hand, jumped up, and in less time than it takes to tell it, the guy had fourteen cuts. The cuts start at the forehead and cheeks and worked down, and although none of them were fatal, they were all maiming and mauling strikes. Now if you are in, or have been in, or know someone who was in the military, I'll bet that you either know or have heard of someone who got torn up by one of these girls— especially if you are stationed in the Far East. Just because someone has a negative rep, don't think that means that you can treat him or her badly.

The other thing about reps is that people think that since you're famous, they can just walk up to you. Normal etiquette for introductions somehow just evaporates. Anyway, if someone has a rep, you don't just walk up to him and say, "I've heard you have a rep. Let me see you do something." It sounds incredibly obvious, but you'd be surprised. If you want to meet someone with a rep, arrange to be with someone he knows or work your way into talking with him gently. Don't just go wobbling up to him.

Notes

[1] My other favorite is when people walk up and ask me to admit to felonies. "Did you ever kill anyone?" Have you ever shot anyone?" Take a hint: don't ask people these kind of questions.

[2] One of the drawbacks that nobody talks about with gang/pack mentality is they have a lousy retirement plan.

CHAPTER EIGHT

Tacking, Scarring, and Piercing

> "I have a rule: don't go to bed with women with tattoos of daggers on their bodies."
>
> —Doctor D

We humans are funny about the things we do to decorate our bodies. People often ask me, if I'm such a badass, why don't I have any tattoos? Well, aside from the fact that I consider someone who wants only to be "tough" to be sort of retarded, I have two reasons.

One is my own personal trip; nothing in my life has ever remained consistent enough that I'd want it on my body forever. I knew a guy who was a real heavy doper who had a tattoo of a joint that went from shoulder to wrist on the inside of his arm. Imagine how much fun he has now that he's left the drug scene. My second reason has to do with the brother of someone I knew in high school. He was facing a murder rap, and he almost got away with it except a tattoo on his right forearm ID'ed him in a lineup. He ended up doing hard time over that one.

Tattooing, scarring, and piercing is very big in the streets and in the borderlands. What's more, it's a language in itself. Let's take a look as to why people do such fun things to themselves.

Say you're sitting in a coffee shop and a guy in the military comes in. This guy is an officer and is in his dress uniform. You can tell just by looking at the guy that he's a lifer. If you know how to read his uniform and insignia, you can tell: the branch he's in, his rank, the campaigns he's been in, the special training he's undergone, the decorations and awards he's received, where he's been posted, if he's ever been wounded, and how long he's been in. You can tell all of this just by looking at his fruit cocktail and hash marks.

TATTOOING

Tattooing in particular is a form of fruit cocktail. If you were to meet a person from a primitive tattooing society, you could tell which tribe he's from, what his rank as a warrior is, what his status is in the tribe, and how many brave deeds he's done—all at a glance. Tattooing is a sworn lifelong allegiance to a particular tribe or system. In exchange the tribe accepts him and cares for him.

The various tribes have certain markings that are peculiar to their group, and they have a habit of getting bent out of shape if they see an outsider with their particular symbols. For example, to this day a certain skull with wings is private property of the Hell's Angels. They have spread the word to all tattoo artists that doing it on a non-Angel is a bozo no no. No respectable tack artist will do it. This also includes many non-respectable artists who have a strong sense of self-preservation.

Depending on the type, coloring, subject, style, detail, and placements, you can tell all sorts things about people by their tattoos: if they've ever been in prison and, if so, what prison; group, or gang alliance; life-style; sexual preference; how long they've been in that system; racial likes and dislikes; if they believe in magic; dead friends; product fealty; musical likes; power animals and totems; if he/she is a warrior, artist, outlaw, musician, etc.; what their self-image is; how long they expect to live; if they were in the service and, if so, where they were stationed; and so on.

Tattooing has become more and more popular over the last few years. In fact, it has gotten to the point where they have tattoo conventions on the East and West Coasts. No longer is a tattoo specifically an indication of being in a trash-can society. The quality and artistic integrity have improved. Now, under Japanese influence, tattooing has become a serious art form.

Reading tattoos is like learning to read a foreign language. You may know how to read the core language, but what about the various dialects? To discover the person under the tattoos, the first thing you should look at is if the tattoos follow a plan and/or pattern, or do they just cover the person like freckles on a bad acid trip?

The sort of person who is tattooed over a large portion of his body in a continuous flowing pattern of swirls and borders is usually different in many (some subtle) ways from the guy who has tattoos scattered all over his arms in no real pattern. I believe that the tattooing pattern reflects how the person lives. The guy that has tattoos of various quality and sizes crammed in wherever there's room generally doesn't really have his shit together in the long run. You may not want to tie your boat to him. While people with tattoos that are either one huge picture or are patterns that swirl and border separate tattoos are generally more stable.[1]

A very good example of people who have massive tattoos that identify them are the Japanese yakuza, the so-called Japanese mafia.[2] These guys are tattooed with clan allegiance and accomplishments. The further into the organization a member gets, the more tattoos he has. If you see the guy without his clothes on you know exactly with whom you are dealing. This is why the police have had such a hard time infiltrating them. The meetings are conducted wearing nothing but a groin strap. If you aren't really one of them, they know immediately. An outsider will see only a Japanese man in a nice suit. From the neck up and on their hands, they have no tattoos. Sneaky, sneaky. As you may have guessed, these people have flowing and continuous tattoos. They also have their shit together, big time.

Another way of looking at this is that people who live inconsistent and sporadic lives also tattoo themselves that way. They generally float along and, when something happens that has relevance to their lives, they often get a tattoo to mark it. This is how you can tell where and when somebody did time. Either they have the name of the prison itself, or they have work done by a recognizable artist of the particular institution. Old cons can spot each other by the style of their tattoos. They recognize the style of the artist. "That's Johnson's work. He was in Folsom between '85 and '90."

People often tattoo themselves to commemorate people as well as events. If a friend dies, they get a tattoo. Often the tattoo is symbolic, e.g., a picture of a snake over a brother named Snake who didn't make it, a picture of the person, or sometimes a name on a tombstone or cross. In short, every tattoo has a story behind it.

While a tattoo isn't always inspired by hard times, it often is. This identifies the wearer as someone who has gone through the toughest of times and still come out alive. You may not think that you'd want a tattoo of a prison on your body, but look at it from the other side. If you knew that there was a likelihood of your ending up in the pen again, you'd want these kind of tacks. If you're just in a level-one for a short haul, the other inmates will leave you alone if you have level-five markings.

Knowing that people tattoo things that are important to them on their bodies can help you spot all sorts of things about a person. A biker swears his allegiance to the symbol of his tribe, the great god Harley Davidson. Therefore, he tattoos either the name or the logo onto his precious body. Another biker tattoo is the mighty V-Twin engine with flames vomiting forth in a symbol of raw power. This is the fabled Harley engine directly applied, skipping the process of words altogether. Another thing that is important to bikers is the image of the Viking warrior. They see themselves as Vikings roaming far and wide—free barbarians who stand apart from the chained sheep of civilization. Freedom is an important issue to bikers, and they have several symbols for it.

A gangbanger tattoos the name "Crip" or "Blood" on his arm, forever sealing himself to a tribe. On the forearm, he tacks the particular sect that he belongs to. Across his biceps, he will often sign his street handle.

A street dude who doesn't expect to make it past thirty tattoos skulls and grim reapers all over himself. Wearing decaying bones and skulls indicates an individual to whom life doesn't mean much. They expect to end up dead from overdoses, accidents, deals gone bad, or just being in the wrong place at the wrong time. Fortunately many of these people are actually more self-destructive than competent in harming others. This is good since many of these people have attitudes that say life is shit. *Hasta la vista, baby!*

In a neighboring area are tattoos that indicate what the person thinks about himself. This may smudge over into his attitude about death that we were just talking about, so you can see that there's a lot of middle ground here. A woman with a tattoo of a spider web is telling you something about how she sees herself, or just as importantly, how she would like you to see her. An example of this is tattos of totems and power animals. By having the markings of the animal on the body, the person supposedly gains the power and ferocity of the creature. The soldier who gets a panther tattooed on his arm is indicating his fierceness. A person who gets a snake tacking is telling the world that he is cold-blooded and deadly and strikes without warning—or he would like to think he does. The guy who gets a grinning death head that's smoking a joint pretty much thinks that it's all over for him. He's in the trash can and is just passing time until his ticket gets punched.

A biker chick who has roses and stars tattooed on her is telling you that, even though she may be in a tough situation, she still has a feminine aspect. She considers herself a soft, caring woman, and, if you don't treat her like a lady, she'll punch your lights out.[3] The guy with a Frazettaesque barbarian on him is letting you know that he considers himself to be a warrior.

All the tattoos can be read like markings on a military uniform to tell you what operating system the person is in. It takes a little bit of practice and research to identify what the symbols mean, but there is a language to tattoos. However, like any other language, it's always changing and evolving. You can tell when someone got a tattoo by the style and subject. There are certain styles from the 1970s, 1980s, and 1990s.

As I stated earlier, tattooing has caught on outside the trash-can societies. Many punkers, young rebels, musicians, artists, S&M'ers, and weekend warriors have moved into tattooing. A tattoo is no longer an indication of how tough someone is. There has always been the guy who got a tattoo to prove more to himself than anyone else how tough he was. Now, however, there are people who are getting tattoos to indicate how far away from the "establishment" they are—an indication of weirdness rather than toughness.

Some people get a tattoo for other reasons, Chris Pfouts, the author of *Lead Poisoning,* got a tattoo of a beautiful woman over a typewriter after he got shot, explaining that the "canvas is ruined anyway." Dear old Chris, a writer through and through.

SCARRING

Scarring is something that surfaces occasionally in odd places. The hard core punk rockers of the 1980s often took razor blades to themselves. They'd sit there while seriously looped and carve the names of their favorite band or some slogan that meant something to them into their arms. There is a famous University in Heidleberg, Germany, that used to have duels with sort of real swords. (Hell, they may still be doing it.) They would wear these masks that protected eyes, lips, noses, and ears but left the rest of the face open. The idea was to slash your opponent across the unprotected part of his face. Once a cut was received, great pains were taken to make sure that it healed in the most blatant scar possible. Everyone was impressed that you had a "Heidleberg Dueling Scar" on your kisser.

In a related vein, another form of scarring is that of wounds. The hardass who has multiple scars on his arms nine times out of ten has been in a shitload of knife incidents. Always check the arms of a Hispanic, an Oriental, an Indian, or a Gypsy before you even consider messing with him. There are fewer white networks that use knives, but they do exist. If the guy has scars, *do not let his hands get out of sight*! If you do, you're volunteering to get either seriously hurt or possibly killed.

Another thing to look for is bullet wounds. Small-caliber wounds are usually small, puckered things going in looking not unlike inoculation scars. Often, what the surgeon has to do to fix the damage usually makes a bigger mess of the skin than the bullet itself. There's a certain commitment that someone has to have to survive a bullet or knife wound.

Generally, these are not the kind of people you'd want to mess with for no good reason. They have survived the worst and often aren't likely to allow you any slack that would risk putting them back there. I highly recommend reading *Lead Poisoning* for a variety of reasons, not the least of which is to see what it takes to make it back when you don't win.

PIERCING

Piercing runs a weird gamut. It used to have a large language, but now it's a purely local interpretation. Misinterpreting it can get your teeth knocked down your throat. The merchant marines used to pierce a guy's ear when he crossed the equator for the first time. Back away if you saw a guy with a pierced ear, it meant that he was a sailor. In the 1950s and early 1960s, pierced ears on a woman meant that she was a slut. That may still hold true for serious backwater areas of the South.

Contrary to some conventional wisdom, these days a guy with pierced ear is nine times out of a ten *not* a homosexual. If you are from an area where men don't pierce their ears, and you meet up with a guy with a pierced ear, calling him a homosexual will likely get your face pushed in. If you are from an area where there is a left/right distinction, be aware that it changes from locale to locale.

In Venice, California, in the 1970s, the rule was: left ear means you're a hellraiser; right ear means you're gay. So not only did I get my left ear pierced, I was such a hellraiser that I got it pierced twice. Imagine my surprise when I discovered that to the West Coast gay community, right ear meant dominate, left ear meant submissive. Yipe! In their language, I was a double submissive. Uh, sorry, guys, not this dude.

However, with the East Coast gay community, the whole thing was reversed: right submissive, left dominate. In other areas outside the gay community, right ear meant that you're a hellraiser, while left ear meant that you're gay. In short, it's very confusing. If you travel with a pierced ear, understand that you could be setting yourself up for some shit. If you have your ear(s) pierced and you are heading into places where violence is likely, wear studs. Do not wear long danglies that make the girls go goo-goo-eyed at you. A common thing to do is to rip an erring out of the ear of the person you're fighting. It hurts like fuck and usually stuns the person. So if you're going to wear danglies (or large rings) wear them when you're not likely to get into a fight.

Nose piercing has also become popular—at least in the cities. It is mostly confined to women, but some guys do it too. It's popular among the "heavily disassociated youth" group, the descendants of the original punk rockers. Don't thing that these people can't fight. Some can't; others will slit you from asshole to eyeball.

An entirely different group of people who are into piercing are the S & M/bondage types. There are some heavy-duty folks here. It used to be if you saw a guy with a pierced nipple, it meant he was gay. Not anymore—bikers and badasses have started doing this too. Again there are some symbols that identify who, what, and what species they're into doing. Generally, these people are into certain sexual practices that I will not excite you with. One common way to spot these people is from their multiple ear piercings. I'm talking about almost to the top.

Occasionally, you may encounter belly-button piercing, usually on a woman with a bare midriff.

You do not want to fuck with people with pierced body parts. Yes, they look odd. Yes, they may look like they crawled out of a freak show, but if you must snicker, do it up your sleeve. Do not hassle them. Remember, these people like inflicting pain, and they have a real big tolerance for it as well. You might not like what you grabbed onto. You may think this chapter had little to do with self-defense. Actually it did. By understanding certain systems, you're not likely to walk up to a guy and say, "What are you? Some kind of fag?" Next thing you know, blamo! The guy then asks you, "What are you? Some kind of shark that can regrow teeth?"

Knowing that the markings have meaning and purpose, you can avoid the mistakes that most people make about these kind of folks. If you meet up with someone from the tattoo/pierce/scar crowd you can walk up and talk to them instead of fighting. I have avoided more than a few fights by complimenting folks on their tattoos and asking for their history. The guy gets so wrapped up in telling me about his decorations that he forgets he was thinking about the possibility of taking a shot at me. This is something to talk about when you're avoiding a problem by making friends with another hardass.

Notes

[1] Although this is not always true about intricate, artsy tattoos reflecting more stability. I am talking about one huge rule of thumb. I've met some serious wackos with vistalike tattoos.

[2] God, I bet they hate being called that. Traditionally, they've been around longer than the Mafia.

[3] I know a lot of tough-ass women who have stuffed animal collections. You walk into their room and their unicorns, puppies, and kittens right next to a sawed-off shotgun. Don't make fun of this aspect of their personality; it's real important to them. You can get seriously hurt by laughing at them.

CHAPTER NINE

Gambling

> "Good?! They were fucking pool sharks!"
> —My mother, explaining to me exactly what my father meant when, after whipping me at pool, he said that, compared to his old friends, he wasn't that good at pool. *They* were good at it.

When it comes to serious gambling, I might as well just hand you my money and save myself time. The only time I've ever come close to being able to win with gambling is if I'm betting on myself. I can go from point A to point B in said amount of time or faster than someone else. That sort of thing I'm good at. However, figuring out what are the best cards to throw away beyond the three that aren't part of a pair leaves me utterly lost.

Needless to say, this gem of wisdom did not come cheaply. In my time I have thrown my money away in some weird ways. Instead of dog or horse racing, I'd bet on tortoise or frog racing (I figured it took longer to lose your money that way). I have no problem with the boys' penny ante poker game. Generally, everybody is as incompetent as me, and no real damage is done. However, I have fucked up now and then and ended up in a serious poker or pool game.

Pool hustlers are not as obvious as Tom Cruise or Paul Newman in *The Color of Money*. In fact, unless you're real experienced, you'll never know you were hustled by a good hustler. They are more like the Forrest Whitaker character in the same movie. Hustling is not cheating per se; it is not letting on how good you are. The guy who cheats at cards is different from the guy who hustles people. They both can end up in an alley with their heads blown off, but one is out-and-out dishonest, while the other relies on people's egos getting involved. You will notice that a good number of fights happen around pool tables in bars. This should be considered one hell of a clue.

Come to think of it, let's look at some categories here.

1) *Professional gamblers.* They have names and reps, guys like Diamond Jim Brady, Jimmy the Greek, Minnesota Fats, the Earl of Sandwich.[1] You'll see these guys on the circuit: Monte Carlo, Atlantic City, Las Vegas, Reno, and Tahoe. If there's a big-money-purse event, they're there.

2) *The smaller guys.* These people aren't exactly major league professionals, but their games are major league, $5,000 and up. What's odd is if you show that you have the cash, the casinos will often spot you all you need. They figure they'll get it back at the tables. These guys not only play the established spots, but the unestablished spots, too—sometimes in motel rooms, other times in the back rooms of certain establishments with these kind of games. Since what they are doing is technically illegal anyway, it really doesn't matter where they do it. They often float between legal and illegal. These guys are serious players, the so-called "lead stick" of certain pool halls or "high rollers." Generally these people are connected in one way or another. Unless you have serious money, they won't even bother to look your way.

3) *The "puffer fish."* These are the guys who are driving a Cadillac one week and living out of it the next. They are

wrapped up in gambling and go from broke to flush to broke again more often than most people change their underwear. These guys constantly amaze me; for every one who blows it and ends up face down in an alley, another one makes it for years. These are the old guys who sit around and tell you what hotshots they were. Most people think, "Yeah, bullshit!" when they hear these stories. It's amazing how often they're true, though. There was a time that a lot of these guys would light cigars with twenty dollar bills. But like puffer fish, they went from small to big to small again.

4) *The hustlers*. These are the guys who prey on the average Joe in the bar or small-time poker player. They go around pretending that they aren't that good, they play a few hands or games, barely winning and barely losing, and then they bring betting into it. They never win by much, but they always win when there's money on the table. They use the other people's greed and ego against them.

Next on the totem pole is the small-time player, the guys who play poker with the boys on Thursday night, the warehouse guys, the guys on the corner shooting craps, and the half-way decent barroom pool players. Truth be told, some sizable money can end up changing hands here; not as much as with the big boys, but when we're talking about rent it is a serious matter. These are the guys that hustlers prey on. In fact, they are the hustlers' bread and butter.

5) *People who make excursions to Atlantic City and Nevada*. These people range in status from the little old grannies who save up their pension checks to would-be high rollers. These people play the game and march along to the tune set down in those places, and, believe me, the tune is well choreographed. You do not get out of line in these casinos.

Now that we have categorized the types of gamblers, let's

look at the situations in which you are most likely to run into them. First, the official version, Nevada and Atlantic City. The first time I ever hit Vegas I was coming back from a week in the back bush of Arizona. My compass had been reoriented a whole lot by being out there. I walked into the place and went "tilt!" I sat there, dumbfounded. The guy with me mistook my expression. "Pretty amazing, huh?" he asked. I looked around for a second more before turning to him and exploding, "This is everything that the cops used to chase me for when I was younger! But out in the open and with bright lights put on it!" Yes, indeedy do, a town that promotes, packages, and glorifies every sin known to man, and it's all legal and controlled.

Having just spent a week looking for snakes and scorpions before I put my feet anywhere, I immediately sent out a radar ping. The reading I got back was not nice: people in a money-spending daze going wee wee wee! What amazed me was that these people were the same ones that spit on the people who run this same sort of operation in their hometowns. Normal folks were running around with their tongues hanging out, lapping up the prepackaged vice. That was fine and dandy. Civilians in an orgy of money, food, sex, drugs, alcohol, and flash is not particularly exciting to me. In short, I've been there, seen that, done that. Ain't no new news here.

It was the operations that got my radar up. Understand, I was involved in the movie industry for years. When the lights go flash, I usually look to see who's running the control board and what the setup is. Call it professional interest. Some hard-core reality is operating in those places. Pit bosses watch every move with eyes that would make an eagle blush with envy. Cameras behind mirrored domes watch every action in every corner. One or two uniform guards wander around, but the real muscle is the well-trimmed large individuals in the immaculate suits. These guys were either standing or moving around, not playing, and watching everything with the same lazy alertness of a very big member of the cat family. I pegged three of them as their scopes dropped on me. Uh umm . . . hi, guys!

Now I had always heard that you don't get out of line in Vegas. Looking at Guido, Vinnie, and Nunzio, I thought to myself, "No shit!" However, let's look at what constitutes being out of line. Is it getting plowed and throwing your money away at a table? Nope, that's why drinks are free as long as you're playing. Is it making a pass at a strange woman? Not exactly, provided you choose the right one, and the system will gladly ensure that you pick the right one. There are certain ladies who cruise the casinos and, for a fee, will keep you company. If you are winning, they are drawn to you like iron filings to a magnet. Make no mistake, the company gets its cut from these ladies' activities. Is getting plastered and barking and drooling all over yourself considered out of line? Nope, that's why they have the shows. At the eight o'clock show, the showgirls have some clothes on. By ten o'clock, the lovely ladies are either topless or nude. As long as you limit your slobbering to those times, you're fine.

What can you do in these places that will get you a free inspection of the trunk of a junkyard car? Rip-offs are a surefire way. Ripping off people in these places is a guaranteed one-way trip, and it's not the cops you have to worry about, either. If you're lucky they will be the ones who find you. Even then your chances of survival are pretty fucking thin. The people you have to worry about have long arms. All a person who gets hustled has to do is complain in the right place and presto! Instant karma!

Cheating is another no-no. The gambling commission will string you up by the balls if it ever hears about cheating. That is, if the people who catch you leave you any. The game is stacked in these places. The flow is going to the house, and the owners will keep it that way. If you start to win too much against the house, they will change dealers. The new dealer *will* guarantee that you lose! Cheating is only allowed by certain parties, and you aren't one of them.[2] If you are able to count cards, you will be escorted from the premises with the express understanding that you are never allowed back.

Violence is one of those things that is verboten in entire sections of town, although control is slipping. In Vegas, the strip and the hotel area used to be off limits, but not any more. The strip is slipping into decay However, do not even think of starting shit in the casinos. Those immaculately suited gentlemen who clink when they walk are guaranteed to be better at it than you are. Even if you had a machine gun, you'd never get more than one of them before they got you. These guys are pros, and they're never together. They're extremely low-key and they have their shit wired tight. In fact these guys, may not shit at all. Instead of feces, I suspect they have balls of wire. If you try to start shit in these places, you will be hammered so hard and fast that next to you a flounder will look obese.[3]

Incidentally, all the casinos/hotels have fax capabilities. If you are barred or bounced from one place, every place in town knows about it within five minutes. If you really screw the pooch, different cities and states know about it immediately, too. The cops are on the same network. These fuckers are prepared to handle trouble if it rears its ugly head.

Robbery is too dangerous to even consider in these cities You can go to north Las Vegas and try it if you're feeling lucky. However, it is a well-known fact that you will suffer a terminal case of lead poisoning if you try for one of the casinos. The last guy who tried was found sitting in his car in Los Angeles with a bullet hole in the back of his head. He knew whoever did him well enough to have him sitting behind him. Trying to jack an individual in certain areas is also pretty stupid. Not only are there police everywhere looking for folks who are not supposed to be there, but the people who own the place do not take it lightly that you are taking money that rightly should go to them.

Generally speaking, when going to gambling meccas, take only the amount of money you can afford to lose. Do not cop an attitude when you get taken. Unlike many situations, these places specialize in kissing you when they screw you. That's why people keep coming back. "Yeah, I got screwed, but boy was it good!" Truck along with the rest of the folks, eating, drinking, and being merry. Don't ever get so bombed that either you can't come back immediately or you lose your common sense. Also if a large, well-groomed gentleman comes up to you and suggests perhaps you should give it a rest, pack it up and put it to bed.

The next most common way to encounter gamblers is the Thursday night poker game. This usually involves people who know each other and are playing for fun. Although, it can move upwards. The basic rule here is if you're playing a "friendly" game with friends, don't take anyone for too much. If it starts getting too serious, take a break or lose some money back to the guy. Of the 21,500 reported murders in 1989, 35 percent of them resulted directly from "arguments." My calculator says that's 6,142. The statistics don't break it down to how many were over gambling debts or losses, but you can see how arguments can get out of hand. Don't try to fleece your friends. If you win $20, that's fine and dandy; just don't let anyone lose his rent money during the game.

Let's move on to a much more serious gambling encounter. There are certain established games that are not friendly. These games are well-known among locals and generally are held in a back room or the local equivalent. I stumbled into one of these and soon found myself down nearly $100. I won a $40-dollar pot and got the fuck out of there. (I was taking a risk, but I'll explain that later.) I knew that I was way out of my league. There were two serious card sharks there, Bob and Gene, and I found out later that Gene was financing his wedding. They were pulling up some obscure-assed games like three-toed Pete, high-low split, and others that I was to learn as I went (read: get screwed as they dealt).

This is a common way to hustle, getting people to play games that they don't know. Until you get the hang of it, you're going to lose. We're not talking the first flush of beginner's luck; we're talking about your getting taken to the cleaner. Don't ever play a game that you don't know for money. If someone starts calling odd games regularly, pack your marbles and go home.

Much of the violence that happens around gambling results from a mediocre player getting suckered into playing in a better player's field. This is what a hustle is all about: some guy who does not want to admit his limitations gets pulled in over his head. Once that happens, the guy starts getting pissed. Generally, he can't put his finger on it, but he knows something is wrong with the picture. Sooner or later he's going to figure out (either right or wrong) that the guy is hustling him.

Of course, you are not being hustled every time that you lose. I have had days on the pool table when I couldn't hit a barn wall if I was inside the damn barn. With cards, there are times when, instead of gambling, you should be in the building biz. The dice are looking toward the snake god. Most people make the mistake of refusing to leave when the game turns against them. They set their heels and try to bull it out. Wrong move, bucko! Cut your losses and run like a motherfucker!

On the other hand, some days you end up getting screwed without getting kissed. The best way to avoid violence over gambling is to avoid serious gambling all together. However, doing that is sort of tricky if you don't know what is going on. Gambling is based in competition. In case you haven't noticed, we're brought up to compete. Sports, grades (especially those fucking curves), positions—from the get-go we are in competition with each other. The purpose of competition is to put two *equally matched* opponents together and see who wins. Nobody expects a regular high-school kid to win a fight with a thirty-year-old iron-working black belt.

The basis of the hustle is that the hustler, through a variety of ways and means, hides the fact that he is of superior talent in a certain area. He makes it look like you and he are neck-and-neck all the way. Then he suggests that you go for a purse, or if he's real good, he manipulates you so that you suggest it. Once money is involved, he always manages to win at the crucial moment. A good hustler will keep a smooth patter going to distract you from what is going on.

The hustler generally scopes out what's going on: who's around, who's got money, who's likely to fall for his game, who's likely to spot his ass, and who would likely rip his lungs out for hustling them. In short:

1) Is there a market?
2) Can he get people involved?
3) Can he get away with it?

A hustler on the prowl will move from bar to bar, off his usual track. The people in his own space know him and know his talent. They're not going to play him, or they're going to get handicaps. If he's looking to line his pockets, he has to look outside. Also, he can't stay long enough to be ID'd as a hustler. Management does not take kindly to sharks fleecing customers. I have met hustlers in all sorts of places. Generally when you think of a hustler, you imagine some guy with a ermine-lined jacket, a purple fedora with an ostrich feather sticking out, and his initials in gold in his teeth—the kind of guy who hangs out in seedy dives in the wrong part of town, with names like "Mr. Divine Prince." Yes, these guys exist. However, it's the guy in the polo shirt and chinos in the corner designer pub or the stranger in the local watering hole that you have watch out for. Street people spot a hustler real quick; nice civilians don't, and it's these nice folks who have the money.

In either case, what you will encounter is a guy who watches the action for a while on the table. I'm not talking about watching the blonde's boobs as she leans over to take a shot; I'm talking about examining the action of the balls, the form of the players, and the interaction of the people. You've heard me talk about doing periodic scans of your surroundings in other books; what I'm talking about now is noticing that the guy was looking your way not once, but three times. There's a look and feeling to people when they are watching someone. People in the spy business are trained to hide the fact that they are watching folks, usually because the people being watched are watching for watchers. However, a hustler generally doesn't cover his tracks that well. Why should he? Officially he was just sitting there thinking about coming over for a friendly game. Yeah right. Bullshit!

The next step is for the hustler to identify his target(s). One, the person will have money. Two, the person will be reasonably competent on the table. Three, the person will be competitive. Now the shark moves.

There are a couple of ways that the hustler can approach. The two most common are either through the ranks or directly to the mark. If the target is hanging around and someone else in the circle has the table, the hustler will walk through these people to get the attention of the mark. This is a sign of a hustler; he blasts through the hanger-ons and slows down when he's getting closer to the mark. If the person he is playing is not likely to bet, the hustler will defeat him in fast (but not suspiciously so) time. A good pool player can clear the table in nothing flat if he has the mind to do so. When he's running full out, you might not even get a chance to shoot at all. A quick defeat catches the eye of the mark. The mark, having just peed on a tree, will notice when another dog sprays the same tree. This usually will draw him back to the table. Sometimes the hustler will make a passing comment to the mark that is mildly challenging to further bait the trap.

If the mark has not relinquished the table, it's easier. All he does is comes up and puts his quarter on the table. That's how you indicate that you want to play the winner.[4] From then on, the hustle really begins, the hustler will control his shots to make it look like he and the mark are close to the same level. During this time, he often keeps up a patter or a conversation to make him seem like a friendly guy. The real good ones stretch it out but continue to lose by one ball through a few games. Then they pretend to get mad and offer to up the ante by placing some money on it. At this juncture, warning bells should go off in your head.

My normal response is that I don't bet with people I don't know. He could be exactly what he appears to be: a normal guy, with some talent who got his dick out of joint because he is losing at a game he thought he was good at. However, there's a fifty-fifty chance that the guy's a hustler. The odds go up if you've never seen the dude in the place before. The appearance of normalcy is the basis of the con. Most people miss that fact entirely.

There you are, on a roll, feeling good. You have held the table for a while, and you've just beaten this guy for three straight games. Yeah, so you only beat him by a few balls— you still won three times straight. Why not take this guy's money . . . *Wrong answer, Buckwheat!*

By getting wrapped up in that sort of thinking, you've just sprung the trap. The guy will nail you for as much as you are willing to bet. He may let you win some back to try to sucker you into another game. It goes on and on until you call a halt to it.

Once you've agreed to play, you're on his turf. Getting pissed about losing is a real common reaction. Generally, these guys know a few tricks about handling themselves, but they often end up in alleys for hustling the wrong person. I've known guys who put themselves through college by hustling, but they were one in hundreds. Your average hustler is a mean slimeball.

Fortunately, most people aren't hustlers. Nonetheless, understand that when you gamble against someone, you are taking a risk, both economically and physically. Some people are sore losers. They can make you sore, too—if not worse. The dangerous times are when you collect the money and when you try to leave. This is why big-time game players have someone else hold the money during the game. You put your money up front into a third party's hands. That way whoever loses can't renege on the bet. (See Chapter 5 for some tips about leaving.)

A lot of shit happens in bars, saloons, and watering holes because someone thinks that he got hustled. Or if he wakes up and realizes that he really needs that $50 and that the old lady is really going to jump his shit for losing it, the situation suddenly gets real ugly. This is why the maxim of gambling is don't do it unless you can afford to lose.

Generally speaking, a good gambler will keep away from games of true chance. The roll of the dice is just too shaky, while the cards and the pool table can definitely be controlled. There is no such thing as a random factor on the pool table. Long after quantum physics has eroded it away everywhere else, $E=MC^2$ will hold true on the pool table. The cards fall within predictable odds and probabilities. Horses have track records, which you can use to compute the odds, but the gamble is still chancy.

The people you meet in crap games and bingo games aren't likely to be trying to make a living at it. Yet, you can see puffer fish here (usually on the down slide) trying to lap up that last bit of wild luck. One thing I've noticed here is that people going for the wild chance games are usually the ones who can least afford to lose, especially on the street. Often they are hanging on by the skin of their teeth, and they are not going to let someone roll away with their welfare checks. A good deal of violence surrounds these street-corner games.

Based on the caliber of the people you are playing with, establish some serious rules. Before you sit down at a table look to see who you're playing with, especially if you are not in a casino. Is everybody at the table willing to lose? Can they really afford it? This is critical. If you end up in a high-stakes game with someone who can't afford to lose, he might just decide to remove you to recoup his losses.

I was talking to a guy some years back who had been in a high-stake game with some coke dealers. He had won $80,000, but deliberately lost $30,000 back to the people that he was playing with. He recognized that he was in a situation where he would not have gotten out alive had he tried to leave. These guys were supposed big spenders, but they really couldn't afford to lose that kind of bread. It doesn't have to be over that kind of money. Someone who can't afford to lose money will turn vicious if he loses too much.

You can win and walk away if you allow the other people sufficient time to win their money back. This is true if you are playing against other people and not the house. With the house, it's a different story. A solid rule when you are playing other people is *you do not win big and immediately walk away.* If you are ahead, you hang around long enough to give anyone who has lost to you a chance to win it back. If you win and hold steady for a period, the other person is not going to feel as screwed as if you won and just up and split.

The semiexception to this rule is what I did. I was losing badly and when I won a pot, I got the hell out of there. I minimized my loses that way. Nobody could complain seriously because I was down $60. One of the sharks did comment on it, but I pointed out to him that he had no right to bitch because he had enough of my money.

Now there are a couple of things that you have to understand about gambling etiquette. Since gamblers have no tolerance for cheaters, you have to act in such a way that nobody can say that you're cheating, much like a guy who might have a weapon has to keep his hands in plain view. In a group of hard-cores, nobody makes a move that can be interpreted as going for a weapon. When you are playing for money, you keep your hands on the table as much as possible. You set anything that you might need on the table up front, cigarettes, lighter, money, etc. If applicable, roll up your sleeves. If you're armed, keep your hands away from the weapon.

Now there is some debate about how much money or chips you leave out in front of you. Some people favor leaving it all out; some vote for putting part of it away as you win. My personal bias is for the latter, but it's up to you. If you leave it out, don't be surprised when a woman approaches you. They don't look like Hollywood hookers, but many of them are pros. I like the squirreling approach because 1) it doesn't attract hookers, 2) It doesn't attract muggers, 3) if someone's losing badly, he can't see how much I've won and blame me, and 4) it keeps people from knowing just how much I have to win or lose. The purpose of a poker face is to keep the other players from knowing what is going on. Same deal here.

In any situation, never play a game that you are unfamiliar with. If someone keeps pushing, get up and leave. Remember the game I told you about with Bob and Gene, when they kept calling for those weird, special-rule games? They won those hands about 75 percent of the time, and the pots were sizable because of the nature of the game's betting procedures. There are some weird-ass variations of games with cards, dice, and pool tables. Understand that often these games are designed to increase the pot size. People can get mighty upset when they realize how much money they just lost during that round.

What I've been talking about is your getting frosted and hustled. One other thing I should mention is that you should always watch your fellow players. If the guy next to you is losing too heavily, watch his attitude. You may want to be somewhere else. Tempting as it is to gather more rosebuds, if he goes ballistic, you might end up getting hurt, not because he was aiming at you but because people are generally lousy shots.

Notes

[1] The guy who invented the sandwich. He was a serious gambler. Once during a card game his servant pointed out to him that he really should eat. Rather than leaving the table, the Earl told him to put a piece of meat between two slices of bread and bring it to him. Voila! The first Big Mac!

[2] A very good book on the subject is *Scarne's Encyclopedia of Games* by John Scarne. It's an older book, but unlike many

books on the subject of cards, it deals with how to spot someone cheating, which is well worth knowing if you go to these sort of places. It gives you an idea of how the handwork is done so you have a good chance of spotting someone trying to do it to you. By the way, don't even think of trying this sort of stuff in the big leagues. I'm not joking about people ending up in the trunks of cars that get squished in the junkyard.

³ I know only one group that ever successfully stood up to these guys.

⁴ Just because someone places a quarter on the table doesn't mean you have to play him. You do, however, have to address it immediately. Running a table is a territory thing, sort of like being king of the mountain. You hold it until someone pushes you off or you leave. If you don't mind playing the guy, nod to him. However, if you don't want to play him, generally you have to relinquish the table. Tell him that was your last game or something. That way you relinquish the table.

CHAPTER TEN

Turf, Territory, and 'Hoods

> "Get off my land . . ."
> —Richard Jones, moments before
> a particularly ugly incident

If one animal from the same species enters the territory of another, you're going to have a squabble on your hands. It is the same with humans. Territory is sort of flexible; it can include personal space, actual turf, possessions, or—the one that cracks me up—women.

Putting it simply, territory is the amount of space that you need to forage, maneuver, and operate to support and defend yourself. Technically, the more bountiful the land, the less territory you need. The harsher the land, the more likely you are to roam and forage.

PERSONAL SPACE

Things are more complicated with humans because people need space around them to feel comfortable. Now depending on where you're from, the amount of space can range anywhere from miles to centimeters to keep from being crushed up against someone in the subway. A lot of aggravated assaults happen over an invasion of space.

There is a distinct difference between what you want and what you need. To live in Los Angeles you *need* some form of transportation; what you *want* is a Ferrari. The same is true for territory. People need space. If you pack them too closely together, they go bonkers. Look at New York. People think Los Angeles is AWOL, but the Big Apple is totally gone.

Generally speaking, there is *external territory* and *internal territory*. External territory is how close you let people get to you physically. This is often called personal space. One of the most common mistakes that people make is to cross accidentally into another person's personal space. People's space requirements differ not only culturally and socially, but also between city and country. There are reasons for the amount of space some people use. Some of these reasons will keep your teeth in place.

Internal territory is much trickier. It is more of a psychological need, and it is what causes most people to end up on the *Uniform Crime Report*'s victim list, one way or the other. It deals with what people will and won't put up with.

Recently I discovered that Colorado had passed a so-called "make my day" law. This law basically says that if someone is in your house and you didn't invite him, you're not liable for suit if you shoot him. In other words, if you shoot a burglar, that's his tough luck. He can't sue you if he lives. My old partner (who lives in California) shot a burglar in the leg. One of the cops who showed up said, "You should have killed him." Sure enough, the guy tried to sue my partner.

Let's look at the attitude behind both of these situations. Can you guess which state has a higher respect for personal space? As you might suspect, there are some folks who do not take kindly to infringement on their personal space. How much people respect someone else's space really depends on a number of factors, but where they live is a biggie.

The first time I got shot at was on a street corner in Venice, California. One gang was cruising a contested border between two territories, and someone thought I looked like the opposition. However, a good number of my country friends were first shot at from doing such quaint little things as moving somebody's outhouse back five feet, which provides a rude surprise in the middle of the night. (I have some rude friends.) In both cases the lead was flying over territory. I was in the wrong area; the others were also in the wrong area. But note the huge difference in circumstances.

Rural vs. Urban Reactions

Generally, in areas where people have more space, they are much friendlier than in areas where they don't. I recently went up to the High Sierras to pick up some inner-city kids who had spent six weeks doing a program in the bush. "When strangers say, 'hello,' they mean it!" remarked one. "When someone says, 'hello,' to you in LA, they're trying to get something from you; up here they're really glad to see you!"

An important safety tip here, though: While rural folks are friendlier and less likely to shoot, when they do, they're prone to be much more accurate than in the city. People are always crowding each other in the city, and shit is likely to explode over smaller things. Unlike out where lizards do pushups, if you explode in the city, the sheer density of the population guarantees someone is going to get hurt—often an innocent bystander, not the person being the asshole. Most gang shootings aren't aimed at a particular person; rather, the gang members shoot at a group that's standing around. The more crowded people are, the nastier they're going to react. This results in the famed New York politeness. You say, "Good morning," and they respond, "Fuck you!" Conversations go downhill quickly after that.

If you've spent much time traveling, you realize that city folk and country fold are very different. In less-populated areas people are much kinder and more polite. In cities people are generally ruder and paranoid and rather ruthless about defending their space. At the same time, the city is also less conscious about infringing on your space. It's okay for people to be assholes to you, but it doesn't work both ways. (Wanna bet?)

On the Navajo reservation, it is customary when you approach a home to sit in your car and wait until someone appears at the door. You don't walk up to the house for a couple of reasons. One is to allow whoever lives there to prepare to meet you (picking up the dirty laundry and stuffing it in the basket, changing or putting on clothes, etc.). This is also customary in other rural areas. I always liked that. The other reason for not approaching a Navaho home is to give the evil spirits that may have followed you time to get bored and wander off rather than infecting the house. Having to wait keeps most New Yorkers out of the Navajos' hair, so there really is something to the evil spirit thing. For either reason, Navajos get bent out of shape if you don't respect their space.

The way you approach someone's space will have a lot to do with how you're received. If you come running at someone you don't know, don't be surprised if he reacts negatively. I have in my time decked skaters and nearly decked skateboarders, joggers, and people running for the bus for no better reason than they were coming up behind me too fast. Oops! Once on Hollywood Boulevard, I stumbled on a crack. A guy saw my sudden movement in his peripheral vision and snapped into a fighting position. I saw him as I recovered and snapped into mine. I had a hell of a time convincing the guy that I had tripped. I apologized and went my way, but that could have gotten ugly. Approach people slowly, especially hard-cores, from the

front and with hands in plain sight to keep them from
getting edgy.

How Much Space Do People Need?

Let's look at something that causes all sorts of problems,
determining how much space people require in certain
situations. Here you have two people. On works in an office
building. All day long he is surrounded by people. Since there
is no parking downtown to be found for less than that which
would make a loan-shark blush in shame, he rides the bus. On
the bus the people are wall-to-wall. In Japan, there are guys
who shove people to pack them into the trains. Things haven't
gotten that bad in the United States yet, but this guy has people
bumping into him all day. On the elevator, people crowd in
and try to ignore the fact that they are jammed up against
someone. When he gets to work, his little cubicle is surrounded
by hundreds of others on the same floor.

After a hard day of skull sweat, this guy decides to avoid
the rush-hour crunch and goes to the local watering hole/meet
market. Surprise, surprise, here are 500 people packed in to
avoid the crunch. This place operates under the "pack 'em in
where you can" attitude as well. He squirms his way to the
bar and orders a round (with that many people you can't
walk; you have to wiggle through them all). Then with raised
drink, he begins his return trek. The same behavior that was
in effect in the elevator and bus is evident here. The way to
respect someone's privacy is to ignore the fact that you've
violated it by bumping into him.

Now let's take a gander at guy number two. In the
morning, he gets up and drives to work. Then he gets into a
truck and drives some more. Now believe it or not, a trucker's
main concern is to allow himself enough space to stop. Most
jack-knifed truck accidents occur because the driver had to

slam on his brakes. Slamming on the brakes is not something that you want to do in a truck. Further, he is suspicious of anyone coming near him at stops because of hijackings. After wheeling around all day, guy number two goes to his favorite watering hole, a rough-assed place where brawls and bushwhackings are common. There, you keep your distance from strangers, and you don't move into people's blindspots. There are certain corridors between bar, pool tables, exits, and bathrooms, which people are expected to use If you come into someone's space, you announce it from a distance by saying, "'Scuse me," then you indicate where you're heading. The you allow the person time to shift positions so he can watch while you're in his space.

What do you think will happen if these two found themselves in the same place? Both of them would be acting in what is considered polite behavior for their proper circles—that is, until the impromptu dental work was done.

Here is a basic law to remember, folks: *The rougher the area, the more space you give and take.* Not only do you allow others more space, you demand more from them! You also do not touch people whom you do not know! What you might consider a friendly gesture can be interpreted as an obstructive preliminary move. A guy could interpret your putting your hand on his shoulder as grabbing his arm so he can't block the shank you're about to put into him. Think you're going to get a pleasant response on that one?

The following is a real dangerous point to remember. When an approaching street person is told to back off, he'll often try to put you on the defensive: "Man, why you being so rude?" This stops most people for a moment. They flash on being packed in the bus or the elevator and wonder why they should object to this person being so close when others are close to them all the time. It is during this momentary hesitation that the scum sucker moves in closer, and when that happens, it's too late.

If someone pulls this shit on you, you tell him, "Cause I'm an asshole, now *back off!*"If someone comes at you after you've told him to back off, you knock his ass into next week—no questions asked. I've pulled weapons, as the third warning.

An effective California prison term I picked up is "gimme five feet!" I usually decorate it with a few colorful adjectives. This tells street people that they've fucked up and picked a homeboy instead of a civilian. A homeboy won't let them get off the first shot; a civilian will. It is critical to remember that these guys know that their asses are on the line. They can't afford to pick the wrong target. If you plant the seed of doubt in their minds, they will hold off until they are sure. While they are sitting there going, "Homina, homina, homina," you're moving out of range. Do it like a pro and don't leave any doors open, and they will wait. Street folks do not like straight-up fights, which is why they're so dangerous. They are going to try to get you in the least-risky way to themselves. If they can't do it, they're not going to risk it. If you keep them at a distance and watch them, they're not likely to move against you.

As I mentioned earlier, different cultures have different personal space rules. Middle Easterners and Hindus generally will get much closer to someone than Westerners do. In America the rule is generally two to four feet for conversational space. Two feet or closer is considered *intimate space*, an area reserved for lovers, close friends, and family. If someone moves into your space, you will begin to feel uncomfortable, if not out-and-out alarmed. You must be invited into this space before you are permitted to enter.

This concept is fun to play with when you're first learning about it. Try moving closer to a casual acquaintance with whom you're talking. As you advance, he or she will unconsciously retreat. You can literally chase someone around doing this. The other person will get uneasy, however, so after awhile you should stop and apologize for messing with him or her. Explain that you're experimenting with a concept, and you're sorry for using him/her as a guinea pig. (By the way other than the pupils getting larger and the voice getting huskier, the best way to tell if you're doing well with a fine lady is if she moves into your intimate space or doesn't object when you move into hers. Oh yes!)

Another aspect of personal space is *spacing*. Say you sit down at a table with someone; immediately there is a line drawn down the middle. That half is theirs; this half is yours. Birds do it on a telephone wire to allow each other necessary wing room to take off. Men do it at urinals. This concept would be easier for people to understand if we still carried swords. To draw a sword, you need you need a certain amount of room. You do not allow anyone inside that space as it might hinder you in an emergency.

Getting too close to someone in a combat situation can get him killed. One of the things wrong with most war movies is that the actors move in a group. Ever since the invention of the machine gun, soldiers space themselves out when they move, especially jungle fighters. A combatant wants to take out as many as he can with one burst. Two or more guys together present a better target than individuals. The guy wanting to get close to you may be signing your death warrant. A lot of FNGs in 'Nam got people killed by doing this, and many vets still have the instinct to keep people at distance in them.

Another invasion of personal space that can get you into serious trouble involves food. The universal instinct to protect food springs from a very basic level, and this means keeping people away from the food source. Ever notice how animals growl at each other when one has food and the other gets too close? A bird or squirrel will grab a big hunk of food that it can't scarf down immediately and run with it. The others will give chase.

This is why you don't reach across the table; you ask someone to hand you something. I've been in some places where snaking out to snatch something off a plate will get your hand pinned to the table. In junior high school, I was sitting in a cafeteria with my friend Tod when another kid kept snatching french fries off Tod's plate. Tod told him to stop, and when the guy went for it again, Tod planted a fork in the back of the guy's hand. "I told you not to do that."

The above are all examples of personal space. It is yours. Unless it's absolutely necessary, you do not allow any strangers into it. People are not allowed in unless you invite them. You're going to get real chummy with your dentist while he works on you, but a guy who just got on the bus is going to have to sit somewhere else if there are any empty seats.

It's odd, but the more successfully you communicate that you can—and will—protect your personal space, the more people will want to be near to you. It's sort of funny the first time you look around and realize that there are people standing under your umbrella of toughness. They look at you, and then they look at some street dude and start edging over to you. They judge that you are less dangerous to them, and they use you to keep the other guy away.

This is sort of like making friends with a knuckle-dragger. They aren't actually asking you to protect them; they're just using the system. This happens occasionally when a woman is being pestered by a guy. She'll walk up and start talking with you. Anytime a woman does this, look around and see who's interested in her talking to you. While I know a couple who was together for ten years after they met this way, I've also known a few fights to start over this trick. If you haven't ID'ed the guy beforehand, he will seemingly come out of nowhere.

DEFENDING YOUR PERSONAL SPACE

Now that you know what personal space is and that the way to cow someone is to invade his personal space, how do you defend yours? If a guy can successfully invade your space and get you to back down, he's won—he's alpha and you're beta. (See Chapter 15 for more on alpha/beta behavior.) However, if you do not back down, fists will be flying in moments unless something else is done. If you feel that you are not in a position to back down, here are five ways of dealing with this situation. Each option has its risks and drawbacks, and you must determine how to proceed based on where you are and with whom you are dealing.

1) *The first option is to deck him him as soon as he moves into your personal space.* As he steps, you swing. Then you keep swinging until he's down and you're sure he's not going to get up. The Japanese have a term for this, but I can't recall it right now (ask Peyton Quinn; he'll know). Basically, it's just a preemptive strike. I've heard it summed up this way, "I knew the fight was going to happen anyway, so I got in the first shot."

As you might expect, this tactic has some serious advantages and disadvantages. The advantage is you're *almost* guaranteed to win if you take him by surprise and keep swinging until he's through. Most fights are short, furious affairs in which one guy immediately gains the advantage and keeps slamming it. This is why so many black belts go down in real fights. In a bar, there is no back and forth sparring.

The disadvantages are twofold. One, and this is a seriously important safety tip, unless the guy was being a blazing asshole, *people only remember who threw the first punch!* Most people will only remember (or see) you swinging at him; they won't know what led up to the confrontation. Unless the guy has seriously pissed in the pool beforehand, you're going to be the one everyone points to when the cops show up and ask who started it. Not only did you hurt the guy seriously, but everyone saw you swing first. The courts aren't likely to give you a friendly kiss for this one.

The other disadvantage is that word gets around if you do this often. If you cross someone, he knows that you have a serious record for fucking up people, and he will not be playing when he comes after you. In *Cheap Shots, Ambushes, and Other Lessons* (available from Paladin Press), I wrote about a dude I knew in Venice who was such a bad ass that nobody wanted to go toe-to-toe with him. He bought it in the back of the head in the alley behind his home. Listen up, I don't care how fucking tough you are, nobody is immune to a shotgun blast while getting out of a car.

While there are times that this technique is fantastic, I recommend using caution with it. Several people I know use binding and locking techniques as their preemptive strikes, which I highly recommend. The guy approaches and is acting like an asshole, and the next thing he knows you have him off balance and in a hold as you escort him to the door. Everyone sees you move first, but you don't really hurt the guy, and they remember this. That is a double juicy fruit for you. First, the cops are less likely to be called, as you didn't hurt him, and if he shows back up and you hurt him later, everyone knows he was the one who came back looking for trouble. Second, people saw you move so they know that you're good, but they don't know *how* good. You never show your full hand in the street.

If you're outnumbered, making the first move is also great. Say there are three dudes who think they've got you.

Next thing they know, you've eaten the face of one before they could move. Then, you either get the hell out of there with much quickness, as they're standing there gawking at what's left of their friend, or you throw number one's body into number three while starting on number two's shit. *Then you run like hell.* Don't ever think you're going to do a standup with three guys. You will not come out whole, even if you win, which is highly unlikely.

2) *As the guy steps toward you, step forward to meet him.* Of the remaining three options, this one leads to two-way punchfests most often. Unfortunately, it is also the natural reaction of an untrained fighter who isn't going to back down. The guy is trying to intimidate you, and you call his bluff. This places him in a put-up or shut-up position. Most people hesitate when you do this. They were expecting to take a step and get into your face. However, they ended up only taking half a step, and you got in their faces with just as much attitude. This spins their head a bit because they were expecting to be the aggressors. The issue is up in the air again. When you do this, you go to Code Red status. If the fucker makes any move, you counterstrike hard. I've blown off blocking before, knowing that I could take the punch because I was expecting it. He, however, is not expecting you to counterpunch. (This is the situation I described in the beginning of *Fists, Wits, and a Wicked Right.*) The other guy is also not expecting better-targeted blows.)

A word of warning: I do not recommend this action if you are up against multiple opponents. If the guy has an audience, he is not likely to back off when you call his bluff. This technique works best with fresh bucks who are young, dumb, and full o' cum, especially if you're older. It's the "young bull who realizes that he's not ready to take a shot at the old bull's title yet" scenario. If you are young, however, this move is a serious roll-of-the-dice proposition. It depends on how much experience the guy you're up against has. If he recognizes the threat, he'll reconsider messing with you. If he doesn't have the experience or the knowledge to realize that it's a different game, you're almost guaranteed a fight.

3) *When he moves you shift your feet into a fighting stance and bring your hands forward about waist level, not far enough for the average person to recognize as a fighting stance, but enough for him to recognize that you're waiting for him.* The rest of this technique has to do with the energy you give off. As that guy cuts into your space, hold your ground (or you can combine this with option two for best results). What stops him is the message in your eyes. When that guy looks into your eyes he sees a large predator who's looking at lunch. You're asking him to make the first move, because when he does, you're going to rip his head off. Let him know that you're the kind of guy who likes the grinding feeling of bones being dislocated under your hands. Don't use killer eyes, which are flat and unemotional. Make sure he sees that you are going to enjoy hurting him. He should realize that he didn't invade your space; he moved into your strike range. Oh, pardon . . . heh, heh . . . silly me.

One advantage to this option is that bystanders don't see you pursuing a confrontation. All they see is you defending your space. If that guy moves, you won't have drawn first, but you will, however, draw first blood. This is an old Navy trick, get the other guy to swing first. After that, it's open season. Remember, popular opinion is generally against the guy who swings first.

Another advantage is that it lets you use people's imagination as your public relations. Never fight in public unless it makes you look good or the witnesses are on your side. My original belief was that you never do anything in front of witnesses, but since the bozos kept coming after me in public, I had to change that a little.

Its disadvantage is that you have to be able to assess accurately the head space of your opponent. If the guy is normal, he'll freak out and usually back down. However, if the guy is missing some parts, he's going to jackrabbit into crazy. Then the only way to win this is to be crazier than he is. He may be missing some batting in the attic, but you've lost the entire roof. This is not easy to do, and, what's worse, it's a bitch coming back. So be careful on who you pull it on.

4) *Go totally cyborg.* I'm talking emotionally dead. This is when you use your flat dead killer eyes. Show no emotion; you're just doing a job. I was taught to do it by imagining mirrors sliding down in front of my eyes. That's why bug-eye sunglasses freak out so many people. All they can see is themselves. They see all the fear behind the bluffing, and they think that the other person sees it too. My face goes totally deadpan, and my body gives off no signals other than the fact that it is there.

If you do speak, your voice should be beyond calm, like Arnie's *Terminator* voice—a flat recording, nothing more, no stress, no fear, nothing. You speak no more than three words at a time. When it looks like the shit is going to hit the fan, you don't want to be jacking your jaw. Keep your mouth shut and locked. Most broken jaws occur when the mouth is open. Throughout, you're sending a message to the guy that you will drop him into the ground and totally forget about it by dinner. This lets him know that you'd waste him as fast as you'd waste a cockroach and with about as much emotional commitment.

This works because the average American still has a deep structure operating system that holds human life sacred. It is only in the far outlands and serious trash-can societies that this is not true. If someone is going to be killed, he wants the person who killed him to feel something—at least the ego gratification that he is a bad motherfucker for killing someone. Being dropped down to bug status freaks them out.

The advantage to this technique is that most people get the message real quick. The disadvantage is that you're not sure which way they're going to jump; that depends on what's inside them. Some people with weak egos will jump on you for this because they can't stand being demoted anymore. Yet the psycho trip works great on them.

This technique is usually best against people who are missing parts. These kind of people are used to bullying people by being out of control. They go apeshit, and everyone runs. When you go frosty, they're going to wonder what went wrong. I had one guy, who later was legally declared 51-50, get froggish with me. He was standing there screaming in my face, and all I did was take my sunglasses out of my breast pocket and toss them into the planter. He got the message that A) I wasn't backing down and B) I was so good I wasn't even worried about him. Crazy or not, he knew he didn't have what it took to do the job. Even though he was feeling froggish, he didn't jump.

I have used all of the above techniques in my day to handle shit. If you can perfect them, I have found that the last two are best for avoiding fights by using the other guy's head to do my work for me. Someone once told me that people, no matter how crazy, know that they are being out of line. That is true. They have a little voice that reminds them that they run the risk of getting hurt. The problem is that most of the time their crazies overpower that other voice. By using techniques that attract their attention to that other voice, nine times out of ten, you can put their dicks in the mud.

I spend so much time dealing with the psychological aspects of fighting because, in the long run, it's easier and safer to mind fuck someone than it is to fight them. If a bull is charging you, meeting him head to head is going to fuck you up. But a matador doesn't meet the bull's charge head on. He uses a red cape to distract the bull, and the bull ends up charging the wrong target. Instead of his ass getting gored, the matador lets the cape take the abuse. Finally when the bull passes for the last time, the matador sticks a blade into its heart. Voila! A giant shish kebab! That is how a man stands up to a bull. He doesn't go head to head with it because he knows he'd lose.

Exaggerated Space

Another aspect of territory is how much space you take up. Ever notice how young toughs swagger around with their arms out? Elbows cocked, they move down the middle of the sidewalk, glaring at everyone who looks at them. When this movement is really exaggerated, it is like the aforementioned cat fluffing its fur. When the swagger is tighter and more controlled, it is like a dog with his hackles raised.

I always found it amusing the way young bucks often jump into each other's faces with chest puffed out and arms thrown back. This is supposed to intimidate their opponents by showing how big and bad they are. What it actually does is leave their dicks flapping in the wind if the other guy moves. Nose-to-nose with arms back is not a good position from which to defend yourself, take my word on this one.

Compressed Space

More dangerous to encounter is compressed space. That is someone's space really isn't that big, but invading it is like reaching down into a badger's den. I recently encountered an someone who used the concept of compressed space in an obscure knife-fighting style from Indonesia called sulate.

The knife wielder had both hands in front and in plain view. His left hand was open, with his palm facing his right hand, which held the knife. His hands were held about four inches from his chest and about an inch apart. I took one look at him and said to myself, "Easy, just take the . . . .uhhh." As I sat there looking at the guy's stance, it got uglier and uglier. I realized it was a total trap. If I went in after one hand, the other would take you out. I finally ended up, standing there with my hands in pocket, saying, "Fuck a duck."

With all of my experience, I found only two possible weaknesses, and neither was guaranteed. The fact that the process is constantly moving meant that those two weaknesses came and went quickly. His form was a perfect example of compressed space. Because it wasn't that big, it looked easy to take—until you got up close and then realized you were in for a serious scrap.

There are a lot of people out there who operate in a similar fashion. They have their territory and mind their own business. The only way to get hurt by them is to infringe on their space. When that happens, God help you.

This guy's technique is a little more sophisticated than most people's, but if you see something in a rough area that looks too easy, check it out carefully. This is a favorite technique of Orientals, who haven't lasted this long by being victims. By the time you realize you're in over your head, it's too late. Often women will also use this technique. This is the female cop cruising for rapists. When the guy jumps, wham!

STAKING A TERRITORY— AND HOLDING IT

Now a lot of young bucks will stake out an incredibly large territory. The truth of the matter is, they cannot possibly hold that much space. A common example of this is the guy who sits on the crowded bus and puts his leg up on the seat to keep others from sitting next to him. Staking a territory and being able to keep it are totally different things. A large number of gang territories are grossly exaggerated. They claim to have this much turf, but they only actively control half of that. If pressed, they will drop the extra territory, but fiercely defend their core territory.

Using Local Camouflage to Pass through Territories

When you must enter an area claimed by a gang, you're best way of getting through is to use camouflage to slip through the cracks. This begins with not wearing the proverbial red flags for the locals.

Flying "colors" in another gang's territory is not real fucking smart.[1] Pay attention to where you are and take off any offending articles before you pass through. You can tell what gang someone is from by the color he wears. If you are in a Crip neighborhood, wearing red is not a good idea. In Blood turf, dark blue is not for you. Wearing an orange ribbon on St. Patrick's Day in certain cities is tantamount to suicide.

What are the local gang colors? I've heard that in Chicago, the preference is black and a color. You can wear all black, or all color, but don't mix them. Unless it's changed radically, you can tell what barrio Mexican gangs are from by their colors. In Los Angeles in the seventies, it was dark blue for Venice, red for Culver City, tan for Sawtelle, and yellow for Santa Monica. The best way to figure out whose territory you're in is to read the graffiti or ask a local kid.

So in the city being aware of colors and their affiliations is vital to your survival. Go out in the sticks, and it's the designer label that will make the natives restless. Pay attention to local fashions, and don't wear things that stand out. This includes hairstyles, styles of facial hairs, clothes, and jewelry. Locals can tell where someone is from by these accessories—most importantly, they can tell that he isn't a local.

POSSESSIONS

The next aspect of territory is possessions. There is only one rule to remember: *If it belongs to someone else, don't touch it.* I have seen so much avoidable trouble start over possessions that it isn't funny.

In low-rent areas, cars are often used as seats. Face facts here, folks: people have a habit of getting bent out of shape when you use their car as a bench. Using it as a table for your coke isn't such a hot idea either. People can, and will, get bent out of shape at you for putting your stuff on their car.

When it comes to territory issues, understand that you are dealing with an issue that basically is straight from our Cro-Magnon days. For all of our fancy posing, territory defense and acquisition is still at the heart of how we operate.

Defining turf depends on what circles you run in. Some people have only their homes; others claim entire areas of the city; while others consider miles of open range as theirs. Trespassing will get you in some deep shit. On the other hand, by knowing that *how* you hold your space against encroachment is so important, you can pay more attention to keeping trespassers off.

Notes

[1] There are certain "neutral" territories where colors are not allowed. Regardless of what club or group they're with, everyone peels off the emblems before entering—*no exceptions.*

CHAPTER ELEVEN

Magick, Religion, and Juju

> "You don't believe in that stuff do you?"
> "Doesn't matter . . . They do."
> —A movie, the name of which I forget, discussing crossing a group's juju.

The further you get from popular culture, the more likely you are to run into people who believe in juju. Popular culture doesn't believe in magick (I use "magick" with a "k" to differentiate occult from stage magic.) The Christian churches did a pretty good form of genocide against the competition. Anything they determine not to be Christian dogma is immediately branded as "devil worship" or a "quaint primitive custom" by most people. I personally find the latter more demeaning and damaging than the former. When it comes to getting slit from asshole to eyebrow, calling something a "quaint superstition" is the fastest way to get the can-opener treatment.

Listen up, folks: It doesn't matter if you believe in this stuff or not. Stepping on taboos, violating sacred spaces, and, in some places, saying or doing the wrong thing can and will get you hurt! The further out into the backwater you get, the more probable and severe this is.

Most street people believe in some form of magick. Where you are determines what forms these beliefs take. Even with the predominant Catholic influences, you'll still find an active, thriving occult network in the Hispanic world. Much of it is paired with Christian icons, but it is pure paganism. Little stores called "La Bonticas" supply all sorts of magickal equipment to the population. *Brujo* and *bruja* (brew-ho/brew-ha) are the terms for male and female magicians.

Although every culture has its forms of religion or superstitions, the two groups most likely to fuck you up physically for messing around with their beliefs are Caribbeans and Native Americans. It is here that their beliefs blend into their etiquette—and you had better fucking not cross these lines.

If you think I'm joking, read *Serpent and the Rainbow* by Wade Davis. Davis went down to Haiti to research zombies and discovered that the local voodoo witch doctors used a drug to "turn people into zombies." He brought the drug back for analysis and discovered that the stuff is seriously nasty. It contains a neurotoxin called tetrotoxin, which is one of the most lethal poisons known to man. If mixed it a certain way, it doesn't kill you; it just drops you into a state of suspended animation.

But what's weird is that, even though you appear dead, you are conscious the whole time. The only way to tell that someone is alive is by slapping him onto a brainwave machine, an electroencephalograph or EEG. The EEG tells the doctor that your brain is chugging right along, even though your body is totally shut down. Any country doctor who doesn't have top-of-the-line medical scanners will declare you dead. Everybody goes, "Oh well," and buries you. Can you imagine what it would be like to be conscious for your own funeral and burial? Even if the drug didn't fry your brain (which it does), when it wears off and you jump up and say, "Hey everybody, I'm back!" do you think you'll get a warm welcome? Ha! Nobody wants a zombie around.

Want to know what that has to do with self-defense? Throw some dust on a Haitian or squirt a Jamaican with a water gun, and you'll find out. That's how this drug and other poisons are administered. That guy thinks that A) you're putting a whammie on him, B) trying to kill him through poison, or C) both of the above. It is extremely likely that he will plant a blade between your ribs before you can say, "Ha ha, it's a joke." To these people, it's not a joke; it's deadly real. If they can kill you before your magick gets them, their spirit won't be enslaved by you in the hereafter.

Believe it or not, there are a substantial number of hard scientific facts to back up some of these people's fears about so-called "black magick." A whole shitload of very dangerous poisons and powerful hallucinogens are hidden behind a lot of mumbo jumbo. Fuck the "eye of newt, tail of lizard" shit; what will kill you is the arsenic on the dart they plug you with.

The reality behind the myth should be enough to tip you off to the fact that you should take care when dealing with people of other cultures. The rest, even if you consider it nonsense, motivates people enough to knock you on your ass for crossing these lines.

The Navajo tribe is the richest and most educated Indian tribe in America. Their etiquette is also influenced more strongly by their superstitions. They really get bent out of shape about "skinwalkers," or witches. They have ways of dealing with witches that make the Inquisitors look friendly. It is impolite to stare into the eyes of a Navajo. The ones who deal with whites are more accustomed to it, but they still are uncomfortable. A Navajo won't stare into your eyes because he believes that a witch steals souls through the eyes.

I saw this in action when I cruised onto a big reservation wearing a pair of bug-eyed sunglasses. I was in Ganado, one of the biggest town on the Navajo reservation. If I had been just a run-of-the-mill white tourist, they would have blown it off, but the way I move, watch people, and look put me in a different category. They were getting seriously uptight. Ever seen a pack of wolves get uptight? It was about the same. I was trying to figure out what the fuck was going on when my friend (who's Arapaho) grabbed me and told me to take off my shades. When I did, their hostility evaporated. Seriously, I was heading for a fight because I was crossing superstition by wearing sunglasses.

The biggest fuckup you can make is to be told of a taboo and cross it anyway. This is that stupid "quaint custom" attitude in action. This culture's condescension toward other people's ways leads to all sorts of trouble.

This is especially true about any area or mountain considered sacred by the group. Sacred places are closed to anyone not of that tribe. If you live near a place or around people who have these kind of leanings, don't let yourself be talked into sneaking over there "just to see what's there." Everybody knows that the area is off limits, but there's always somebody who thinks he can get away with it. Every three or four years you hear about a couple of people who "disappear" around these sacred places. The angered ancestor spirits come in the form of a 30.06 slug between the eyes. There ain't no defense against sniper fire out in the open. Respect their beliefs by not messing with their sacred places.

Another violation that often gets people in trouble is ignoring taboos about ceremonies. The Hopi Indians allow visitors to attend certain ceremonies but not all. You can watch them, but cameras are not allowed. They will *ask* you not to take pictures. If you persist, they will *tell* you not to do it. Push it and you will get bounced. Often, the guy who crushes your camera is a Hopi cop. If you try to be slick and they catch you, you will trip many times before you get off those mesas.

Now before I go on, I want to point something out. A devil worshipper is a Christian. It's the same game; you're just rooting for the other team. There is a big difference between the occult and satanism. The reason that I mention this is that you will run into both on the streets, and you had better be able to figure out the difference.

A satanist will be an asshole, just to be nasty. I'm talking using poison darts and putting water moccasins in your bed. If you have something these people want, they will go for it, and whatever twisted logic these people use decides what it is they want. Mostly, these people are about the melodrama of being evil. These people (along with so-called "black magicians") are relatively easy to spot. The real obvious ones will wander around dressed in black, trying to look ominous. If they don't get their way, they'll wiggle their eyebrows and make spooky sounds about calling up the "dark ones" right up to the time that you deck them.

Yes, folks, I said deck them. So-called black magick, 0. Right hook, 1. The story about these people is the same as about scum. You don't let them whip themselves up to make the first move. Their first moves are back-stabbing and poison darts. Generally speaking, if you drop one of these bozos, there won't be any witnesses. There will be a lot of people laughing and buying you the next round but no witnesses. Nonetheless, it's better if you can heel hook the guy and plant an elbow in the short ribs on the way down. These people aren't accustomed to other people making the first move. While he's sitting on his ass gasping for breath, let him know you don't appreciate that sort of shit. Then for the next few weeks, watch your ass. You don't have to worry about bombs under your car half as much a scorpions in your mailbox.

Oddly enough, the biggest area of satanism in the United States is the Bible Belt in the South. They go to such extremes down there with fundamentalism, that they drive a lot of people to the other team. Mix that in with voodoo up from the Caribbean and you get some weird shit. New Orleans is another planet altogether. Anywhere you have Haitians and Jamaicans, you have juju, the magick attributed to the charms or fetishes of West African people. Also anywhere you find people who have come out of the backwoods, you'll also find believers. Hillbillies call it the "shining" or the "gift." You run into a lot of them in Chicago these days. Out west, Indian reservations and Mexican barrios are filled with people who believe in and/or practice some form of magick or superstitions.

More than likely what you'll run into on the street are occult symbols for protection and luck, which get mixed up with other stuff that floats around in the trash can. A biker will have all sorts of tattoos, often of death heads and warriors, usually mixed with some occult protection symbol. Saxon Wican (English witchcraft) and Nordic (Viking magick) are the two most common, with Celtic (Irish, predominately) thrown in now and then. If you do run into this sort of stuff don't A) laugh at them or B) call them satanist/devil worshippers. People don't take kindly to your sharing your ignorance so loudly. Bikers especially have a habit of punching first and asking questions later.

Another thing which you have to contend with these days is Muslims. Black Muslims are an out-and-out pain in the ass. They can be as bigoted and vicious as any white supremacist. They have taken aspects of Islam and mixed them with racial hatred and U.S. black culture. Like radical feminists, their hatred and anger spur them on. Avoid them if you can; if not, don't let them get the first move. Also, let them know up front that it's not a racial thing; it's because they're being assholes who're hiding behind religion.

By the way, do not mistake U.S. black culture for Haitian, Jamaican, or African culture. They are wildly different, and they do not particularly like each other. Throughout this book, I have avoided differentiating between white and black cultures for the simple reason that what I say goes for both. There exist as many different networks and operating systems among U.S. blacks as for Caucasians. A Texas black is as different from a New York black is as a white Texan is from a white New Yorker.

Muslims are another problem. First off, what Muhammad taught is not what Islam has now become. Islam has been bastardized into a warrior religion. Those fuckers go on *jihads* (holy wars) at a drop of the hat. Science and reason are what the West used to knock off the holy war shit. We used to be just as bad as they were. (Most people know about the crusades to win back the holy lands from the Muslims, but most don't know about the Catholic/Protestant wars that ripped Europe apart for centuries. It was an ugly time.) Muslims still have the gusto when it comes to religious wars.

How does this relate to your self-defense? Muslims believe that dying in a holy cause is a guaranteed ticket to paradise, and this influences how they fight, particularly if they see a confrontation as religious in nature. Muslims, particularly from the Middle East, also consider nonbelievers, or infidels, to be on the same level as a dog. They have a term for these people, "farenggi," which means "unclean." (The word supposedly comes from the root word "French" and was first used during the crusades when the crusaders were busy slaughtering Muslims. *Star Trek: The Next Generation* used the term to represent the slimiest creatures in the galaxy.) Anyone who is not a Muslim, or not of their particular sect, is a farenggi. Muslims don't fuck over other Muslims, but anyone who is farenggi is fair game.

So if you're dealing with a Muslim, you're dealing with someone who A) is from a warrior culture and B) thinks he's superior to you. Often what happens is Muslims get accustomed to bullying Americans. An American tries to be reasonable and negotiate, while Muslims are going to go as far as they can. The last guy I put into the hospital for personal reasons (not professional) was a Palestinian. He pushed, and I didn't move. I tried to be reasonable even when he was attacking me. I kept on saying, "Damn it! I don't want to fight you," while he was firing away at me. Finally, I got pissed and took him out.

The way to deal with a warrior is as another warrior. As long as they know that they can't get away with being pushy or there is profit in it for them, you can deal with Muslims. If you show weakness, they will walk all over you, especially the young bucks.

CHAPTER TWELVE

Eye Contact

> "I didn't start the fight. I just don't let people look at me like that."
> —Tim Toohey

It took me a few minutes to get off the floor when I heard my bro' say that. He was dead serious, and I was on the floor in hysterics. Every time I tried to get up, I would see him, glaring at me like what he had just said made the most sense in the world, and I'd lose it again.

He was, in a way, correct. I, however, had never heard anyone put it quite so succinctly. If I had a dime for every time I saw shit start over hard looks, I'd be able to hang out with the Rockefellers. With most people, you can tell before the shit actually hits the fan that it's in flight. Way ahead of fists flying, hard looks are zooming around the room. This is the biggest indicator that trouble is brewing.

There is something about a guy's eyes when he's thinking about starting shit or he's locked in male pride syndrome (MPS) that is immediately recognizable. He's over in the corner throwing out these batwaves that you learn to spot long before the actual fight starts. When he locks in on a target, you can lay money that something is going to go down right quick.

CONTROLLING EYE CONTACT

People get nervous if you look at them too long. The amount of time you can look at someone or maintain eye contact depends on who you are, who the other person is, what you're doing, where you are, what culture(s) you are dealing with, what time of day it is, and, of course, who you are with.[1]

What do people do if they perceive that your eyes have overstayed their welcome on them? That depends on what type of people they are. Some get nervous and run around in circles going, "Oh me, oh my," while others drive your nose through the back of your head. If the latter type did not exist, I would not have to mention this subject.

People's stare quotient varies according to whether you're in the big city, medium city, or the sticks. If you're walking down the street in the big city, generally you are expected to avoid looking at other people. This is why in America we all face the door in an elevator of strangers. If you fuck up and accidentally look at someone, you both flash a quick little smile that says, "I'm not dangerous." If you live in, or have seen movies of, New York, you'll notice something about the crowds. Everyone looks straight ahead. If they do glance at each other, it's for no more than a second. You can look at an attractive woman longer than you can a man, but still the look is usually no more than two seconds.

These rules apply when you're are in neutral territory (downtown is not anybody's neighborhood) and during the day. At night, the rules are a little looser. There are individuals who want to be seen and noticed. The people with purple hair and clothes that would make a blind man flinch want to be looked at. However, the snicker tolerance is usually about five seconds before they turn hostile.

They know people are looking at them and are very sensitive to it. Any attention longer than five seconds gives them justification to sneer and flip you off. You will find out that a number of them excel at monkey kung fu, hurling shit and insults while scampering out of range.

I've seen a lot of people get jacked up this way. Some clean-cut middle-class guy is with his date. He sees the "freak," and laughs. The punker sneers and says something that makes the American boy look like a dork in front of his date (or maybe the punk insults the date). Our clean-cut boy steps forward to defend mom, apple pie, and the American way, and the punker flings a chain in the guy's face. Punker beats feet while All-American bleeds on his date's dress.

People who make up the freak show aren't interested in doing a toe-to-toe with everyone who laughs at them. They're usually more interested in proving what dorks the civilians are. Why fight some jock and get hurt when you can nail him and run? By looking at them longer than five seconds, you invite them to express their hostility. Don't expect a standup fight. They're outnumbered, they know it, and their fighting style reflects that.

The time you are allowed to look at certain people goes up in designated areas. For instance, in a fast-food joint you can look at the people behind the counter as long as it takes them to come over and take your order. You can still watch them while you are waiting but for shorter periods.

Perhaps most important in terms of self-defense, the rules of looking at people change when you are in someone else's territory. This applies to your looking at people as well as their looking at you. If you are walking through someone else's 'hood, you are going to get stared at. Depending on the place, they are either just interested in what's going on, or they are sizing you up. People watching you from a window are easy to ignore. The three dudes who are trying to decide if you're victim material are another thing altogether. In some shitty areas, everyone is sizing you up to see if they could get away with it. In other areas, the young bucks look you over to see if they can use you to prove themselves, while other places, you only have to worry about the criminals.

How can you tell if someone is looking at you out of curiosity or if his intentions are more sinister? Someone who is merely curious will watch you for a moment and then go back to what he was doing. That is radically different than the way someone who is looking for trouble looks at you. Again it boils down to "batwaves." A group of young bucks out to show their nuts "feels" different than a group of guys who are going to jack you for drug money. How you deal with these situations depends on what you're up against. Often if you don't bite their bait, young bucks will leave you alone. However, reacting that way to somebody "interviewing" you for a mugging guarantees that he'll go for it. In his little cretin mind, he'll have pegged you as a victim.

LOOK INTO MY EYES

Eye contact is an important nonverbal communication, one that we all use every day. It's a lot more complicated than avoiding making eye contact with strangers on the street. For example, when you're talking with someone, it is acceptable to look into their eyes, right? Maybe. Here's where it gets complicated. In America, the way you show someone you are honest and sincere is to look into his eyes when you speak to him. To show that you are listening, your eye contact is not as intense, but you still meet their eyes a fair amount of the time. This is something a person with "shifty eyes" doesn't do. The supposed shady character won't look you in the eye in a "manly" way.

A lot of trouble starts over this miscommunication. Number one, people who have survived the shitstorm seldom if ever leave their eyes on one thing for too long. They are always scanning to see what's going on around them. It's not that they are being rude, they are just doing what they know how to do to survive. If you ever talk to me, don't be surprised if I spend a lot of time looking elsewhere. I've cooled it considerably (I once got yelled at for doing it during sex), but the habit still remains. This also caused a lot of trouble for guys I know when they came back from Vietnam. They had stayed alive for a year by watching what was going on around them, and then people thought they were being rude when the vets wouldn't look at them all the time.

Aside from the Navajos, a number of oriental cultures also have different eye contact rules. A Filipino will look at the floor when he is being sincere, thus honoring and respecting you by averting his eyes. Most Americans think that the guy is lying through his teeth when he doesn't look at them. This often leads to misunderstanding, and a misunderstanding with a Filipino can be lethal. There are literally thousands of variations of kali, the only fighting form I know of that *starts* with weapons training and gets uglier from there. They've made knife fighting almost a science. Almost every neighborhood has its own style.

HANDLING HARD LOOKS AND AVOIDING TROUBLE

There are a lot of different ways to handle people giving you hard looks, but I usually recommend the one that avoids trouble. However, in some place, you avoid big trouble by getting into little trouble.

If you end up in the cage and are put into a group cell, everybody is going to be sizing you up. In this situation, you should look around and pick one of the middle-line guys— not too tough, not too weak, but just right. These guys are easy to spot; they think they're tough, but they only move in groups. You know, the guys who stand behind the mouth and go, "Yeah!" Walk up to this guy, get right up in his face, and demand, "You got a problem?!" If the guy averts his eyes, let it go. Take a bunk and let it be. If the fucker so much as hesitates, you floor his ass right then and there. Drop him fast and retreat fast.

Your concern is not the other prisoners half as much as having the guards land on you. You'll get in shit with the guards, but everyone will know where you stand. Even if shit starts later, it will be half as much as it would have been otherwise. By nailing the first guy you let everyone know where you stand. Unless you are really fucking good, do *not* try to do this on the cell's toughest guy, who's just as likely to move first as you are. If you challenge him, he *has* to move because he's got his reputation on the line. All you need to do, however, is to get through until they spring you.

In case you haven't noticed, I've mentioned ignoring people a lot in this book. This is good advice here as well because eye contact is an invitation to further contact. Most people think a hard look will warn hardasses off. What they don't realize is that the message they are trying to send may not be the one received. Most people don't really know what they look like when they project "tough."

Tough comes from deep down in the soul, not from the mind. Standing in front of a mirror practicing your truculent sneer may impress the shit out of you, but the guy on the street is going to see something else. When you're standing in front of the mirror admiring how tough you are, you're seeing you want to see. The other person will see things that you don't realize you are showing. Your posturing is analogous to a cat's fluffing its fur rather than a dog raising its hackles to get ready for a fight.

It's amazing what we broadcast unconsciously. It's like hearing your own voice on a tape recorder. "Man, that ain't my voice. I know my voice is deep and resonating. I hear it every day." Never mind that what you hear is radically different than what is going out to the masses. Shit, that's why I can't sing. I think I'm on key, when the truth of the matter is I'm in the next state.

The same thing can be said for hard looks. A would-be tough guy gives me this look that tells me he's unsure of himself enough to glower. He thinks he's projecting full-bore toughness and that the very smell of testosterone will knock me on my ass. On the other hand, getting a look from a serious hardass is like getting a .50-caliber pointed at me. In case you don't know, there is no place to hide from a .50 on most blocks. A .50-caliber round will go through entire houses before it even considers slowing down.

To see what type of message you're really projecting, use a video camera. Study your unconscious signals and drop them if necessary. These are the things that really shoot you in the foot. I saw a guy get into it at the beach once, and his tough-guy act would have worked if it weren't for the fact that his kneecaps were trembling—a fact his shorts didn't cover, whereas his pants would have.

Watch people when they are nervous to learn what their body signs are. There are lots of them. Swallowing is a common one that tips the other guy off. If someone is standing there looking bad and then he gulps, man, I know the dude is sweating underneath.

Discover what your body language is when you get nervous, and then drop these indicators like hot coals. That's what really differentiates between would-be toughs and hard cores. The guy facing me off throws two sets of signals: one, how tough he is, and two—which totally invalidates the other—how scared he is. What wigs people out is I don't show any signs of nervousness. I send one message and one message only. Inside I may be saying to myself, "I want to run fiercely," but nobody is going to know that by my expression, my tone of voice, or my body language. That's the .50-caliber look I mentioned earlier. All this guy sees is someone who will not only go to hell to get him but make the return trip when the job is done. Anybody who remains calm when you are in his face is not someone you want to fuck with.

ALPHA/BETA BEHAVIOR

Now the following is going to seem like a diversion from our discussion of eye contact, but bear with me. Alpha/beta behavior is directly related because it explains why some people react to eye contact as if it were a challenge and why eye contact so often leads to further contact.

Have you ever held a dog when another dog enters its territory? It's weird, all of the dog's attention targets on the other animal, and it sort of quivers in anticipation. It wants to beeline it over to the other Rover. You say no, but it shakes in anticipation. I was walking with my brother-in-law, on whom I've got ten years, through a tough-assed part of town when we saw a group of young bucks hanging out near a liquor store. I swear to God, this kid got the same liver-quivering reaction. He was watching them with everything he had. I told him to quit staring at them (we were there on business), and he told me, "I can't, there's something about guys like that, that I just gotta stare at them." I sighed and remembered when I felt the same way. Fortunately, we were near our truck, and we got out of there before trouble started.

The most common way for shit to start is that exact "he looked at me once, he looked at me twice, if he looks at me again, there's going to be a fight" mind-set. You put two bucks together in a place and, sure as shit, quiver, quiver, quiver, blamo! A fight erupts.

Eye contact is the first step in announcing that you are an active player in the game. That's what my brother-in-law was doing when he was giving the hard eye to the group of guys. In a situation like that, it's like a magnet. Someone shows the signs, and you have to keep looking at him. He's probably looking at you too.

This is because of a thing called alpha/beta behavior. In simple terms, it means who's top dog? This program controls a whole shitload of lives on this planet, human as well as animal. Alphas are top dogs, and betas are the rest of the pack. As you get older you find your niche, settle into your place, and get on with your life. However, when you are young, there still is a lot of jockeying to be done.

A friend and I went round and round about whether alpha/beta behavior is instinctual or voluntary. To tell you the truth, we're smart enough to break away from this behavior if we want to, but it is rather convenient. I'm not sure if it's hard-wired instinctually into us, or if it is just a learned habit these days.

The true reason for alpha/beta behavior is survival of the species. The purpose of it is to protect the tribe from outside attack and to protect women and children. Face it, guys, from a biological standpoint, we're expendable after we impregnate a few females. After we've contributed to the gene pool, if we get eaten by a lion, it's no big deal. So it should come as no surprise that the alphas are the defenders of the group. Now, countercharging an attacking lion is not the smartest thing to do. The equation of "lion that way, me go other way" has a whole lot to recommend it. Yet, when the shit goes down, the alphas go out to face it. It kills them a shitload of the time, but they do it.

Many a time I have found myself jumping into the shit while a part of me was screaming, "What the fuck are you doing, fool?" This is no bullshit, I have saved people's lives. When everybody else was turning the other way, I and others charged. If our lives had to be risked to buy time for others to get away, so be it.

Machismo is the alpha instinct gone wrong. Actually wrong is not right; it's more like this instinct with no place to go. Without a focus, this instinct runs amuck. When the tribe no longer needs protection from outside threats (such as in a civilized society), this instinct begins to turn in on the tribe and you end up with gangs, macho men, and wife/child beating.

The American Plains Indians (particularly the Cheyenne) had a group of warriors living outside the camp who ran the buffalo hunts and protected the tribe from attacks. They were referred to as dog soldiers by the cavalry because they lived with the watchdogs and performed the same function. Any attack on the camp or raid on the herds was met head-on by these guys. To be a dog soldier was a great honor, but it also meant that if the camp was attacked, they were going to be the first to go down. Everyone in camp recognized the status of the dog soldiers and honored them.

In this culture we have lost not only the concept of the dog soldier, but also respect for the guardians. Therefore, we have no constructive place to put this energy.

Gangs are this energy carried to the extreme. They're fighting for territory, respect, and livelihood. It's a sick parody of what the instinct is actually about, but it's the best that they can do. It's no wonder we're ass deep in gangs. What's amazing is that it didn't happen long before this point.

So the desire to be top dog still drives a lot of people and results in a lot of fights. And eye contact is usually the first step toward those confrontations.

AGE AS A FACTOR

Did you know that more fights happen at college weekend hangouts than at biker bars? I was talking with some other guys in the field, and they were amazed at the number of fights in college haunts. One place averaged about three a night. When I was doing event security, we handled 30,000 people a day and had six beer stands, each the size of a small house. In 100-degree weather, a lot of beer is chugged. The people who got into the most shit were the young bucks. We even had a term for them, "No Shirts." You'd see some young buck with a stack of sixteen-ounce beer cups, his shirt off, and a glazed, dangerous look in his eye, and you knew you were in for some shit. They were young, full of juice, and had no concept of self-preservation.

Fortunately, these very guys who are most likely to fight are the ones least likely to be good at it. When I was growing up in Venice, I was amazed at the number of fights that the jocks got into. These guys were supposed to be the best and brightest, and yet they were into group stompings. They thought that a one on six was a stand-up sort of thing. As long as they were the six. Those of us from the wrong side of the tracks were less interested in looking good than in surviving. We used weapons, so one on six took on some interesting angles. They thought we were chickenshit for using weapons. Somehow the chickenshitness of six on one eluded them.

I got cornered in the locker room once by four jocks, but they stopped when I flipped out a straight razor. While they were deciding what to do, the coach walked in. Now, I know the motherfucker saw the razor, but he also saw that I was about to get jumped. Instead of doing anything he roared, "Shower check!" They backed off, and the razor disappeared. I owe that coach.

Eye contact was a primary cause of that close encounter. They had looked, and I hadn't looked down. That meant that they had to show me the ropes. That was back when longhairs were supposed to be peaceful and passive. I failed Peaceful 101. When one of the jocks gave me the hard eye, I held my ground.

Knowing what I know now, I probably could have avoided that scrap. Four against one is something that still scares the shit out of me, but I'm not going to show it. The way things work, because there were four of them, I should have acknowledged that they had the upper hand. Unfortunately, teenage testosterone said I had to stand up regardless of the odds. The fact that I looked back at them meant that I was challenging them. There is no doubt that there was fear on my face. If I was that scared, and it showed, they thought there was no way in hell that I had the right to challenge them.

Often guys in that position are looking around for someone to mess with. The fact that there is a pack makes it "safe" for them to be assholes. They look for someone who will look back, yet have enough fear to make it safe. This is why it is so dangerous to look back unless you know exactly what you are transmitting yourself. I've heard it said that people will mess with you just to see if they can do it. Generally speaking, however, I have found that people won't mess with you if you don't give them some sort of indication that they can get away with it. You don't need to issue a challenge, per se, but rather a plain declaration that tying up with you is a painful proposition.

GROUP ENCOUNTERS

You have to be careful when you see a group of guys throwing hard looks around. Because they feel safe in a group, they're more likely to start shit. This belief in their safety leads to some stupid-ass decisions on their parts. It's best not to tangle with them, and this is usually done by avoiding eye contact. If you must look, make sure that they are looking at a Terminator, who will leave them alone if they leave you alone.

This shouldn't be mistaken for bravado. You don't need to show the world that you're not afraid of them. If you do you'll call the shit down on yourself. I have seen a lot of fights start because someone takes this too far. He walks out and makes a production of showing everyone that he isn't afraid. This is the bozo who sticks his jaw out and walks through their hangout or stands up and makes an announcement to everybody that he doesn't think the group is all that tough. Good going, guy. I can't think of a better way to force the other team to move. Because of the group mentality, everyone is more concerned with not looking bad in front of their friends than they are with getting hurt. Shit, they're in a group, they're safe. As long as you bow before them, they're happy.

Since that episode in the locker room, I have locked horns with groups on a number of occasions. The largest group I ever backed down consisted of ten guys with their girlfriends. I got out of that by letting them know, "I'm gonna die doing this, but I'm taking some of you with me." As you might have guessed, there wasn't much fear showing when I did that one. That was one of those when the little voice in the back of my head was saying, "Other way, fool!" yet alpha behavior was driving.

Now as you may have guessed bowing and scraping was never something I was very good at. The way that I keep the young bucks out of my way now is to ignore them until they bring it into my territory. When I have to move I don't give them any time to work themselves up. It's going to go to combat right up front. I might even show up with a weapon and an attitude to match. That weapon is going to be pointed at the ground until I use it on one of them. There is no gesturing or pointing of the weapon as a threat. That way from the get-go they know when I point it, I'm about to use it on whoever is at the other end.

(Incidentally, aiming it at the ground or their knees is the sign of a pro. The average civilian will point a gun and be just as scared as the person on the other end. They say intelligent things like, "Don't make me shoot you!" Gee, you think this guy is a cold-blooded killer or what? The bad guys know that. They also know that a whole lot of people won't pull the trigger. Point it at their knees, however, and a different signal is sent and received.)

One thing that youngin's don't understand quite yet, is several alphas can exist in one area. They don't have to rumble to see who is top dog. Each has his own area of expertise and/or is good enough not to mess with. They can work together. I've been in teams where no one needed to give orders; we all instinctively covered the open areas. This is a matter of accepting that they have their space and you have yours, and respecting it. Youngin's have a habit of biting off more turf than they can actually hold. Instead of claiming the entire club, you should only try to keep your table and the area around you.

STARING AT WOMEN:
AN INVITATION TO TROUBLE

Looking at women who Neanderthals consider "theirs" is also an invitation to a fight. Most women get bent out of shape when a guy acts that possessive, but there is a small group of women, I call them low-brow breeders (LBBs), who encourage this sort of shit. My guess is that they are outnumbered by normal women by about twenty to one. The bad news is that the LBBs are attracted to their counterparts in the male world. By tying up with Neanderthals, they keep this game going. While you can run into this program anywhere, it usually happens around high schools and the lower classes. People who run this number often gather in a particular place. This is why you should always scope out what's going on in a place before you start drooling at the women. (In the next chapter, we explore in more detail how women can initiate, or be the objects of, fights.)

Much more could be said about the rules of eye contact, but you should go out and start checking this out yourself. It is, in many ways, more complicated than I've made it out to be and, in many ways, much simpler. Rules change, and you need to be able to pick up the cues for wherever you are.

An important safety tip to remember is: *Looking away first often indicates that A) you're not looking for trouble or B) you're submissive.* The trick is in which direction your eye moves away. If you look away by looking down it means you're submissive. If you slowly look away to the side, it means you're not looking for trouble, but you're not afraid of him either. It's that subtle, but that real.

For more information about eye contact rules and body language interpretation, contact Neuro Linguistic Programming (NLP). It was the first to decipher the meaning of eye-movement direction. Based on the work of Milton Erikson, this organization made some incredible jumps. This information is critical for making it out in the borderlands and in Boomtown. Most people out there know this stuff unconsciously, yet they use it every day of their lives. When I was there, I saw this communication going on and I wondered if anyone else had noticed it. When I got into places where they had names for it, I went, "Ah-ha!"

Remember I said one of the skills you need to make it in Boomtown is that of an actor? Not only will this stuff allow you to interpret correctly what the other fella is going to do, but it will give you the edge when it comes to making sure he decides what you want him to decide. Good stuff, Maynard!

Notes

[1] I've never figured out how a woman knows when you are looking at another woman, but, man, they immediately know. They must have some sort of radar that I don't know about.

CHAPTER THIRTEEN

Women

> "A stiff cock ain't got no conscience."
> —American provincial wisdom

Let's take a gander over to the *Uniform Crime Report* again. What's this we see? Under "Murder Circumstances by Relationship," it has a category for "Romantic Triangle." Gosh, what a surprise! In 1989 there were 385 murders committed for this reason. Let's dice up that 33 percent "Unknown" and sprinkle a few of the "Other Arguments" as possibly undeclared hanky panky just to spice it up. Hmmm . . . could it be that we could learn something from these numbers about putting our dicks in the wrong places? Could be, Buckwheat!

That's just the number of *murders* that happened over women. I don't even want to guess how many *fights* happen over women. Remembering that the ratio of aggravated assaults to murders was slightly higher than forty-four to one, you end up with a whole shitload of fights.

Old-timers generally agree that most fights are over money or women. Despite everything I've said in this book, I still have to nod my head and go, "Yep," to that one. I might modify it by saying, "Money and women are often used as excuses to fight."

SOMEONE ELSE'S DATE OR GIRLFRIEND

If a man is looking to pick a fight, your looking at his woman is all the excuse he needs.

If the guy is not real self-assured, his concern is less that you might make a move on his girl than that she might take you up on it and dump him. You must understand that this guy is motivated by the fear of losing something. He's not going to be terribly rational as long as he feels threatened. Allen Sherman touched on this in a book he wrote some years back called *Rape of the A.P.E.* (A.P.E. stands for American Puritan Ethic). It's one of those "laugh while you are receiving some thought-provoking ideas" types of book. I'm going to have to paraphrase because I lost my copy, but he said that a woman gets up every morning with the solid knowledge that, no matter how ugly she is, she can get laid. Somewhere, there is a guy who is desperate enough to bed her. A guy, however, gets up each morning and faces the horrifying realization that he may never get laid again in his entire life (especially in Alaska where men outnumber women by ten to one). The guy who overreacts to a look at his girlfriend is panicking because he's not sure he can attract another female. So he's going to defend what he's got with tooth and nail. The odds are his approach is going to be one of pyrotechnic rectumhood until he feels safe.

You have to be able to size up the guy's motivation. A guy looking for an excuse to pound someone will not accept your saying, "Sorry, man, I didn't mean to cut in." He's looking for a fight, and you've just volunteered. On the other hand, if he is just afraid of losing his warm fuzzy, he will often chill out if you back away and don't look at his woman again. Hell, if he pushes it, she may dump him. Few women smile at being fought over. Those what do have popped a few rivets from their plating.

LOW-BROW BREEDERS

I mentioned low-brow breeders in the previous chapter,

but let's delve deeper in to this subject. These women act on instinct, as do alpha and beta men, but there are a few new wrinkles attached to their behavior. An LBB is one of those wrinkles; we are talking about near Neanderthal level here. Of course, you have to remember, by the nature of statistics, half of the population is below average. Yike!

There is not a woman today who was not bombarded with the "Prince Charming" bullshit while growing up. As we were shafted with the "be a manly man" crap, women got nailed with "wait for your Prince Charming, who will ride up on his white stallion, sweep you off your feet, and take you away to his castle." I don't know about you guys, but my armor is at the cleaners this week. Even though it's been fluffed up a whole lot, if you boil it down to the absolute lowest grunt level, what all this translates into is "breed with the best alpha you can find."

LBBs are women who have not gotten past the Neanderthal stage themselves. You're less likely to run into LBBs after high school, unless you run in certain circles that attract these women. They play a very immature and dangerous game. Essentially, the game consists of finding a potential alpha male, who shares the same dysfunctional pattern but in a complementary role, and then testing him.

These girls are usually hotter than a three-dollar laser; there's something about them that makes even the most gentle male want to crack heads together and climb over the bodies to screw her.

If another alpha enters the area, LBBs flirt with him to see which one is a better protector. If her alpha wins, she'll stay with him. If he loses, she'll go out and find another. She usually ends up marrying and having kids with the best fighter she could attract. In short, these women are the type who start shit to see the fight. It is on a basic sexual level, I'm talking neanderthal stuff here.

The reason that these women cause so much damage is they are usually running around when hormones are the highest. (This and PMS have done more damage to women's quest for equality than anything else.) When you are gripped in a testosterone frenzy, it doesn't matter who they belong to, a pair of tits stuck in your face will start you drooling, slobbering, and barking if you're like most guys. However, if they belong to an LBB, there's a gorilla hanging around somewhere who is going to get pissed. All he's going to see, by the way, is your hitting on her. He's going to edit out the fact that she may have approached you or signaled her availability.

For those of you thinking that you can use this to condemn all women, they don't do this consciously. They don't get up in the morning and say, "I'm going to test to see if my boyfriend still is the biggest cock in town." With the proper stimulus (often an unidentified alpha walking into a room), a bell seems to go off, and when that happens, women unconsciously start up the pattern. After they have wiggled enough to get you barking and drooling, their boyfriends show up.

At this point, you should watch the girl with a critical eye. If she jumps on his case and tells him to back off, odds are that you're not dealing with an LBB. If she climbs all over him, rubbing her boobs in his back, and starts sweet-talking him, you know you've been set up.

There are songs about women like this; the one that stands out in my mind is an oldie where the woman says, "Come a little bit closer, you're my kind of guy . . ." After she says it to one guy, her old man shows up, the guy who is singing the piece makes a hasty exit, and as he's leaving he hears her say to her boyfriend the same thing she had said to him.

When this happens, you're not likely to walk away without a fight. The combination of your cutting in on his woman and a hot crotch grinding against his thigh does not lead to rational thinking on his part. I have avoided fights in situations like this in one of two ways. I either have pointed out to the other guy, man to man, that we've been set up, or let it be known that the woman was going to be mine after I won the fight—after all, if she's going to act like a spoil of war, she's going to be treated as such. Loot is not treated nicely. In the first scenario, the aggressor started thinking, and in the other his encouragement evaporated.

It is unfortunate that women such as these exist. They seriously pee in the pool for all other women attempting to gain equality. I'm not referring to the radical, man-hating femi-nazi-ists, who hide behind the women's movement's rhetoric to attack men; they cause enough damage on their own. I'm talking about women who are seriously working to gain balance and equality between men and women.

One bad experience with a LBB could leave a man with a bad taste for his entire life about female sexuality and motives. And it's pretty deeply anchored that an attractive woman coming on to you means deviated septum in certain circles. Unfortunately, when they usually cause the damage is in high school when kids are uncertain what the hell is going on anyway and are, thus, more impressionable.

OUTSIDERS AND WOMEN

Some guys also have a problem with outsiders hitting on local women. You come in and some sweet young thing starts talking to you. Next thing you know, some local buster shows up and gets in your face. Often the guy has been trying unsuccessfully to get a date with her for awhile. Then he sees you cutting in on "his territory," and trouble is on its way. This involves the same emotions as the guy who is not really sure he's got what it takes to attract another woman. Again watch the girl's reaction; if she tells him to bug off you know you haven't been set up, and she's really interested in you. Incidentally, try to avoid these kind of fights at all cost; if she's interested in you and you get in a fistfest, she's gonna lose interest right quick.

A similar, but more understandable situation arises when you are an outsider to a group. You do not mess with their women. When I was first being trained by the old street fighter who taught me (his handle was Oberon, we saw a Japanese girl, who he he remarked nice looking. I glanced over, grunted, and looked away. Oberon asked me what was the matter—in a tone that implied I was nuts for not drooling by just looking at her. She was fine. I told him that in Venice you left the Japanese girls alone, unless you wanted to come home one day and find five guys waiting for you. He told me to date anyone I wanted to, and if there was a problem, we'd handle it together. Well, back then I was willing to take on the world, so I did exactly that.

What I discovered was that the group gets very bent out of shape if you come in like an outsider who threatens to take their women away into your culture or if you cruise through for a quick fuck and move on. If, however, you come in, learn their culture and are accepted by them, then you can date their women. This rule applies to the men and the older women, who watch out for the young, unmarried women. In certain cultures, if grandma doesn't like you, you're history.

Remember the power behind the throne? Granny says no, and all the young bucks come gunning for you. This is true of almost any ethnic group. If you start messing with a woman from a different culture, you had better be able to face brothers, cousins, and uncles because they will protect her. If you show, by learning their customs and rules, that you are not just looking for a quick piece of ass, you're less likely to get into shit. Even then it's kind of risky. A friend of mine went to a Navajo gathering and was talking to a woman, next thing he knew, he was surrounded by about twelve guys looking very perturbed. This guy has about thirty years' experience and clan ties by marriage and adoption. Before you even start thinking about their women, start learning their culture.

WHAT IF IT'S YOUR GIRL?

When the shoe is on the other foot and it's your girl who is being ogled or approached, you must remember this incredibly important point: *You do not own the pink slip on her!* A woman is not property, and the normal woman does not appreciate when you treat her as such. If you come over and growl at a guy she is talking with, she is going to get pissed at *you*. This situation calls for a certain amount of balancing on your part.

My motto for dealing with it these days is: "I don't get upset until she does." If a guy hits on her, I let her handle it until she gets pissed, then I get bent. Getting flamed before she does usually will result in the two of you getting into a fight. I don't know about you, but I'd rather get in a punchout than a row with my old lady.

Also, the guy may be simply talking with here. When you're young it's hard to imagine talking to a girl for reason other than trying to get into her pants, but as you get more time under your belt, you'll discover it happens a lot. If you come roaring up to some guy who isn't trying to score with her, he's likely to take offense (as, of course, will she). The fight that ensues is not over a woman; it's because you were being such an asshole.

Always check out what's going on with women before you jump to conclusions. Women really do think differently. I've said it before and I'll say it again, "For all the times I fought over pussy, I ended up not getting any!" A sane woman really gets pissed off if you fight over her like she is a piece of meat to be had.

MARRIED WOMEN ARE ALWAYS TROUBLE

Not long ago I was talking with two women, Ina, the wife of my bro', and another woman. The conversation was about men thinking with their dicks. The other woman looked at me and said, "You don't do that sort of stuff, Animal." Ina, who knows me rather well, and I looked at each other and cracked up. She looked at the other woman and said, "The reason he doesn't do it now is because he's done it before."

Let me tell you, people, the one-eyed trouser snake has led me into some serious shit in my time. She's hot, I'm hot, she's married, and I'm not. Bad fucking combo! If you want to prove that you're smarter than I was: *keep away from married women!* This is why I started the chapter with numbers from the *UCR*, which undoubtedly reflects many homicides directly related to someone doing someone else's wife. When it comes to marriage, possession is nine-tenths of the law. A man who will just get bent about your messing with his girlfriend will shoot you for messing with his wife.

I personally am not very proud about the times that I messed with married women. They were fireballs, but it just was not worth the hassles. One of the most uncool moments of my life occurred when a married woman, who'd just had a fight with her husband, crawled into a van I was sleeping in. It was after a party, and everyone was smashed. I found myself in a closed-in space with someone else's wife, whose husband had two 9mms and a clear field of fire into my position. Lady, I'm sorry that you're having trouble with your marriage, but don't use me as an escape—especially when your husband is armed!

Someone once explained to me that married people who have affairs are looking for the romance and fire that have gone out of their marriage. What you get during an affair is about five years of lust and passion all vented at one time. We are talking a level of passion that is every man's fantasy. If you've found a woman with that kind of passion who isn't married or involved, doesn't have a hidden agenda, or isn't an LBB, let me shake your hand and buy you a beer!

But, guess what? Cuckolded hubby can show just as much passion and fire as there was in the affair, vented in an angry, dangerous way. Every year tens of thousands of people end up in divorce court, and it's a safe bet that at least a thousand end up in the hospital on the way there and another four hundred end up in the morgue. Don't ask me why, but it seems that men instinctively want to go after the other man. Some guys won't hit a woman—they'll come after you instead. Some guys hit women and still come after you. Very few guys conveniently commit suicide, leaving you all the goodies.

As tempting as it is, as hot as the sex promises to be, as passionate and torrid as the looks may be, don't do it. Wait until after she leaves the guy before you fall in bed and make like wild puppies. Not only does it fuck up friendships, but it might end up fucking up your life.

Beware of the sob story in this situation. This not only goes for married women, but for women with boyfriends as well. She's distraught about her relationship, and you want to comfort her. Comforting does not mean going to bed with! Capiche?! I guarantee that—if you are more sensitive than a turnip—you will find yourself in this situation at least once in your life

If, despite all these warnings, your pecker gets you into an affair with a married woman, go to code-yellow status. Jealous husbands follow wives they suspect are messing around on them. A night at the bottle might convince him that shooting you is a good idea. Southern boys do not like being cuckolded. Their Rebel honor demands that they revenge themselves for the hurt you've done to them. One of the things that amazes the hell out of me is how often Mexican and black cultures demand that the husband cheat on his wife, but the woman can't return the favor. When wives do, guess who goes hunting? Jealous lovers and husbands do all sorts of damage. According to the *UCR*, in 1989, 28 percent of female murder victims were done in by their hubbies or boyfriends.

Another unpleasant aspect of having affairs is that you're not going to get much sympathy from those around you. If you get into trouble and call for backup, their support is going to be halfhearted when they find out what you did to deserve the wrath of jealous husband. Not only that, but even if you beat him to the draw, you could have some serious problems with your defense in court. "Well, why were you having to defend yourself from him?" "Uh . . . 'cause I was fucking his wife." Good, good, that's going to win you lots of brownie points with the jury, let me tell you.

BEWARE OF OPEN RELATIONSHIPS

Now another thing that has put my ass on the brink of disaster is the so-called open relationship. That's when someone *supposedly* has the okay from her spouse or significant other to mess around. Number one, don't just take her word for it. Come on, guys, let's get real here. What kind of lies have you told to get laid? Anytime someone tells you she's in an open relationship and her attached won't mind, check it out with other sources. Get the skinny from other places before you waddle up to the guy and ask, "Can I fuck your old lady?"—or just proceed without asking. I once had to pull a friend out of some deep shit because it turns out that she had lied. It wasn't an open relationship.

Even if the spouse says that yes, the relationship is open, and no, he doesn't mind, don't just listen to his words; watch everything about his body language. The guy who says yes, while his eyelid is twitching has a part of him saying, "I'm gonna kill this son of a bitch."

Under stress, people return to the basic programming that they were reared with. Anytime someone says something, watch him like a hawk to make sure he doesn't revert to form. A part of him may do the talking, but, when it actually goes down, another part takes over the driving.

I was once deep in Boomtown, where sex was an open forum, and this woman and I had been flirting around. I knew her old man, but she said, "Open relationship." I said, "I'll check your references." After doing research, I approached her old man about it, and he said it was cool. I won't go into where we were that we were sleeping outside with weapons around the bed, but after a wonderful evening with the lady, I got a rude awakening the next morning. When I opened my eyes, he was standing there looking down at us with two sharp Chinese butterfly knives in his hands. He said he wanted to show them to me. Inside, I was asking who was he going to carve first? Then I grabbed my bowie knife.

I may laugh about this stuff now, but, at the time, they weren't funny. Those were two times that if the guys had decided to move, I would be dead. Plain and simple, they had me hands down, and there wasn't shit I could've done about it—especially in the van. Not that I objected to jumping her bones, but I would not have chosen a place where we could have been shot so easily. I had a roommate once who was messing with another man's wife, and the dumb motherfucker left the front door unlocked. Her hubby is a Vietnam vet and a gun collector. I jumped his shit big time for that one.

Another factor to consider is that, on a subconscious level, the woman may want to get caught. She's bored or unhappy with the relationship she's in, but she's also scared to leave. She sets it up so that she gets caught, and the matter of her leaving is settled. She gets out; who knows what you get. This is why you play it supertight and don't leave a trail—even if you think it's cool. People use this sort of stuff to get out of relationships that they don't have the balls to just up and leave. Unfortunately, if she called the game wrong, it could turn ugly.

People don't plan to get involved in assaults and attempted murders. It's not something that they get up in the morning and say, "Hey, I think today I'll go out and do something to piss someone off enough so he'll try to kill me." Yet, everyday at least three thousand people get assaulted and sixty bite it. Do you think they planned to get killed that day? It is the day-to-day stuff that gets you hurt in this life. That's what you have to watch for. This is especially true if women are involved. Any time that there are strong emotions, you run the risk of violence. I don't know about you, but I don't know of any source of stronger emotions in men than women.

VIOLENCE BY WOMEN

Okay let's change tracks here for a second. I want you to pick my story out of the following true stories:

• Waking up in the middle of the night with her sitting on his legs, muttering to herself, and with his balls in one hand and a knife in the other.

• Waking up with her sitting on his chest with his .25 caliber pointed at his face. When his eyes opened, she pulled the trigger. Fortunately, she had forgotten to chamber a round.

• Sleeping in the walk-in closet with one foot against the door and a hand on a weapon in case she decided to come through in the middle of the night.

• Walking through the door after getting off a motorcycle and meeting her standing beside the door with a hammer. Her blow punched a one-inch hole in the helmet. Ordinarily, he took his helmet off before he came through the door.

• A woman gouging an eight-inch gash in a guy's back with a nail when he turned to walk away from during a fight.[1]

Women are not helpless. Not all of them are sane either. There is an incredibly important thing to remember. You have to sleep sometime! I swear I know a lot of guys who have been mauled by women. More than a few of them deserved it, too. So let's look at some of the things you can do to keep the woman in your life from getting a piece of you.

First off, I have a personal rule: I do not use violence against people with whom I am intimate. If I ever get so flamed at someone that I want to hit her, I walk away. Not only that, but I require the her to abide by that rule also. I am off limits. Break this rule, and I am gone, forever.

If you ever find yourself in a place where you are so angry that you strike the one you love, there is something way wrong, not just in the immediate situation either, *but with the whole picture.*

I believe that men are programmed instinctually not to hurt women—sort of like a battleship has stops in its big guns so it won't blow off its own bow or bridge. From a survival standpoint, it is counterproductive to attack females. However, this programming can be overridden. Once it is overridden, all hell breaks loose.

I don't say that hitting women is wrong based on the "girls are weak and helpless" bullshit we were brought up with. I'm saying it because the internal programming has a virus that has run amuck or it would not have gotten to the point. That you would raise your hand against the woman you love means that somewhere way back either your safety stops were pulled out about this or they never developed. There is something wrong with the program.

The problem is that there are certain networks that not only condone violence against women, but rather expect it by the man as well as the woman! In these operating systems, a willingness to strike her shows that you love her. If you don't hit her, you don't love her. This is sick but true. If you do not voluntarily strike women who believe this, they will proceed to make you hit them! I have seen this in action too many times for me to deny it.

I am not saying all women want to be hit, because that is

bullshit. However, there is an abuser/abused syndrome running inside certain people. If you find yourself in a situation in which you are hitting (or want to hit) a woman, or being attacked by her, the problem is not in the violence. It occurred way before then. If you find yourself resorting to violence, the relationship is over. Goodbye, so long, sayonara! Cut your lines and split. Do not famous final scene. If you stay it will only get uglier and more vicious.

Women fight differently than men. However, they are, in their own way, just as ruthless, hard-hitting, and low-blowing. Since they don't often break jaws when they fight, it's sometimes hard to see the immediate damage that they can do. There needs to be serious damage before men remove those safety stops. It is important to realize how different we are. After a particularly vicious fight, I once admitted to a woman that a verbal shot she had taken had really hurt. She looked at me in honest amazement and said,"You never showed it."

Great, I don't show emotion, she gets scared that she's powerless, and she hits harder until she gets a response. By that time, I'm nearly torn in half. This is how these stops get pulled out. If I said, "Ouch," would you stop? This is the price of being men of steel, guys.

Women who come from fucked-up backgrounds, in which violence is acceptable, are just as likely to go ballistic on you. The different war stories I told you about earlier are examples of how violence can go both ways.

It takes two people to play these games. If you find yourself in a relationship in which domestic violence occurs, or if you grew up with it, understand that a very important safety stop has been ripped out of you. The damage was done a long time ago. Fall back and regroup on this one. You have to look at your patterns and then look at hers. I've left some interesting relationships because I would not strike someone I loved, and I knew the situation was heading that way.

As warriors, it is our duty to protect our clans, not to turn our violence against them. Just because we don't do violence to them, however, doesn't mean they can do it to us. I don't hit you; you don't hit me. The street runs both ways.

Notes

[1] Did you guess? Mine was the foot against the door and the hand on the weapon.

CHAPTER FOURTEEN

Untouchables

> "Certain professions transcend social, racial, and economic boundaries."
> —Ruth Lawrence, a former roommate of mine

I have a friend who goes by the name of Minstrel. Give this man a guitar and he'll charm a snake out its socks. Minstrel has kicked around the United States since before I was born. He has a story that illustrates the point of this chapter.

Minstrel was playing a biker bar in the Midwest when the natives got restless. A full-scale barroom brawl was brewing. Minstrel is no small puppy—I'd guess about 6'2", but the sergeant at arms of the involved bike club walked over, picked him up under his armpits, and placed him on top of the jukebox. He then turned and announced to all and sundry, "The Minstrel's off limits!" What ensued was a classical barroom brawl straight out of a movie, which Minstrel watched from his perch. Nobody touched him.

It may sound weird, but there are people who are off limits to violence by group consensus. These people are outside of cast, creed, status, and alpha/beta jockeying. According to the Geneva conventions, which all "civilized" wars are to be fought by (cough), medics are classified as noncombatants. The guy with the big red cross on his helmet is not to be shot at. Of course, some nations have been very creative in getting around some of the Geneva agreements. Back a few years ago Israel did some ass kicking on Palestine Liberation Organization (PLO) strongholds in Syria, and U.S. television stations NBC and CBS were all over Israel's shit for blowing up hospitals and schools. Months later, it came out that the PLO had been storing munitions in the school and had a headquarters on the top floor and munitions stored in the basement at the hospital. If someone doesn't play by the rules, there ain't no sobbing when he gets slapped.

On a personal level, some people still believe that certain people should be considered noncombatants. They are off limits, the kind of off limits that forces an aggressor to fight everyone else in the place before he can fight them. Generally, people who are considered off limits provide some sort of service that transcends all sides and serves humanity. It's almost as if these people can go anywhere, and their services will be needed or welcomed, as in the case of Minstrel. Their usefulness provides them a passport to travel anywhere safely. It's sort of the cosmic press pass.

I'm Scottish by descent (with Scot/Irish and Indian thrown in). There's something to be said about a people who dress in skirts and throw telephone poles as a national pastime. It also should be noted that Scots have a national instrument that sounds like someone torturing a cat. It may be because I did research into Scottish history, or it may be because I'm a member of a clan, or it may be something that is just buried in my genes, but when I hear bagpipes, I either want to wail and cry or go out and slaughter people and steal cattle. That is weird but true.

Recently, I was with my lady, Tracy, in a shopping mall that had a bagpiper playing while people shopped. All of a sudden there was a crash, and the pipes quit. I spun around saw the piper squared off against three Mexican punks that my radar had zeroed in on when I first arrived. I heard someone roar, "Ya dinna touch tha piper!" and I felt Tracy's hands trying to hold me back as I charged across the mall. Fortunately, security landed on the kids before I got to them. I didn't care that they were underage; I was in such a serious rage that I was going to hospitalize the little fucks. Later Tracy asked me "What were you yelling about?" It took me a second to realize that I had been the one yelling.

In Scotland, the piper is off limits. Traditionally, the piper/bard was a wanderer who was given shelter wherever he went. He played for kings and peasants, told stories, and brought news. No man's hand would be raised against him, or every man's hand was raised against the offender. It was that serious: kill a piper and you had better leave the country, and even then you might not be safe.

Maybe because of my heritage, it is easier for me to understand the concept of an untouchable. I don't mean this term in the way it is used in India to mean someone who is on the same level as slime. By untouchable, I mean someone off limits.

I can give you an example of what I mean that might make it clearer. Let's say you get in a jam with someone. He stands up and says, "Oh yeah?" When he stands up, five other guys stand up to back him up. This guy is not an untouchable. On the other hand, if, when you stand up, about four people step between you and your prospective sparring partner and say, "Leave him alone," then the guy is an untouchable. Although it is possible that you've found someone's little brother, if you're out of high school that's unlikely.

UNTOUCHABLES BY CATEGORY

The main untouchables are musicians, healers, holymen, specialists, and leaders.

I don't know if protecting certain people is instinctual or evolved out of necessity. What I do know is that untouchables provide necessary services that keep the whole sheebang running smoothly (or actually, a whole lot smoother than if they weren't there) and that every society has people it protects. Stop and think, what type of person would you automatically step in to help if he were being harassed? I'll bet you that the person would fall into one of these categories. (Many people might also consider the elderly as a category that is off limits to violence, but I can no longer categorically exclude the elderly because of what some older people in the cities have degenerated into.)

The untouchable theory works in all but trash-can systems, and it even functions there to a degree. However, there are some freak systems that are totally beyond anything that the average person will ever dream of. People can be so warped and twisted that they literally aren't human anymore. While anyone else would understand (though perhaps not consciously) the necessity of untouchables being left alone to do their stuff, these freaks are so twisted that they don't care.

Musicians

Since people are more familiar with seeing musicians in a potentially violent setting than the other untouchables, let's start with them. Let's take a trip down to the sleaziest, down-and-dirty honky tonk in Texas. We're talking sweep-up-the-eyeballs-at-closing-time sort of place. Want to know how to tell you're in one of those places? There is chicken wire around the bandstand. Officially, this is to protect expensive equipment in case trouble starts, but it also protects the musicians. When the nightly brawl starts up, the band is safe from thrown bottles, chairs, and bodies.

I have seen these brawls start because some drunk throws

something at the band. If the band is bad, others might just join in. However, if the band is good, the guy who threw the bottle is going to get nailed by the other patrons or the bouncer. That's the difference between a musician and a noise maker. It was the latter situation that I saw. A guy launched a bottle and needed stitches damn near before it hit the wire.

Everyone was enjoying what the musician had to offer. If one guy hurts the musician, everybody suffers. I do not know anyone who does not like some form of music. Music plays to our souls, and the person who supplies that connection is not to be messed with—not because he can't fight but because others can who enjoy his music.

Healers

Healers are sort of a blanket category. It includes medical doctors (and, to a degree, nurses) who really help people. I'm not talking about Beverly Hills practitioners; those fuckers would get mugged in a New York second. I'm talking about doctors who work in hospitals in the poorer parts of town. Unless you're talking a real combat zone or zombie land, these people are off limits. Medics are also people who others stand up and fight for. That medic is the guy who's going to save your ass if you get hit. You don't want to risk him in a punchout with some bozo.

There is also another kind of healer, the guy who always listens without judging you and gives good advice. This is the guy who sits on the group member who gets too bombed to drive until the taxi comes, or the person who helps you get back on your feet.

These kind of people are usually more attached to a group, but they also travel in Boomtown. When you see someone fucking with them, something inside you reacts along the lines of: "Wrong sucker, you're messing with the guy who helped me get through the breakup with my old lady. You're not going to play with him. You're going to deal with me instead." Outside, you're telling Hopalong Casually to do just that.

Holymen

Holymen are also off the hit list. The very idea of punching a priest will send most staunch Catholics to confession. Usually, priests, pastors, reverends, or ministers can travel through territories untouched, and often they are called in to be mediators. They bring comfort and consolation to people who need it.

Medicine Men

Medicine men or women are also untouchable. These people have the juju. They bring magick to the poor or have big medicine. Since most street people and backwater folks are superstitious, messing with someone who has got the magick is a no-no. Who knows who's going to take you out, the local who is affronted that you are messing with the holyman or the boogie man? If you offend a juju man, everyone will avoid you like a leper. They don't want to be around when the magick gets you. It sounds silly, but it happens. What's worse, if you accidentally cut off our thumb or trip down the stairs, or if your car throws a rod, people will say that the evil spirits did it.

Specialists

Specialists are also off limits. Trying to jam with a wizard who performs a vital function for the group could lead to your death warrant. The first example that pops to mind is the master wrench in a bike club. This is the guy who can make a Harley sing. Everybody can work on their ride, but this is the guy who makes magic with the V-Twin. Cross this guy and you are in for shit. Likewise, a fence serves an important role for certain people. If you rob him, who's going to fence your hot goods? Of course if he tries to rip you of, that's another story. Drug dealers aren't off limits, but munitions dealers usually are. Not only will they shoot back, but if you pester them, where are you going to A) get your clean guns and B) turn in your hot ones?

Leaders

The last category is not based on appointed rank; rather it is predicated on the real thing: leadership. The number of fraggings that took place in Vietnam indicate that leadership is not something that can be appointed or commissioned.[1] Nor can it be inherited. I always thought that the so-called sacredness claimed by the upper classes was something put into effect to keep the peasants from stringing up their snobby asses. But it worked for a long time with a lot of peasants, and there is still a trace of that kind of thinking floating around. If not, there would be more lower-class assaults on the upper classes.

Not all people in positions of leadership are off limits, only *real* leaders. The difference is that a leader has the good of the group at heart, while a pseudo leader has his own interests or some sort of goal in mind. The lieutenant who wants his platoon to score a high body count so he's guaranteed a lifetime cushy position does not have the best interest of his men at heart. The sergeant who tears a new asshole in someone who did something that could have gotten them all killed actually is looking out for the group.

True leaders are people the group will step forward to protect because they rely on the guys to lead them through serious situations; at times, their lives may depend upon this guy. I once knew a guy who was a doorgunner in 'Nam. There were usually four-man crews on choppers, but the guy flying the bird was the one everyone relied on to do the right thing to keep them alive. A doorgunner could get hit, and it was a loss, but if the pilot got hit, they were all fucked. Anyway this guy's pilot was good; he'd saved their shit more than once. He was also smart. Also in the wing was a dumb-assed Southern boy who went by the name of Cobra. This guy was not only dumb, he was mean and he hated anyone who was smarter than he was.

One night while the rest of the pilot's crew was somewhere else, Cobra decided to stomp my friend's pilot. The crew got there in time to hear Cobra threaten, as he was being pulled off the beaten pilot, "One night, I'm going to come after you, and you won't wake up!" Cobra made a fatal error with that comment. He was a killer, and he had just threatened the life of a man who kept other people alive. Everyone knew he was the sort to do it, too. During a mission a few days later, while receiving fire in flight, the doorgunner looked up and saw that they were parallel to the slick that Cobra was on. With no hesitation the guy snapped his '60 up and blew Cobra away.

I don't consider this murder. What's more, everyone who has been through the grinder would understand why he killed Cobra. He did it for self-preservation and the protection of one of his own. I would have done the same thing in his place, as I am sure thousands of others would have. This is an extreme example of a leader being off limits, but it does exemplify what people will do for a true leader. Learn to differentiate between a leader and a boss—there is a big difference. A boss leads by having the biggest dick or by appointment from some organization. He is not off limits.

AFFILIATED VS. UNAFFILIATED UNTOUCHABLES

In addition to being categorized by their function, untouchables can further be broken down by their affiliation.

One type is affiliated with a particular group, while the other is not. Being unaffiliated allows the latter to travel anywhere. An unattached rap musician can travel through any gang's territory. He pays the toll by performing for the gang, and they let him pass. If, however, he is attached to a particular gang or has strong ties with it, he does not get his travel visa.

To be a universal untouchable you have to be neutral. This could mean that you stand outside the game or you belong to a group that is declared neutral by all teams. Unaffiliated untouchables are valuable because they contribute to all without consideration of local sides. Untouchables must respect the rules of neutrality (too complicated to go into in this book), or they have to take their chances like all the rest. If an untouchable who conforms to the rules is threatened, people will say, "Hey, he wasn't doing anything wrong. He's a musician. Leave him alone."

BORDERLORDS AND BOUNTY HUNTERS

Certain people are outside of the game but very much involved in it. Their roles are well defined but understood by very few. Years ago I began to see hints and bits of patterns in operating systems that made no real sense. It was as if I were looking at a giant jigsaw puzzle and some pieces just didn't fit. I then began to track these pieces down, and when I began to see these people and their roles, I went, "Naaw! It couldn't be!"

To understand the concept I'm about to explain, you need a little biology refresher. Go back to the analogy of the giant living network and the spaces in between (described in Chapter 1). Remember, I said that each network was a living system. Well, guess what? Each network has white corpuscles, which—much like our bodies' white blood cells fight off infections—kill off system contaminants. These immunizers, if you will, are rare, but they do exist.

I call these people borderlords. I know of no designation for these kind of people in American culture. There are references to these type of people in other cultures, but none here. Borderlords are the people who hunt down those who maliciously or repeatedly break the rules. You really have to fuck up to get one of these people on your trail, but if you do, God help you. I know I sound like I'm talking about a fantasy character, but I have talked with a lot of oldtimers about them. Most of whom have sat there with intense looks on their faces and then said, "You know what? You're right. I have seen that!" I'm talking about street fighters from Detroit, San Francsico, New York, L.A., and Philly.

To illustrate, let me tell you a true story that I got from an FBI agent when I mentioned this concept to him, about Cleveland in the late 1950s and early 1960s. This was back when the Mafia ruled supreme, before the Colombians, Jamaican posses, Japanese yakuza, and Oriental triads started giving them a run for their money. There was a man by the name of The Jockey who was the arbitrator for any mob situation he was asked to mediate. If you and another family had a problem, you took it to The Jockey, and his decision was final.

Well it seems that a couple of goons walked into this after-hours club with machine guns and robbed everybody inside, including a member of the crime community, who told them, "Hey, you can take the money and the rest of the jewelry but leave this ring. It has sentimental value." One of the goons responded, "Fuck you," and took the ring. Since this was an after-hours club, nobody ran to the police. The man who had been robbed went to The Jockey and said, "I want the ring back." The Jockey sent an invitation to the partner of the goon who'd taken the ring and, at their meeting, instructed him to carry the message back that the ring was to be returned. The goon who took the ring refused to return it. The Jockey had the messenger goon brought to him again. What transpired is a mystery, but a few days later the partner stepped out of the car and asked the beringed goon if he would return the ring. The goon refused.

At that point, the partner pulled out a gun and, in broad daylight, blew a hole in his associate's chest. A few days later The Jockey called the ring's owner to his place and returned his ring.

Borderlords can track people through networks. Imagine that you could move across dimensions. If you do something wrong in one, you just shift over to another, and you're scot-free since most people don't or can't leave their dimensions. A borderlord, however, can track you wherever you go. The closest contemporary example to illustrate what I'm talking is a bounty hunter.

Most people are familiar with bounty hunters. They often work for bail bondsmen. A bounty hunter does not need an order of extradition like a law enforcement agency. He doesn't have to read you your rights or have a warrant, but he must obey the laws of the states in which he tracks you to bring you back. A borderlord may not be interested in obeying laws or in bringing you back. He may simply punch your ticket.

Borderlords aren't untouchable, per se, so if you're feeling lucky you can try to nail one of them. That is highly unlikely because they are good. It's odd, but borderlords are often recognizable when they are on the hunt. An old Detroit street fighter (I'm talking Cass Corridor here) buddy of mine pointed out something that I hadn't consciously noticed. Borderlords can come right into your home territory and take you out. What's more, their mere presence lets everyone know that you really fucked up. My friend has seen people wasted by these guys in their home territory, and nobody did anything.

In addition to taking out troublemakers, borderlords also prevent trouble. I've seen these guys literally come out of the woodwork when trouble is brewing, much like good bouncers. They walk in and say to the potential combatants, "We're going to sit down and talk about this." An agreement is reached, trouble is avoided, and the borderlords vanish. If someone refuses to compromise and decides to play maverick, he has not only the other team after him, but the borderlords as well. Based on the quality of the borderlords I've seen, you should worry more about them than the entire other team.

How do you know if someone is a borderlord? If someone walks in during an escalating confrontation and tells everyone to sit down and shut up, check to see what the locals do. I'm not talking about the guy who comes in wringing his hands saying, "Gentlemen, please! Let's talk about this!" I'm talking about the guy who suddenly appears and looks like he is going to gouge out the eyes of anyone who doesn't do what he says. If the locals all go, "Yipe," and sit down, you're up against someone serious.

Borderlords also set rules for how a fight is going to proceed. They might agree that a fight is for the best, but they establish limits: Go ahead, but keep it out of this area, and don't cross this line. These limits are deadly serious.

Andrew Vachss, who writes the most realistic fiction books about the street that I have ever read, has a series about a guy called Burke, who I would consider a borderlord. Vachss really brings this kind of character to life. I highly recommend this series to you for enjoyment and enlightenment.

Most people don't see these guys because they don't fuck up far enough. A borderlord is not a minion of the law. In fact, in many ways the law considers them to be criminals. However, since the judical and prison systems are so fucked up in this country, these people serve a serious need. Cops have a habit of looking the other way when these people have done a job. The body of a repeat-offender child molester is found tied to a chair, shot three times, stabbed so as air doesn't bloat the body cavity and turn it into a float, and thrown in the river with rocks tied to it, and his death is called the worst case of suicide they've ever seen. When I said most people don't fuck up bad enough, I meant that they don't sexually molest twenty kids and then jump bail and run to another state. If the guy is lucky, all he'll get is a bounty hunter after him. If the child is related to or has family that is connected to a borderlord or a dog soldier, the chase will be on.

Personally, my only problem with these borderlords that is there are too few of them. Society has become too civilized and, at the same time, too twisted. I have always believed in personal responsibility and an eye for an eye. The people who bemoan the conditions of so-called abused, deprived, misunderstood, and mentally ill offenders have never seen those cases from both sides. Capital punishment may not have worked well for society as a whole. However, if you want to be safe on the street, you'd better make it clear to anyone in search of a victim that you are capital punishment personified, and he had better look elsewhere if he wants to live. In short, you have to be a giant mirror. If someone comes at you with respect, you treat him with respect. If someone comes at you with no regard to your life or well-being, you do the same.

Notes

[1] Often fraggings were not meant to be lethal. A grenade outside the hooch was used as a warning of what could happen if an officer didn't chill out. For every lethal fragging, there were about three warnings.

CHAPTER FIFTEEN

Awareness Building Techniques

> "The mind involuntarily rejects any information not in line with previous thoughts and/or actions."
> —Leon Festinger
> *Cognitive Dissonance Theory*
>
> "1)The overriding of ignition system by alternative means.
> "2) By passing locks, barriers, or other systems that interfere with operations by any means possible."[1]
> —My theory on hot-wiring

About nine years ago, I was helping a friend out on a construction job. One guy I hadn't seen for a few years came wandering by. The guy was never really tightly wrapped, but he was really off into hippieland that day. He was wearing a pair of dark glasses. He handed me a plastic hiking water bottle full of liquid when I said, "Hi." It was a very hot day so I took the bottle and said, "Oh boy, water," as I took a swig.

He looked at me and said, "No, acid." Well, I looked at this guy, and his nonverbal body signals said he was totally relaxed. That and his smile convinced me that he was bullshitting.

To show that I was able to hold my own with funnin', I said, "Oh, boy!" and took another chugalug.

About a half hour later, I suddenly experienced an incredible body rush. The closest thing I can liken it to is the feeling you get immediately after great sex. Part of me went, "Oh yessss!" while another part of me went, "Wait a fucking minute!" I sat there for a moment thinking about what could have caused the particular set of symptoms I was experiencing. Suddenly, a bell went off inside my head! The dude had been telling the truth!

I did some quick calculations to figure out how many hits I had accidentally consumed. My rational brain was still functioning enough to figure out that I was going bye-bye for a long time. I told my friends what had happened and that I needed them to keep an eye on me, just in case . . .

We had a moment of concern because the people we were going to be staying with were throwing a party for us that night. Hey relax, I survived the Los Angeles drug culture of the 1970s, and I'm told I had a lot of fun, so I wasn't worried. After making sure all of my ducks were in row, I kicked back and went with the flow. I went south for the next fifteen hours. Generally speaking, one hit lasts for about four hours, so you can guess how much I had ingested.

At this time I was studying neurolinguistic programming and Jungian psychology. On top of that, I had been a drug dealer in the past, so I was not particularly worried about being whacked. No new news here. However, what occurred at the party was of particular interest. It is also why I bring up this particular story. The combination of street experience, the current research I was doing, and enough acid in my system to give chromosome damage to a bus knocked me into a particularly bizarre place.

The best way for me to describe where I was is "in between." If all that went on at the party was music; I was in the time between the notes. I'm not claiming I disappeared or anything, but if there is a point A and a point B, mentally I was halfway between them. I sat there blazing away and watching people when they didn't think anyone was looking. When everyone looked at the person who was speaking, I looked at the people who weren't speaking. I didn't have any stupendous hallucinations or revelations. God didn't speak to me, nor did I discover any cosmic truths. Enlightenment was still over the hills and far away.

However, as I wandered around the party, I watched people in a way I had never seen them before. I saw what was behind and around the images that people projected. If someone wanted to be considered something by everyone, they put on a mask and set it forth for all to see. It was what was going on behind the masks that made me go, "Whoa." Of course, there were people there who did not project these facades—what you saw is what you got with them. I vaguely remembered from my psychology courses that 80 percent of all communication is nonverbal, but I was too frosted for that to make much sense.

When I landed much, much later, I thought, "That was weird." I would have written it off as merely the drug had I not seen it occur later when I was straight. I took another look at NLP and said, "Holy shit! This is what they were talking about!" What I had experienced as a drug trip, I later verified as aspects of the cutting edge of modern psychology, anthropology, and sociology. At this discovery, someone else may have shined their fingernails on his chest and looked smug. I was happy to get back with most of my marbles intact.[2]

HOW TO INCREASE YOUR AWARENESS

What I'm going to share with you is ways to shift your awareness without the use of drugs. I should point out to you,

I haven't done drugs in about five years, and, because of an ulcer, I have seriously cut back on my drinking. So you're not getting the ramblings of a drug-crazed maniac.[3]

As you may have gathered, people who hunt other people have a slightly different perception than most folks. The following techniques will bring you into closer alignment (or at least understanding) with the thinking processes. For any of them to work, you have to practice them. I'm not guaranteeing that you will become a kung fu wizard, able to hear the heartbeats of an assassin lurking behind the wall. However, you will be able to spot the most common mistakes that people make when it comes to awareness—mistakes that identify them as victims to muggers, slime, and would-be tough guys. Most of these techniques are relatively easy and actually rather fun to do. You get to mess with people's heads while you're practicing, and, unlike whacking off, you're not going to go blind by doing them. Also what I'm going to do is give you the exercise and then explain its purpose. This is straight-up, what you're doing and why, with no hidden messages or pointless tactics designed to trick you.

Become the Hunter

The first and foremost technique is to put yourself in the hunter's shoes. For a month, pretend you are a mugger. How would you bushwhack someone in the various places in which you find yourself. If you live in an apartment, where in the building or the parking facilities would you hide if you were going to jump someone? If you have a friend around, hide there and check if he can see you. Lying in wait around a dark corner that has a hidden safety mirror revealing your presence isn't real effective, is it? Hiding in the little cubbyhole near the elevator might be a good spot, though. How would you nail someone getting into your car? How would you nail someone at your automatic teller machine?

Essentially, what you're doing is programming your mind to do a search model—to search subconsciously for certain signs, patterns, and situations. If you're wandering around in the forest trying to find food, knowing what it looks like is the key to success.

For example, there is a type of bump that a certain edible mushroom makes on the forest floor. These suckers are huge. One of these mushrooms will feed you for an entire day. Unless you know what that bump looks like, though, you're going to wander right on by and stay hungry. By ingraining the search model into your psyche of potential ambush sights, your eyes will check it out whenever you walk by one. Even a glance is sufficient to determine if you should be careful. This exercise also begins to break your conditioned eye-scan pattern, which you will see has a whole lot to do with it all.

Bang! Diving for Cover

I call the next exercise "Bang!"It's simple: if you'd just been shot at, where would you dive for cover? As you walk along every now and then, pretend that someone took a potshot at you. Pick a direction that the shot came from and figure out where you would rabbit for cover. At first, you'll probably always get sniped at from a place where diving behind the brick wall is the best recourse, but after a while, the imaginary sniper is going to get a little trickier. There will be occasions when you're going to look around and say, "Shit, there ain't no cover here!" Odds are, you'll quickly scurry away from (or, even better, avoid) situations like that.

The objective of this exercise is the same as the mugger technique, but it is more defensively oriented. After a while you will immediately begin to pick out places to get out of the way of trouble. This is especially important if you are with a loved one. While he or she is still wondering what is going on, you're dragging him or her to the best cover around.

Soft Focusing

The next technique is called "soft focus." Basically, it consists of seeing out of the corner of your eyes. Stop and look at some object in the room. Now, without moving your eyeball, what do you see out of the sides of your eyes? Top and bottom? What you are doing is opening the shutters of your eyes. Your focus goes from a 20-degree arca to one around 200 degrees. As you may have noticed, you are no longer focused on the object you were looking at before. This is good. At first your mind will object to this. It will keep on trying to drag you back to one-point focusing.[4] This you should not allow to happen. You should practice this technique until you do it subconsciously most of the time. When you need to focus on something, visualize a hose nozzle that you can adjust from a wide spray to a concentrated stream. Then adjust your vision go back to wide spray.

This technique is especially important for a number of reasons. The primary reason is that, by simply turning your head, you can check your blindspot. If you twist a little further, you can scan the entire 360 degrees around you. In case you haven't realized it, this makes it pretty fucking hard to sneak up on you. You like? You walk down the street turning your head now and then, and you can spot somebody trying to set you up.

Another advantage of soft focusing is it allows you to discern movement much better than if you are narrowly focused. When you focus on one point, it's literally like looking through a paper-towel tube, everything else falls away. Just as our brains color in the areas in our peripheral vision beyond which we are color blind to make them look right, when we focus on one object, our brains also fill in the rest of the screen with a fuzzy pseudopicture. We are not seeing what is actually there. Unless someone is jumping up and down and waving his arms, your brain is going to edit him out.

Mi hermano taught this technique to people at a mountain retreat who immediately freaked out. They thought they had been invaded by animals. Actually the critters had been there all along; they had just edited them out. Critters in the wild who move as boldly as humans quickly become lunch. Their movement had been too subtle to distract the singularly focused attention of the people.

Limiting your search model to one object is learned behavior. Your operating system teaches you do this. It is kind of like a physical version of dragon-blocking sunglasses. Try soft focusing on a street in the suburbs. All of a sudden, you'll see all sorts of birds, cats, bugs, and trees waving in the breeze. Also, when you do this in a crowd, you will begin to spot movements that are not in sync with the rest of the environment—like the guy who sees you coming around the corner and quickly drops his hand out of sight. Wrong! Soft focusing is a major step in widening your awareness. The shock of seeing exactly how much you've been missing makes you want to double check other areas into which your operating system may have installed blindspots.

Aside from overall improvement in your awareness, this technique is applicable in two different areas of your self-defense. One is if you're nose-to-nose with someone you can immediately spot any body shifts or hand movements that an untrained individual usually broadcasts when he is about to attack. This is how most experienced fighters know when the other guy is getting ready to move, and they usually don't even know they're doing it. Two is by doing periodic visual sweeps behind into your blindspot, you A) have advance warning if someone tries to maneuver into the danger zone and B) broadcast to would-be attackers that you are aware enough so that, if they try anything, you're going spot the attempt long before it would be a guaranteed success. Read: they ain't going to get away with it.

Following People

The next few techniques are a lot of fun; you get to skulk. I'm talking about sneaking, slithering, and tiptoeing. The first exercise consists of going to a mall or other public place where a lot of people gather, sitting around for a while and then picking a person who looks as if he is off in his own little shopping world—oblivious to everyone and everything around him—and then following that person. Don't go commando or ninja on him, just tag along. Stick your hands in your pockets and whistle as you wander along. At first, don't try to get too close. If your subject goes into a single-exit store, hang out across the way until he comes out, then pick up the trail again. Don't wear bright neon colors or sinister-looking clothes—you're not trying to scare him; you're just doing an experiment in awareness.

It is appalling how unaware most people are. I've tagged after people for more than an hour without them catching on. My presence is such that, when most people actually see me, they clutch their wallets and beloved ones closer as I pass by. It is important that you keep it light as you do this. If you go into a Rambo mode, people will spot you faster than if you're just hanging out cruising the mall. Cops, security guards, and tough guys will also spot you faster if you play ninja.

Next, try to get closer to your subject. Not only follow him, but also slip in and out of his blindspots. This is like stalking a deer. When the deer looks up, you freeze; when it puts its head down, you sneak some more. When your subject is walking, come up behind him and fade back when he turns a corner. If you're real good, you can take the corner with him by staying in his blindspot. When he goes into a store, pace him the next aisle over. At first, you won't be able to keep this up as long as you could when you were following him at a greater distance. In fact, you're probably going to freak out some people, so I don't recommend you do it too much at once. Tagging behind seven people in one day at the mall is a little much. Sooner or later somebody is going to notice. The other thing about this is, with the rising crime rate, people will think you're a would be if they see you doing it too often. Once you get spotted, quit playing the game and move far away from that person.

The purpose of this exercise should be obvious. To hone your tracking and observing powers. You really have to be on your toes to get away with these exercises. You learn to watch people in a different sort of situation. By actively looking for what they are doing and trying to second guess them (which you have to do in order to be good at this) you get all sorts of valuable information about how people work.

The other thing that this exercise does is by seeing exactly how unaware people are, and what are the most common blindspots people have, you'll begin to drop those things from your own personality. It's similar to a girlfriend who is always locking her keys in her car; your very pride demands you can't do the same thing. Instead, you end up being hyperaware about taking the keys out of the ignition. You can't bitch about her doing it if you do it yourself.

The next surveillance exercise is to be done with a friend who is similarly inclined. Have him do the skulking. What you do is walk along watching him as he does it. You take turns sneaking and skulking. When you're doing this you really have to be careful not to look like you're muggers or rapists. Two people are easier to spot than one. The next step is have him try and trail you.

This one is a definite giggle to do for two reasons. One, you can laugh at each other's attempts to sneak. Two, you can play superspy. This is such a valuable exercise because it teaches you what a person looks like when he is trailing someone and, more importantly, trailing *you*. As you might guess, this could have important benefits.

The final exercise in the skulking department is the most fun. It's sneaking up on your friend. If you manage to do it, you get a cookie. If you get snuck up on, you lose a cookie. This exercise really hones your abilities. If you don't know why it does this by now, forget self-defense and become an accountant.

Watching and Eavesdropping

The next exercise is to go someplace where different types of people congregate and simply sit down, watch them, and eavesdrop. Yes, I'm talking about sitting there and listening to people's conversations as you watch them in all kinds of settings. I'm talking about plopping your ass down at a mall and people watching. This is the going to a party and standing in a corner with one beer and watching people get smashed. What are they like at one level of drunkeness? At the next? And so on.

By actively watching people you know and people that you wouldn't generally hang out with, you begin to get a feel for what people are like. Inside your head you are compiling profiles of people types. The way they move, the way they act, the way they watch other people. I recommend going to the local criminal court and pulling up a chair for a few days or nights. Kick back and watch the floorshow for a while.

You will see literally hundreds of criminals. Watch them, study them, and learn to identify the "type." Learn their strengths and weaknesses. Ninety-nine times out of a hundred their major strength is that they are willing to strike first over boundaries most people would have to be seriously pushed before crossing. A normal person would have to be desperate to do something like trying to rob a store. These guys are willing to do it rather than work.

The next exercise also involves people watching. For it, I recommend a mall or a busy street. As you sit and watch them, say the first impression you get about them. Make it one word if possible, if not a short phrase works too. If you see someone who is all pinched-faced and glowery, say, "Angry." If you see someone bebopping along, say "Happy." Not all your descriptions are going to be positive. You'll be amazed at how many terminally fucked up people there are. Whiner, bitch, asshole, mean, sadist,[5] punk, slimy, backstabber, shallow, sneaky, etc. You're going to see them all. In fact, you might want to cruise the dictionary for new terms. Somehow "sneaky" doesn't describe some people as well as "Machiavellian"does. Don't get into details or elaborate descriptions about the people. Keep it simple; go with your first impression. "Sadist, I wouldn't turn my back on him" is about as complicated as you should get.

Oddly enough, in time you will be able to tell the difference between someone who is momentarily pissed and someone who is terminally constipated. There is a visible difference. Also, I know it's hard, but instead of saying, "Nice tits," try and see the person behind them. Women are people. People have character flaws and failings. Until you get past your initial dick-twitch reaction, you're not going to be able to see that.

This technique accomplishes the first step in "spotting" or "pegging" someone. When someone walks into a room, I immediately know if he is looking for trouble. I have a search model established for certain types. When I see them, I generally know what to expect. I used to work with a guy who could stand at a gate and watch crowds go by and, as they did, pick the people who would be security problems later on. Like fucking clockwork, we'd end up clashing with these people. I'm good, but entire crowds? This also lets you radar-ping the real hardasses—not the little whipdicks, but the people you should not cross for any reason. At first, you are going to have to work on this, but after a while, it becomes subconscious reflex.

Physical Imprinting

The final techniques are actually physical imprinting. I do not recommend doing them unless you are in some serious turf. You don't need this kind of program in Grant's Pass, Oregon, but you need it in Hell's Kitchen. For the purpose of this exercise, they consists of dropping into a fighting stance whenever you get frightened or spooked. To this day, if someone frightens me by popping out of nowhere, I'm someplace else with one hand cocked to strike, one hand set to block. I still duck when a car backfires. Deep imprinting.

You're going to annoy some people with this. You're going to hear all sorts of shit like, "Stop overreacting!" That's fine, let 'em bitch. When you get this imprinted into your deep reflexes, you have taken a major step toward protecting yourself.

The next step calls for some internal rewiring. Instead of leaping and landing with wide eyes and shaky knees, you land ready to rip someone's throat out. If it were a surprise attack, you wouldn't have time to prepare your spirit for combat, but you'd better be ready to rock and roll when that attack comes. That's why so many black belts go down in actual confrontations. They think they're going to receive a warning and have time to prepare for battle. It would be nice, but don't hold your breath. What actually makes this work is a small but critical safety catch. When you move, you wait a split second before you attack so you can see if you are actually faced with a threat. Is the person standing there still in the same position, doing nothing? Often, when someone accidentally scares you, he freezes. This has saved many a person's teeth, let me tell you. The difference in body language between an "oops" and an attack is obvious. Learn to spot the difference. If you get to this point with your imprinting, I highly recommend establishing some sort of identifying signal with your loved ones when they are about to enter your area. This sound or word disengages your crunch response.

All of these awareness-building techniques come into play when a slime bucket (who you've learned to spot from your people-watching techniques) tries to sneak (which you've learned to spot from your skulking exercises) into your blindspot (which you've learned to monitor from your soft-focus exercises), and you can identify what he's trying to do (from your mugger exercise) and react accordingly. If you land in a fighting crouch and are ready for combat, that boy has to be seriously stupid to try to continue. And, if dufus still tries, you can tear him up using all the fun techniques you have learned from my other books.

Notes

[1] Underhanded and sneaky are my personal favs.

[2] I later tracked the individual who had spiked me. It turns out he was blazing when he gave it to me. Had I been able to see his eyes, I would have known not to drink from the bottle. He panicked when I caught up to him. I put my arm around

him and said sweetly, "First, I'd like to thank you for the best acid trip I've ever had. Second, if you ever do that to me or to anyone else again, I'll break your fucking legs."

[3] I may be slightly off-kilter by the normal person's standards, however, the fact remains that I'm still alive after coming through some of the worst shitholes imaginable. That I'm alive and well, while so many of the others I started out with are dead, in prison, or busted beyond repair, indicates that I'm doing something right. Nor are you going to get some mystical, oriental mumbo jumbo. You will be able to verify the basis for everything I mention in the bibliography. These techniques are backed up with solid, respectable, academically backed works and studies by professional headshrinkers; also known as Viennese head thumpers.

[4] This tendency of one-point focusing was developed to combat motion sickness brought about while riding in an automobile. The passenger pretends to be driving, which focuses his attention on one point on the horizon, and the passenger ignores the stuff flashing by. This prevents him from becoming queasy. This single-point focusing is instinctual while in a car.

[5] There is a subtle but distinct difference between someone who is mean and a sadist. A mean person will hurt you if he has the chance. A sadist, however, will go out of his way to set up a situation in which he can inflict pain. They both enjoy it, but the person who is mean is usually unimaginative about how he hurts people. A sadist is not only mean but sneaky.

"Look, you probably can kick my ass on the mat. That ain't no big accomplishment. Also, it doesn't mean shit. If you want to prove how good you are, let's go for thirty days to different dives that I choose. If you get out of those hellholes alive, that will mean something . . . It ain't about fighting. It's about surviving."
—Me, to a martial artist who wanted to see if he could take the "Animal." Oddly enough, he didn't take me up on it.

I was sitting alone, minding my own business in a topless bar and killing time before I had to meet someone. (How's that for an opening line?) The main entrance to this particular establishment was through the parking lot in the back. In fact, you couldn't exit through the front unless it was an emergency. So there I was, kicking back, drinking a beer, and admiring the lovely ladies.

The door opens, and three white-trash boys come walking in. Inside I went "click." The bozos came in far enough to see the entire bar. They then began to zero in on anyone who was alone. They pegged me and ignored the fact that I was looking back at them. Then they turned around and walked outside. Had they held up a sign reading, "We're here to rob someone," they could not have been anymore obvious. I laughed and went back to some delicious fantasies.

About ten minutes later, it was time for me to go. No one else had left so I was first out the door. The three dickslaps were leaning against a car in the first parking space. It was quite a distance away from the door because of fire regulations. I saw their little antennas go quiver when I stepped out of the door. I smiled to myself and turned left. I hadn't driven to the bar so my car was a few blocks away. They sat there as I walked away, trying to figure out what had gone wrong.

I walked down the driveway that led onto the main street. When I turned the corner, I glanced over my shoulder, and, sure enough, there they were. I stepped out of sight for a moment and then stepped back into sight. I got a big dopey smile on my face, and I waved to them. (I swear to God, this is a true story.) I then continued on, thinking that any thug in my old neighborhood would have gotten the message. They'd been spotted; they should back off. I cruised down to the corner and looked over my shoulder. The three musketeers were still coming after me.

I thought to myself, "What fucking amateurs." They tried to look casual as they came toward me, but they failed miserably. I waited for a second more and then crossed the street. As they got to the corner the light turned red. We now had a boulevard between us. I sat there looking at them in amusement as I checked my knife for position and speed draw.

Across the street from me was a bowling alley with a big parking lot in front. (Those of you from the San Fernando Valley will know where this place is). I crossed the street and stepped into the parking lot, heading for the bowling alley. When I got out of the light, I dropped and zigged over three parking lanes towards where I was actually heading. From the other exit, I watched these guys try and figure out where I had gone. I then turned and slipped away into the night, laughing my head off.

I have to tell you, though, that I had a serious contingency plan cued and ready. If the ditch hadn't worked, I had an ambush spot picked out. All these guys would have known was that there had been a blur with a knife and at least two of them would have been in some serious shit. I wasn't worried about fair play; my plan was a blitzkrieg attack from behind with crippling and killing targets. I don't care how tough you think you are, a knife buried in the outside of your thigh affects your iliatibial tract, which supports your knee. You don't walk for a long time. A thrust to the left side of the spinal cord under the rib cage pulls the plug of the inferior vena cava, and the person bleeds to death inside of a minute. (That's why you take out a sentry with the knife in your left hand.) I was ready for combat, and I was not going to let these guys get the first move. I was going to give them the same chance they would have given me: none.

Yet, here I stand with a funny story and no extra scars. I'm absolutely convinced that I got the best deal imaginable out of that situation. By keeping my awareness up, I managed to spot the trouble on the way. By knowing how things worked, I tricked the would-be muggers. Hell, I reckon I did pretty good there.

I had been robbed when I was younger (about 14) and have experienced several attempts since then. I must admit that the previous ones ended up in bloodshed and violence. (except for the guy with the knife in the Hollywood Laundromat—but that's another story). I don't consider the times that I have hurt people funny. On the other hand, I don't have much sympathy for those people either.

In my first video with Peyton Quinn (*Barroom Brawling: The Art of Staying Alive in Biker Bars, Beer Joints, and Other Fun Places*, available from Paladin Press), I pointed out that of all the guys I used to run with, only two are left. Looking back at all those deaths, I realize how many could have been avoided. I raise a glass and toast the memory of dead friends, but to tell you the truth, I would rather have them alive, sitting here next to me.

What I hoped to do with this book is to show you, in an organized fashion, some of the things you're going to need out there in Boomtown. I sort of look at the organized part with a raised eyebrow. Hell, if you think I ramble in my books, you ought to see my sock drawer. Most of what it takes is far removed from what normal people are knowledgeable and proficient in—or even know exists. Chris Pfouts in his book *Lead Poisoning* said it best, "I'm kind of Philistine by nature, but following a trauma like that [a gunshot wound] you will look for relief in places other than where you sit. You have to."

Much of *Violence, Blunders, and Fractured Jaws* is designed to jingle your bells. Stuff is out there for you to see and make up your own mind about. I'm less concerned about your agreeing with me than I am about your thinking about it. If I get you to say, "Aww, bullshit, Animal! It ain't like that; it's like . . ."—I've done what I set out to do. Every time someone says that, I'm off in a corner hopping around in glee because I got that person to think about the subject. I've always said make your own decisions about self-defense, and I've always meant it.

All I've done with this book is to show you a filing system and point you toward new information that you might not have heard of before. I've always maintained that conventionality should be pissed on from a very great height. Ever since I found out that the guy who fills your work order at a car dealership gets a commission on that order, I've known that there's a lot going on out there that isn't on my side. This is what really led me to being an outlaw. Don't piss down my back and tell me it's raining. If it's going to be a free-for-all, tell me that up front. That I can live with. What is even better is if I'm informed that I am going to face one of eight different games and I'll know which one when I get there. That way I can pack for any situation that arises.

You've got to float your own stick in this world because nobody is going to do it for you. When they tell you that you have to play the cards that are dealt you, they're right. Of course it helps you to know that only a fool or a masochist doesn't learn the real game rules and cheat just as much as the dealer. When they tell you to play by the rules, you smile at them and keep one hand on your gun under the newspaper.

It all boils down to being able to pick and choose the game that you play. If you never know that there are different games or unspoken rules you're going to get hurt. If someone goes renegade, you have to be ready for that as well. Take this information here and go out and see what you can do with it, or more importantly, not do with it—like get your ass kicked.

Fly low and stay cool.

Animal
1992

BIBLIOGRAPHY

All right, kiddies, as promised here is the bibliography. I've broken it down by category for easier access and understanding. (I don't know about you, but I'm often totally lost in bibliographies—that is if I even bother to read the damn things.) I'm not going to go into who publishes the friggin' things, just the titles and authors. Any good bookstore or library can find these books for you without your having the other info. This listing is the shortened version. Ever since I got grounded once for two weeks without TV, I've been a voracious reader. So here are some of the highlights.

War/Strategy/History

The Art of War. Sun Tzu. To hell with Clausewitz, this guy makes more sense—even if he did write this in the sixth century, B.C. I highly recommend this.

On War. Carl von Clausewitz. This book is often referred to as *Clausewitz on War;* by any name, it still comes out boring!

Mastering the Art of War: Zhuge Liang and Liu Ji's Commentaries of Sun Tzu. If you liked Sun Tzu, these guys are almost as much fun.

On Guerrilla Warfare. Mao Tse-tung. From a leader of the Chinese Communist revolution and a founder of the

People's Republic of China, this is one that the U.S. government should have read before committing our asses to Vietnam.

The Civil War. Julius Caesar. Written about 49-48 B.C., this is recommended more for seeing how long shit has been happening and how people react to it than for tactical purposes.

The Prince. Niccolò Machiavelli. I love this guy. Just as the Marquis de Sade's name got hung on sadism, Machiavelli's has become synonymous with "sneaky." Get an annotated version; he does a lot of referencing of local events in Italy in the sixteenth century, and the footnotes make it a lot easier.

WAR! Gwynne Dyer. First off, Gwynne is a guy. Secondly, he has written one of the most comprehensive and in-depth looks at the phenomenon known as war. It was also made into a PBS documentary for video types.

Europe Divided, 1559-1598. J.H. Elliot. This one is pure history, but it validates some of the claims I made about European history. Not for the easily bored.

A Distant Mirror. Barbara Tuchman. Another history book but with a twist. Instead of just giving you the facts, she wraps the events around what's happening in one real guy's life so you've got someone to root for. Unfortunately, he dies in the end. Highly recommended if you want to take a jab at the calamitous fourteenth-century in Europe.

Road Kill Cookbook. B.R. "Buck" Peterson. Just thought I'd throw one in there to see if you're still on your toes.

Chance and Circumstance: The Draft, the War, and the Vietnam Generation. L. Baskir and W. Strauss. Sort of dry, but the authors talk about some eye-opening stuff as to how the system works.

Manual of the Mercenary Soldier. Paul Balor. I resisted reading this one until my editor threatened me with a vicious edit. When I picked it up, I read it all in one night and loved it. This guy is so real, it makes your tongue sweat.

Book of Five Rings. Miyamoto Mushasi. The so-called "Sword Saint" of Japan, this guy gives a good introduction to another way of looking at conflict other than what we were taught. Written in the seventeenth century.

Neurolinguistic Programming
NLP was sort of shot down as an original concept by the psychiatric community. This is funny because the way the founders came up the system was by watching those psychiatrists who were the best in the field and then organizing what they were doing into a system. Where this gets funny is that who the NLP proponents were teaching it to were other psychiatrists. Regardless of the debate, NLP is still a great starting point for learning body signals. Truth be told, these books are dry and require concentration to read, but they are well worth it.

Structure of Magic I and II. Richard Bandler. This examines the deep structure of language, what ideals are conveyed by a language, and how language shapes our outlook on what we see.

Frogs into Princes. Richard Bandler and John Grinder. Here the authors veer away from he textbook approach and begin simply to write their seminars.

Trance-formations. John Grinder. This goes further into

hypnosis. Hypnotizing someone before you deck him is an acceptable technique. I've used it and so have others.

Reframing. Richard Bandler and John Grinder. How to break the chains of bad memories and operation system knee-jerk reaction.

Anthropology/Sociology/Body Language

Life among the Apaches. This book, written in 1868, is not bad if you remove the cultural and professional biases.

Navajo Taboos. Jon Budlow. A good introduction to how to avoid stepping on your privates on the reservation.

The Hell's Angels: The Strange and Terrible Saga of the Outlaw Motorcycle Gangs. Hunter S. Thompson. This is still the best description of the biker life-style ever written.

Do or Die. Leon Bing. What Thompson did for the Hell's Angels, Ms. Bing has done for the L.A. Crip and Blood gangs in this book.

The Greening of America. Charles A. Reich. This look at social conditions in America will rattle your chain a bit.

Manwatching: A Field Guide to Human Behavior. Desmond Morris. This is a library special. It shows how gestures and space change from culture to culture and also how to read people's body language.

Body Watching: A Field Guide to the Human Species. Desmond Morris. This one is about bodies and what they tell us.

Body Language. Julius Fast. The first voice the public ever heard about body language.

Humankind. Peter Farb. This is a good introduction to anthropology.

Body Language of Sex, Power, and Aggression. Julius Fast. The sex is more about gender standards than how you look while having an orgasm. Nonetheless, it's damn good reading.

Signals. Allen Pease. Still more body language.

True Believer: Thoughts on the Nature of Mass Movements. Eric Hoffer. An astounding work, this was written by a longshoreman on the nature of mass movements.

Contact: The First Four Minutes. Leonard Zunin, with Natalie Zunin. This one is about how we present ourselves and the most common social oops.

Psychology

Man and His Symbols. Carl G. Jung. Jung's works generally translate better through someone who is a Jungian psychologist.

On Aggression. Konrad Lorenz. This book is boring, but the information is sound.

The Parable of the Beast. John Bleibtreu. This guy deals with the relationship between mankind and the animal aspect that we have lost contact with. It makes for interesting reading.

A Primer of Freudian Psychology. Calvin S. Hall. This is a good introduction to the old boy's works. Personally I think Freud is a dinosaur, but the academic world still thinks he's great.

A Primer of Jungian Psychology. Calvin S. Hall. This is another good primer, and I like Jung better than Freud. That's okay, Jung didn't like Freud either. Ex-friends make the worst enemies.

Taboo Topics. Norman Farberow. Why we don't talk about certain subjects.

Your Many Faces. Virginia Satir. This book about self-perception is a great starting point for learning about the masks people wear.

The Quiet Furies. Elton McNeil. This is based on case studies of mental disorders; it also includes explanations.

Family Operating Systems

The Family. John Bradshaw. His videotaped seminars are also shown on PBS. Never have I encountered anyone who describes the roles of dysfunctional operating systems so well. Be forewarned, this book will rattle your cage.

Healing the Shame That Binds You. John Bradshaw. This tells how to break free of the dysfunctional programming that ruins most people's lives. I recommend Bradshaw carte blanche; he speaks the truth, and it isn't hidden in pomposity. You don't have to be a psych major to understand.

Politics of the Family and Other Essays. R.D. Lang. This is more academically oriented but still good.

Politics of Experience. R.D. Laing. More of the same.

The New Peoplemaking. Virginia Satir. How families affect the way people behave.

Growing Up Absurd: Problems of Youth in the Organized System. Paul Goodman. Ya think the problem is new? It was around in 1960, when this was written.

Male Issues

Castration and Male Rage: The Phallic Wound. Eugene Monick. Great concepts, but the academic delivery is ZZZZZZZZZ.

Iron John: A Book about Men. Robert Bly. This is must reading for any male. It's easy reading and informative.

Passive Men, Wild Women. Pierre Mornell. This discusses different roles and behaviors of men and women and why they collide.

King, Warrior, Magician, Lover: Rediscovering the Archetypes of the Mature Masculine. Robert Moore/ Douglas Gillette. This is another must read, especially if you're young.

The Hazards of Being Male: Surviving the Myth of Masculine Privilege. Herb Goldberg. Our manly-man mythos is killing us—heart attacks, high-blood pressure, burnout, all the real tough-guy stuff.

Pop Psychology

These are books that haven't fossilized into accepted academic dogma. They're new, they're hot, and they're untested in the long run. Then again, unlike the dinosaurs, they also seem to work and are usually easier to read. They're also guaranteed to get you into an argument with psych majors at parties.

Don't Say Yes When You Want to Say No! Herbert Fensterheim/Jean Baer. Learn the difference between being assertive and aggressive. Be assertive rather than aggressive, and you have to punch fewer people.

Stop Running Scared! Herbert Fensterheim/Jean Baer. More assertiveness training.

When I Say No, I Feel Guilty: How to Cope Using the Skills of Systematic Assertive Therapy. Manuel Smith. Assertiveness! Assertiveness! Everywhere I look, assertiveness.

The Intimate Enemy: How to Fight Fair in Love and Marriage. George Bach and Peter Wyden. Setting rules for dispute with your loved one is probably the smartest thing you can do. Especially with a loved one, fight fair, and demand that she/he does the same.

I'm Okay—You're Okay. Thomas Harris. Transactional analysis, it's still a good rule of thumb as to how some people think.

How to Win Friends and Influence People. Dale Carnegie. Written in 1936, this was the first (and still the best) book for the average Joe on interpersonal interaction.

Nobody's Perfect: How to Give Criticism and Get Results. H. Weisinger/Norman Lobsenz. This offers a great way to avoid screaming fights and black eyes.

An End to Innocence: Facing Life without Illusions. Sheldon Kopp. Responsibility without blame—what a novel idea.

Looking Out for Number 1. Robert J. Ringer. This one I highly recommend.

Winning through Intimidation. Robert J. Ringer. More for business, but the man has insights that can be applied to self-defense, namely covering your ass.

Stop! You're Driving Me Crazy! George R. Bach and Ronald M. Deutsch. Thsi book deals with double messages and how they affect your sanity.

Under the Influence: A Guide to the Myths and Realities of Alcoholism. James Milam and Katherine Ketcham. Alcoholism and its myths are the subject of this book.

Read anything you can about adult children of alcoholics, adult survivors of sexual abuse, substance abuse, twelve-step recovery programs, obsessive/compulsive behavior, etc. It is fucking amazing that we haven't been wiped off the face of this planet.

Fighting/Self-Defense

I assume that you'd guess my books and videos are on this list without my having to list them.

Championship Fighting. Jack Dempsey. This book took years of martial arts mumbo jumbo and turned it into easily understood terms to explain power tranference and punching.

Lead Poisoning: 25 True Stories from the Wrong End of a Gun. Chris Pfouts. Getting shot ain't no fun, This details what it takes to make it back. (Available from Paladin Press.)

A Bouncer's Guide to Barroom Brawling: Dealing with the Sucker Puncher, Streetfighter, and Ambusher. Peyton Quinn. Peyton and I sound like two old philosophy professors bickering over the finer points of Eskimo philosophy when we get together. He comes from a different school than I, and I highly recommend that you read him to catch some points I miss and to get another viewpoint. (Available from Paladin Press.)

Put 'em Down, Take 'em Out! Knife Fighting Techniques from Folsom Prison. Don Pentecost. All I can say about Don is, "Oh, yes!" (Available from Paladin Press.)

Fiction

Sometimes it's easier to pick up some ideas in story form. Here's a couple of writers I highly recommend.

Skinwalkers, Listening Woman, Blessing Way, Ghostway, and *Dancehall of the Dead.* Tony Hillerman. Two Navajo policemen chase the bad guys in these mystery books. All of his books contain good information on the background of various Indian customs and beliefs.

Blue Belle, Flood, Strega: A Novel, Blossom, and *Sacrifice: A Novel.* Andrew Vachss. This guy knows the freaks like no one else I've ever run across. His descriptions of the street are the best I've ever read.

Any Louis L'Amour book by, believe it or not, Louis L'Amour. There are very few authors who knew the rougher side of life and could write about it better than he did. While the plots are straight out of the 1950s and 1960s, this man lets more accurate and good information about awareness and tough guys ooze out of the cracks of his westerns than most mystery writers even know about.

· · ·

There are other books that should be included in the bibliography, but I'm tired of typing. If you want more information, write me in care of Paladin Press, 7077 Winchester Circle, Boulder, CO 80301, and I'll tell you about them.